WHERE
ON EARTH

ARE WE
GOING?

JONATHON PORRITT

BBC BOOKS

JONATHON PORRITT has been involved in the Green Movement since the early 1970s and joined the Ecology Party (now the Green Party) in 1974. In 1979 and 1983 he both wrote the Green Party's election manifestos and co-ordinated their campaigns.

From 1984 to 1990, Jonathon Porritt was Director of Friends of the Earth, an independent, non-party political pressure group. During this time he became a well-known figure through his writing and his appearances on radio and TV. His previous books, *Seeing Green* and *The Coming of the Greens* (with David Winner) were acclaimed as major contributions to the green debate.

This book is printed on environmentally friendly paper. The text is printed on Precision Matt blade produced at Papyrus Grycksbo Papermill in Sweden. This paper grade is classified as environmentally friendly by the Swedish Association for the Protection of Nature and by the Environment Society. The colour sections are printed on Precision Gloss produced at Papyrus Nymölla, a sister mill which recovers 97% of all chemicals used. Both plants use dioxin-free pulp (non-chlorine bleached) from carefully managed forests.

Published by BBC Books,
a division of BBC Enterprises Limited,
Woodlands, 80 Wood Lane, London W12 0TT
First published 1990

© Jonathon Porritt 1990

ISBN 0 563 20847 3

Set in 11/13 Bembo
Designed by Stuart Walden, Bridgewater Design Ltd
Printed and bound in Great Britain by Butler & Tanner Ltd, Frome and London
Colour separations by Dot Gradations Ltd, Chelmsford
Colour printed by Lawrence Allen Ltd, Weston-super-Mare
Cover printed by Richard Clay Ltd, Norwich

CONTENTS

ACKNOWLEDGEMENTS

PHOTOGRAPHS (BLACK AND WHITE):

HEATHER ANGEL page 184; ARDEA pages 65 (John Mason), 69 (John Daniels) and 143 (Jack Bailey); BARNABY'S PICTURE LIBRARY pages 30, 33 (R. Rixon), 128 (top, E. N. Issott) and 206 (Oliver); CAISSE NATIONALE DES MONUMENTS HISTORIQUES, PARIS page 191 (bottom); CAMERA PRESS pages 212 (John Manning) and 213 (DPA); COLORIFIC page 128 (bottom, David Levenson); NIGEL DICKINSON page 229; ECOSCENE page 145 (Sally Morgan); MARK EDWARDS page 14 (bottom); ROSEMARY & PENELOPE ELLIS page 71; ENERGY ADVISORY ASSOCIATES page 46; FOOD FROM BRITAIN page 79; GREENPEACE page 222; THE GUARDIAN page 85; ROBERT HARDING pages 117, 165 and 182; HOLT STUDIOS pages 61 (Nigel Cattlin), 123 (Mary Cherry) and 185 (Nigel Cattlin); HUTCHISON LIBRARY page 169 (Richard House); ICCE page 139 (Mark Boulton); THE INDEPENDENT page 202; ISLINGTON COUNCIL page 105; DAVID JACKSON page 60; KENTISH TOWN CITY FARM page 109; LIBRARY OF CONGRESS/V. & A. page 14 (top); LONDON BOROUGH OF TOWER HAMLETS page 207; MAGNUM pages 131 (Bruno Barbey) and 148 (Paul Fusco); NATIONAL PORTRAIT GALLERY, LONDON page 191 (top); THE NORTON SCHOOL page 100; REX FEATURES pages 28 (Carrero) and 53; DONNA RISPOLI page 152 (both); DAVID SOUTH pages 108 and 188; 3M page 142; TROPIX page 181 (Martin Birley); UPI/BETTMANN NEWSPHOTOS page 132; DAVID WILLIAMS page 83.

PHOTOGRAPHS (COLOUR):

ARDEA page ii (bottom, J. Swedberg); ASHRAM COMMUNITY SERVICE PROJECT page vi (bottom); BARNABY'S PICTURE LIBRARY page xiii (bottom, Anthony Cooper); BRUCE COLEMAN front cover (meadow, K. Wothe); COLORIFIC page x (bottom, Black Star/Dan McCoy); C.R.O.W. page vi (top); SUSAN CUNNINGHAM page xii (top); ECOSCENE pages vii (Ian Harwood), viii (top, Gryniewicz), xiii (top, Sally Morgan) and xiv (top, Sally Morgan); MARK EDWARDS page i; ESA/METEOSAT page xvi; FAGOR page x (top); ROBERT HARDING pages iv (left) and v (top, Geoff Renner); HOLT STUDIOS page viii (bottom, Nigel Cattlin); HANS HULTBERG page xiv (bottom); ICCE page xii (bottom, Mark Boulton); MAGNUM page ii (Bruno Barbey); NATURE PHOTOGRAPHERS page iii (top, Paul Sterry; bottom, Maurice Walker); NHPA pages v (bottom, S. Krasemann) and xi (top, James Carmichael); PANOS PICTURES pages ix (Bruce Paton) and xv (top, Trygve Bølstad; bottom, Sanjay Acharya); REX FEATURES page iv (right); DAVID SOUTH page xi (bottom); SPECTRUM front cover (inset, David Bailey).

TEXT AND ARTWORK

ASSOCIATION FOR THE CONSERVATION OF ENERGY page 27 (top); CERES page 148; COUNTRYSIDE COMMISSION page 106; THE DAILY TELEGRAPH pages 76, 137 and 198; THE EVENING STANDARD page 213; FINANCIAL TIMES pages 19 (centre), 155 and 159; FRIENDS OF THE EARTH pages 43, 55 and 144; THE GUARDIAN page 31; DAVID HENCKE page 170 (top); THE INDEPENDENT pages 19 (top and bottom right) and 48; MAIL ON SUNDAY page 66; W. W. NORTON AND CO. pages 27 (bottom), 172, 178, 179 and 182 (from State of the World Report, 1989 by Lester Brown); DEBBIE OBIED page 137 (cartoon); THE OBSERVER pages 53 and 61; TIM RADFORD page 168; WALTER SCHWARZ pages 85, 176, 177 and 223; MICK SMITH page 50; ROBIN STAINER page 166; THE SUNDAY CORRESPONDENT pages 44, 201 and 203; TIMES NEWSPAPERS LTD pages 19 (left), 93, 170 (bottom), 178 (bottom) and 195; TODAY page 64; WORLD BANK page 165 (chart)

Every effort has been made to trace copyright holders but the Publishers would be glad to hear of any omissions.

INTRODUCTION

WHEN I TOOK over as Director of Friends of the Earth in September 1984, very few people seemed to be genuinely concerned about the environment. Indeed, environmentalism was seen essentially as a minority pastime for a few well-meaning fruit-and-nutcases, deserving little more than the occasional token reference in party manifestos or weighty editorials. Despite the many honourable exceptions to that state of dereliction, from the highest in the land to the most anonymous activists slogging it out at the grassroots, it was a disheartening time.

What a transformation there has been in just six years! Throughout the developed world, millions of people have come to accept the overriding importance of environmental issues. Though many politicians are still just playing at being green, assiduously cultivating the dubious art of 'media green-speak', others have set out with sincerity and enthusiasm to adapt their somewhat fragile political and economic beliefs to the very different perspective which inspires today's Green Movement.

It is almost impossible to keep track of the different initiatives contributing to this transformation, for they come in all shapes and sizes, in every sphere of human interest. Their cumulative impact has been to open people's eyes, both to the inherent contradictions of our current way of life, *and* to the existence of a compelling, but as yet largely untried, alternative.

It is that alternative which this book, and the television series which it accompanies, are all about. From my own experience of countless public meetings the length and breadth of the UK, and from the increasingly emphatic findings of opinion polls and social surveys, I became aware several years ago of the hunger for *answers*, for positive ideas, for practical alternatives. Media coverage of the environment still tends to be depressingly gloomy, disaster-oriented and subconsciously disempowering. There's never enough good news to balance the bad.

I have been lucky enough to experience at first hand some of the solutions to that overpowering sense of doom and gloom, and to hear and read of many more. By an even greater stroke of luck, I was able to persuade the BBC that all these examples of 'best ecological practice' were as worthy of their attention as their continuing coverage of all the things still going wrong with Planet Earth.

I do not discount the importance of that kind of coverage. It has shocked and gradually drawn many people into a state of awareness about our fragile environment without which little progress can be made. At the end of 1989, a new series on the 'State of Europe', from the BBC's Natural History Unit in Bristol, opened with a programme on air pollution in Poland. In its own way, it was as shattering as any environmental documentary I have ever seen, rudely dispelling some of the new-found optimism that had built up in me over the previous two years. Even hardened environmental campaigners were shocked by Michael Buerk's account of the province of Zabrze:

> 66 *This province has the highest infant mortality rate and the most sickly children in Europe. Doctors showed us results of a study they have just completed on 11 000 children in the town. Half the four year olds, two-thirds of the six year olds and three-quarters of the ten year olds have chronic illnesses. The number of cancer cases has doubled in the last twelve years.* 99

If the Green Movement's solutions are not as relevant to these Polish children, and to the millions of children in the Third

World whose suffering is even greater, as they are now held to be for children in the so-called 'First World', then they are not worth putting down on paper. I profoundly hope they are, but I cannot guarantee it. There is very little evidence to go on. What you will find here is not, therefore, the definitive 'greenprint' for the future, but rather an account of what has already been achieved and a glimpse of the vast potential that, with the right kind of vision and political will, is there for the taking.

As of the first few months of 1990, the straight answer to the question contained in the title of this book, *Where On Earth Are We Going?*, is 'into the abyss of ecological collapse'. The problems outlined in Chapter One reveal a planetary life-support system pushed almost to breaking point by the undiminished demands of humankind. By any standards, that is a somewhat gloomy opening for what is meant to be a very optimistic project! But the whole point is that there *is* an alternative, some of the details of which are sketched out in these pages.

Some will continue to deny that this alternative provides a suitably definitive response to our current predicament. But it needs to be set against the cast-iron guarantee of disaster looming if we do not learn to change our ways over the next few years.

It is *always* better to light a few small candles than endlessly to curse the darkness.

JONATHON PORRITT

Chapter I

WHERE ON EARTH ARE WE GOING?

AT ITS SIMPLEST, to be a 'Green' today is to put the environment at or near the top of one's list of priorities, and to recognise that we can never genuinely enrich ourselves or properly protect our children's future without first protecting the natural wealth of the planet.

Put like that, it sounds so reasonable and obvious. How could anyone possibly disagree, let alone seek to live in a way which imperils our very future as a species? Yet that's exactly what the majority of human beings alive today either choose to do, in the developed world, or are compelled to do by chronic poverty in the Third World.

In evolutionary terms, the impact of humankind on the rest of life on Earth has been a very recent phenomenon, taking up just a few thousand years of a life process that goes back over 13.5 billion years. We only really got into our destructive stride at the start of the Industrial Revolution, 250 years ago, at exactly the time when our capacity to transform the Earth's raw materials into goods and services began to liberate millions from lives of grinding hardship and poverty. And we only started to realise the implications of what we were doing a mere 20 or 30 years ago.

This awareness (and the Green Movement that has sprung from it) is only just beginning to permeate our political processes and value systems. It seems to be taking an agonisingly long time to sink in, but when an individual can only count on an average three score years and ten, it's very hard to have to think in evolutionary terms!

There is still no guarantee that we're going to make it. By all accounts, ocean-going tankers (of the kind that devastated Prince William Sound in Alaska) need about 8 miles to stop, even with the engines in reverse. The industrial juggernaut that we have created has gained a similar momentum, and there is as yet no desire at all to engage reverse gear as far as most world leaders are concerned. It's daunting enough for them just to confront the need to slow the beast down.

There may be some out there who fondly imagine that just because everybody is talking about the environment, there's nothing to worry about any longer. Just as garlic is supposed by some to ward off marauding vampires, so the inexhaustible stream of hot air from politicians is thought by others to be a sufficient antidote to impending ecological collapse. Most of this book is resolutely optimistic about the potential for change, if not about the extent of the change to date. But optimism is a facile quality if it is not rooted in a thoroughly realistic appraisal of what's *really* going on out there.

It's worth making a lightning review of the twelve most important factors, at the international level, that threaten our future well-being – the 'Dirty Dozen' of the ecological crisis.

1 OZONE DEPLETION

Ozone in the upper atmosphere protects us from highly damaging ultra-violet radiation from the Sun. The 'ozone layer' is now under attack from chlorofluorocarbons (CFCs) and other chemicals. Once released (after use in aerosols, or as refrigerants and foam-blowing agents), they can remain active in the atmosphere for at least 100 years.

In September 1987, the Montreal Protocol set in train international negotiations for phasing out some of these ozone-depleting substances. The Protocol was reviewed in June 1990, but the delays in achieving total phase-out are extremely worrying; every *five*-year delay sets us back *fifteen* years in terms of reducing chlorine in the atmosphere to acceptable levels. Meanwhile, the seasonal hole in the ozone layer over the Antarctic gets bigger and bigger, and in 1988, a three per cent thinning was detected over densely populated areas of the Northern Hemisphere, ensuring many thousands of extra deaths from skin cancer in the next century.

2 GLOBAL WARMING

The small amount of carbon dioxide in the atmosphere makes life possible by trapping some of the Sun's heat reflected back off the Earth into the atmosphere. However, the more there is of it (and other so-called 'greenhouse gases'), the more heat is trapped and the warmer it gets. Since the Industrial Revolution, we have steadily increased our use of fossil fuels (the largest source of man-made carbon dioxide) and destroyed more and more of our forests.

International scientific consensus now predicts temperature increases of anything between 1.5 and 4.5 degrees Centigrade by the middle of the next century. This would have a devastating effect on agricultural production and gradually raise sea levels – possibly by as much as three metres by the end of the century. Weather patterns the world over will become unpredictable and there will be more storms, hurricanes, floods and droughts.

3 ENERGY

Meeting the energy needs of more than five billion people is putting a huge strain on many of the Earth's life-support systems. Fossil fuels are still plentiful, but they are a finite resource; yet even now there are more than 400 million cars on the planet, each using an average of 2 gallons of fuel every day. Burning coal and oil not only accelerates global warming, but gradually acidifies the environment. Acid rain has now affected over 7 million hectares of forest in over 20 countries. It has eliminated trout in rivers across 35 000 square kilometres of Norway, acidified 90 000 kilometres of brooks and 18 000 lakes in Sweden and severely affected over 50 lochs in Scotland, 700 000 lakes in Canada and many in the Adirondacks in the USA. The situation is becoming just as grave in many Third World countries.

Nuclear power provides no escape from this dilemma, not least because we still don't know how to dispose of the waste. By the end of the decade, there will be 100 000 lorry loads of

radioactive waste in store in the UK alone. In many
developing countries, firewood is increasingly difficult to find.

4 AIR POLLUTION

According to a major report published by the World Watch
Institute in January 1990, more than a billion people (one fifth
of the world's population) are now breathing air contaminated
by pollutants in excess of international safety limits. Air
pollution in the United States is estimated to cause up to 50 000
deaths a year; deaths in Athens rise by up to six times on days
of heavy pollution. Ozone levels in Europe are dangerously
high, causing many chest and lung problems.

One day's breathing in Bombay is equivalent to smoking
10 cigarettes. Many other Third World cities, such as Cubatao
in Brazil, and Mexico City, have been very seriously affected
by a rapid growth in industrialisation, and an almost complete
disregard for proper environmental standards.

5 DESERTIFICATION AND SOIL EROSION

Around 6 million hectares of new desert are formed every year
through poor management and changing climatic patterns.
The Sahel, where population growth, over-grazing and the
disruption of nomadic lifestyles have steadily increased
pressure on marginal land, has been particularly badly affected.
An inch of soil takes at least 200 years to lay down, but can
be swept away in just a few years. Worldwide, an estimated
20 billion tonnes of topsoil are washed or blown off croplands
every year; more than 3 billion hectares (around 25 per cent
of the world's total land surface) are now at risk.

6 DEFORESTATION

Forty-five per cent of the world's rainforests have been
destroyed in the last thirty years; tropical rainforest destruction
has nearly doubled over the last decade, and 1.8 per cent
(around 140000 square kilometres) of the remaining rainforest
disappears every year. The carbon dioxide released in the
process contributes around 15 per cent of total global
warming. By the end of the century, most of the world's
rainforest will be gone, with the exception of Zaire, Papua
New Guinea and Western Amazonia.

Tropical deforestation is also the single greatest cause of
species extinctions as the rainforests are home to more than

13

ABOVE: The American 'dust bowl' of the thirties: a glimpse of horrors to come?

RIGHT: Soil erosion in many Third World countries represents the gravest threat to their ability to feed growing numbers of people.

60 per cent of the millions of species on Earth. Astonishingly, scientists estimate that, given current rates of deforestation, as many as 100 species a day may be disappearing.

7 WATER SHORTAGES

Water use has at least quadrupled in this century, and could double again over the next two decades. In more than 80 Third World countries (with 40 per cent of the world's population) serious water shortages are undermining the livelihood of millions of people and holding up sustainable development.

Since 1980, more than 30 countries have been involved in international disputes concerning the use and control of diminishing water supplies. In China, more than 200 cities are without sufficient water, and the water table under the North China Plain is dropping by more than one metre a year. California is in an equally bad situation, and serious pollution of the Ogallala Aquifer is threatening agricultural production throughout the Western States.

8 CHEMICALS

Worldwide, some 70 000 chemicals are in everyday use. Between 500 and 1000 new chemicals are added to the list every year. The use of pesticides in agriculture, and the disposal of industrial wastes, releases hundreds of millions of tonnes of hazardous substances into the environment every year. Pesticide use in the United States tripled between 1965 and 1985; it is estimated that 80 per cent of pesticide-associated cancer risks come from 15 foods, with tomatoes, beef, potatoes, oranges and lettuce leading the list.

In the Third World, pesticide use is also increasing very rapidly. The World Health Organisation estimates that pesticides poison more than 500 000 people every year, with one in ten cases resulting in death or permanent disability.

9 TOXIC WASTES

Toxic waste dumps litter the landscapes of the developed world. There are more than 4500 toxic waste tips in Britain alone, at least 1300 of which have been identified as posing serious risks to the environment. Imports of hazardous waste into the United Kingdom have increased sixteen times since 1984.

In the United States in 1987, the Environmental Protection Agency identified 950 sites as needing urgent attention, and set up an $8.5 billion 'Superfund' to finance the clean up. Experts now reckon that final costs could exceed $100 billion. Surveys in West Germany and Denmark have revealed similar problems.

Between them, EEC countries produce 50 per cent more waste than can be disposed of at existing facilities. As a consequence, thousands of tonnes are disposed of in the Third World. It is impossible to estimate total volumes of hazardous waste in Third World countries, as there are very few regulations or appropriate disposal facilities.

10 ARMS SPENDING

Military budgets currently amount to around one trillion dollars a year, which is a larger sum of money than the entire income of the poor half of the world's population. It works out at $2.75 billion a day.

On average, 6 per cent of nations' GNP is spent on defence; developing countries have increased their arms budgets five-fold in the past twenty years.

The share of public research and development outlays that goes on military expenditure is as high as 70 per cent in the United States, 60 per cent in the USSR and 50 per cent in the UK. Half a million scientists work in the arms business. By contrast, the United Nations' Environment Programme has received $30 million or less a year from governments around the world since it was established in 1972. Three days of global military spending is the equivalent of funding the Tropical Forest Action Plan for five years. Two days of global military spending equals the entire annual cost of the United Nations' plan to halt Third World desertification.

11 INTERNATIONAL DEBT

The cumulative debt of developing countries has now reached more than one trillion dollars. Interest payments are $60 billion a year. Beginning in 1984, the traditional net flow of capital reversed itself: in 1982, $18.2 billion went to developing countries; today $52 billion a year is transferred from developing countries to the rich North.

This inevitably puts massive additional pressure on the natural resources of debtor countries, as they seek to accelerate export-led growth in order to pay back the debt. Without due regard to environmental protection, it is impossible for these debtor countries to achieve sustainable development.

12 POPULATION

Today, there are around 5.2 billion people on Earth. By 2025, there will be 8.5 billion. Of the additional 3.2 billion, 3 billion will be in Third World countries where millions already live on the edge of survival, on marginal and unsustainable land.

Lower birth rates in the developed world are off-set by disproportionately high consumption of energy and resources. Long-term reductions in population levels, both North and South, are therefore a pre-requisite of achieving sustainable development.

For all the rapid growth in awareness about the environment over the last few years, that remains one hell of a catalogue. There are, of course, many encouraging factors on the other side of the balance sheet: new energy-efficient and resource-saving technologies; far greater ease in communications and exchanging information; the end of the Cold War and the democratisation of Eastern Europe; a clear understanding of trans-boundary issues (like the thinning of the ozone layer) that demand a new level of international cooperation; the exhilarating acceptance of sustainability as the key principle in devising economic and development strategies for the 1990s. All these positive aspects, and a great many more, are covered at some point in this book.

For all that, the gap between the debits and the credits is not noticeably narrowing. Too many of the credits exist as little more than ideas and theories; lip-service is paid to them at every turn, but they are still inadequately developed and deployed. It is this continuing gap which has provided the main stimulus for the huge surge in environmental organisations and initiatives throughout the world. In the UK, the 'growth curve' for many organisations has been phenomenal, as detailed in Chapter 8.

The United States and many other European countries have experienced a similar green surge. Even more encouraging, after years of suppression and persecution, environmental organisations are springing up like mushrooms in Eastern European countries, which now face environmental problems so devastating as to make ours look like an exercise in litter-picking.

Simultaneously, throughout the Third World, there has been a marked shift in attitude, so that 'environmentalism' is no longer seen as a callous effort by Northerners to 'pull up the ladder after them' and keep the Southern poor in their place; environmental protection and population restraint are now accepted by the vast majority of developing countries as preconditions of a more prosperous and sustainable future for their people.

But will it all last? Or will the bubble burst, and all today's whipped-up green froth be dispersed on the winds of economic recession, changing political priorities, or even some new fashionable cause? Even the best-maintained bandwagon can support only so many self-serving fellow-travellers. And there is only so much marketing hype that the punters will put up with before smelling a rat, albeit a green one. The most uncomfortable question for all those environmental organisations currently enjoying their hard-earned influence is a simple one: is contemporary greenery just a fashionable fling for those who have done so well out of the decade of Mrs Thatcher, or a somewhat chaotic manifestation of something much more durable and radical?

There are, of course, a few noisy cynics who do indeed think it's all a load of nonsense, a zany mixture of exaggeration, scare-mongering, economic illiteracy and advertisers' hype, dreamed up by people like myself to put the wind up people like you, and make our names or even our fortunes in the process. By contrast, there are those who saw the green light long ago, and who now believe that we are witnessing the first stirrings of a new age, in which humankind will make a 'quantum leap' in awareness, banishing poverty, eliminating war and assuming our rightful mantle as stewards of creation.

Most of us just carry on living our lives rather more prosaically, oscillating somewhere between profound despair and inspired hopefulness! All the frenetic green activity of the last few years has left everyone feeling a little breathless and understandably bemused about what the future holds. And it is indeed fair to ask what makes today any different from the last significant surge of environmental concern in the late sixties and early seventies.

Disease rife in 'most polluted city in Europe'

BITTERFELD in Saxony announces itself from the train with a vista of coal heaps and smokestacks. The station sign is covered in grime.

The station cleaner shrugs. No matter how often he cleans it, he says, the dirt comes back straight away. In East Germany, the town is a byword for pollution and neglect.

Two-thirds of the 130 000 residents work in the chemical plant, power station or coal mines dominating Bitterfeld.

The stench of chemicals, coal dust and diesel hits you at the first intake of breath. Half an hour of walking in the town left me breathless. The old brick houses are caked in black soot and the dust lies so thick on the streets that the children draw patterns in it.

The West German magazine *Der Spiegel* carried out its own research this month and found dioxin and other poisonous chemicals in the water, which is drained from factories into the Elbe via open channels.

It concluded that Bitterfeld was 'the most polluted town in Europe'.

ANNE MCELVOY, © THE TIMES 10.1.90

Worse than Chernobyl

IN SOVIET central Asia an ecological catastrophe is crippling and killing uncounted thousands of people: in some ways, it is a disaster greater than the nuclear fire at Chernobyl.

The cause of the catastrophe can be summarised in one word: cotton. For years, huge overdoses of chemical fertiliser, pesticides and defoliants have been poured on the cotton fields. The chemicals have seeped into the water supply, poisoning tens of thousands. At the same time, great quantities of water have been siphoned from the region's two main rivers, the Amudar'ya and the Syrdar'ya (the Oxus and Jaxartes of classical times), for irrigation. Starved of water, the Aral Sea is disappearing.

In the Karakalpak region bordering the Aral Sea, two-thirds of the people suffer from hepatitis, typhoid or throat cancer, according to an article last month in *Socialist Industry*, an official Communist Party organ. It said 83 per cent of the children had serious illnesses. Andrei Sakharov, the famous physicist and liberated dissident, claimed a few weeks ago that more than half the children living near cotton plantations in Uzbekistan suffer from serious liver complaints and that most of the young men called up for national service are rejected as unfit.

© THE FINANCIAL TIMES 30.7.89

Why the Black Sea turned bright red

LEADERS of the fledgling Romanian Ecological Movement said yesterday that they knew of at least 625 cases of serious pollution around the country and fear 'an ecological disaster'.

They are demanding stringent controls to clean up after 20 years of unfettered industrialisation under the late President Ceausescu, for whom massive chemical plants were an obsession.

'The Black Sea was turned bright red last year by chemicals poured into the Danube from Sulina and Tulcea,' said Mr Silviu Palalau, a vice-president of the movement.

© THE INDEPENDENT 19.1.90

Huge pollution bill for Poland

POLAND will need some $25bn this decade just to arrest the pollution of its air, water and land, but there is little prospect of a clean-up until the overhaul of the Polish economy is well under way, according to the World Bank.

Its estimate for arresting environmental damage in Poland – which suggests that the bill for the whole of Eastern Europe could easily exceed $200bn – dwarfs the money currently earmarked for the environment.

© THE INDEPENDENT 25.1.90

Though my green crystal ball is no more reliable than anyone else's, I consider it extremely unlikely, if not impossible, that green issues are going to nose-dive off the political agenda as rapidly as they were forced on to it. There is a huge groundswell of concern behind the international Green Movement today, motivated not just by the state of the Earth itself, but by the response it has evoked among key groups in society.

First and foremost among these groups are the scientists. Our collective knowledge base is now so much greater than in the late sixties and early seventies. What was hypothesis then (about ozone depletion or acid rain, for example), has now been emphatically demonstrated, even though there still remain many variables and uncertainties on several scientific issues.

Scientists are also playing a much more influential role on the world stage – setting the pace on global warming, for instance – in such a way that pressure groups are often left trailing behind. As an indirect result, the biological sciences have shed their Cinderella image and achieved higher status within the scientific community.

We face a particular problem in the United Kingdom, however, which can only be described as the 'Where is the pile of bodies?' approach to the environment. Unless it can be proved 'beyond reasonable doubt' that x per cent of our trees are dying specifically because of acid rain, or y per cent of our rivers are now seriously polluted by pesticides, or z children have died of leukaemia specifically because of exposure to radiation from power stations, the government just doesn't want to know. The notion of sensible, precautionary, preventive action remains alien to many British decision-makers, though there have been some encouraging signs of a change of heart at least within the Department of the Environment.

It is right and proper that politicians should be able to call on the best scientific advice when making decisions. Unscientific political decisions are of no more use to the Green Movement than they are to the established political parties. But beyond the science, politicians have also come to realise that 'the environment' matters a great deal to people in other ways, be it in terms of huge global issues like the rainforests or global warming, or, more commonly, of local concerns about familiar landmarks, favourite walks, litter and general environmental deterioration. Coupled with the growing influence of the Green Parties throughout Europe, this has accelerated the 'greening' of established political parties; a very different scenario from that of the early seventies, when politicians were often dismissive and contemptuous about issues affecting the environment.

Unfortunately, most politicians are still very badly advised by their economists, who find it difficult to locate the environment anywhere in their abstruse and abstracted world. The idea that all man-made wealth still depends on the natural wealth of the planet (in terms of energy, raw materials, food, climate regulation and other life-support systems) is barely worth a mention in most economic textbooks. There are precious few environmental economists in the UK, and the whole dyed-in-the-wool profession needs hauling somewhat abruptly into the real world of the nineties.

The other big problem is that everything has to be *economic*, in terms of making money. That is the all-powerful criterion: if something is *not* economic, it is judged to be of no value, regardless of any long-term benefits it may bring. If something *is* economic, then that's fine, regardless of the long-term social and environmental costs. The consequences of this are dire: we strip away our irreplaceable ecological assets as if there were no tomorrow because that is what makes the money today. The idea of drawing an annual interest payment on that ecological capital – through the optimal management of our resources – simply doesn't square with contemporary economics.

Most people have now come to realise that we gain little in the long term by making war on the planet in the short term. Yet all too often behind the glossy front of 'growth', 'development' and 'aid', there has lurked the much grimmer reality of resource depletion, environmental destruction and human exploitation.

Are politicians merely driven by the wishes of their constituents, or are people positively led by politicians into new patterns of thought and behaviour? This is a debate that seems to rumble endlessly on. But in this case there is little doubt that ordinary people have provided the motivating force. One opinion poll after another has shown the astonishing strength of feeling on environmental issues.

21

Given such evidence, it's hardly surprising that industry has begun to adjust to a different set of priorities for the 1990s. Many companies are now committed not just to cleaning up their image, but to cleaning up their act, with the Green Consumer Movement providing an additional and very powerful spur in this direction. Large sums of money are now being invested in environment-friendly technologies and products, and in cleaning up some of the errors of the past.

Informed, cajoled, and occasionally inspired by the environmental organisations, this combination of science, politics, commercial self-interest and consumer power has set in train a mutually reinforcing process of change in society, which is, again, quite different from anything we saw in the late sixties.

Very belatedly, one final ingredient is now being added to the melting pot: religious and spiritual leaders are realising that they can no longer sit tamely by while their respective gods' Earth is pillaged and vandalised by humankind. What, after all, is the point of worrying about life after death when we're busy creating a living hell here on Earth?

For reasons that will become clearer in Chapter 8, I personally believe that this final ingredient is of crucial importance. The kind of transformation that we're going to have to achieve is so far-reaching as to put it way beyond the realm of conventional political change – unless that process is preceded by a profound and lasting change in our values, attitudes and lifestyles.

To achieve such a transformation in one country might seem challenge enough, but the daunting truth is that it has to be done across the whole Earth. It matters not a jot whether ozone-depleting chlorofluorocarbons or greenhouse gases are released here or in India or China or Botswana. Their impact, and the threat they pose to life on Earth, is the same. It matters even less whether the polychlorinated biphenyls (PCBs) killing the polar bears in the Arctic are British PCBs, Canadian PCBs, or Russian PCBs. The polar bears themselves certainly can't tell the difference, nor can the scientists who have to carry out the autopsies on them.

The notion of 'One World', that great emotional cry of so many broad-minded internationalists over the years, is changing before our very eyes from a theoretical, unattainable ideal, into a dynamic, demonstrable reality. There is, of course, a paradox at work here: the greater the scale of the environmental threat, the greater the potential for international cooperation. For it is astonishing that so many people have for so long so successfully averted their eyes and shut down their minds to the truth of what is happening around them.

It is really not so very complicated. The human species has been formidably successful, from an evolutionary point of view. Through our collective ingenuity, the use of tools and the subsequent development of advanced technologies, we have colonised almost every available ecological niche on Earth. But for all that, like every other species, we are still constrained by certain fundamental laws of nature.

A more domestic analogy can be drawn from the time-honoured pastime of baking a cake. We are all familiar with the variables involved: the basic ingredients, their availability and nutritional value; the energy required for baking the cake; the skill of the cook; the waste that has to be disposed of at the end of the process; the number of people amongst whom the cake is to be shared, and the relative size of the slices that people receive!

For the first time, there is now a general awareness that shortages and inadequacies in terms of the basic ingredients, pollution from the energy used in the 'baking', difficulties in disposing of the waste and an ever-greater number of people rightly demanding a fair share of the cake, are threatening our wealth-creating bakery with total collapse.

There is a *lot* we can do: we can install more energy-efficient ovens to reduce energy waste; we can all but eliminate many of the waste products involved. We can dramatically increase the cake's nutritional content, so that people are satisfied with a smaller quantity than before; we can improve our own skills in gathering the basic ingredients and can seek out new sources or vary the mix. However, at the end of the day, if the number of people involved exceed the cake's capacity, then people die.

They are dying right now. Mostly, it is true, because of the inequitable distribution of wealth rather than because of any fundamental shortage of the basic materials required. However, as population continues to soar, this won't last long.

The upshot of this lengthy comparison is simple: we have no choice but to share our wealth more fairly, and no choice

23

but to find ways of limiting the number of people who will in future be calling on that natural wealth to feed, clothe and house them, let alone to satisfy a host of other demands.

This remains the rock on which all conventional party politics still founders. Not even the most gung-ho growthist seriously supposes that the five billion people on Earth today (let alone the eight billion in 2025) could enjoy the same material standard of living as we do without the Planet literally falling to pieces. To some, that doesn't particularly matter; inequity is a 'fact of life', and if the poor people of the poor countries go to the wall, whilst we continue to prosper, that's just too bad. To others, it matters a very great deal, for it seems to us impossible to talk of 'progress' unless the benefits of that progress accrue to all people rather than to a tiny, favoured minority.

If one holds to that view, the implication is clear: 'wealth' must be interpreted differently, created sustainably, and distributed more fairly. That is exactly what the 'green alternative' is all about.

Chapter 2

ENERGY
WITHOUT END

'ENERGY FOR LIFE' proclaims the advertising slogan. Fair
enough. But for once, the ad-men would seem to be
underselling their product. For energy *is* life. And the source
of all that life-giving energy is the sun – not British Coal, nor
British Gas, nor even British Nuclear Fuels.

The history of our species has been closely tied to our ability
to exploit different energy sources. The Industrial Revolution
was fuelled by the development of vast reserves of coal, and
our modern society owes its very existence to the discovery
and accelerating depletion of oil and gas. But our attitude to
these stores of natural wealth has always been astonishingly
profligate. Until the oil shocks of the mid-seventies, few
questioned the wisdom of acting today as if there were no
tomorrow. The tripling of the price of oil in 1974 did wonders
to shatter such complacency, but the lesson was relatively
short-lived. 'Gas-guzzlers' were back in fashion by the mid-
eighties, and low oil prices have steadily devalued the business
of promoting energy efficiency.

The main concern in the seventies was how long we had
before 'the oil ran out'. Bestselling books like The Club of

Rome's *Limits to Growth* and The Ecologist's *Blueprint for Survival* laid it on the line with lashings of doom and gloom. Oil junkies all, we were warned of what would happen to us when deprived of our regular fix of black gold.

Though the point about these reserves being strictly non-renewable is as important now as it was then (in one year, humankind consumes as much oil as it took a million years to lay down geologically), such predictions were somewhat naïve. Oil reserves, even at current depletion rates, could *theoretically* carry us through the first quarter of the next century without undue inconvenience. Reserves of coal promise even greater long-term security, even though fossil fuel usage is widely predicted to double between now and 2025 as the population grows and demand increases.

But as we all know, and a few brave souls were saying even in the seventies, it's not the fact that our oil and coal will one day run out that matters most. Rather, it is the fact that the Earth's capacity to absorb the pollution arising from their combustion will be exhausted long before that distant day. There is a threshold beyond which our lakes, rivers and forests can no longer absorb the sulphur dioxide and nitrogen oxides from our coal-fired power stations. And there is an even more critical threshold beyond which the atmosphere can no longer absorb the carbon dioxide from burning fossil fuels without dramatic disruption to our climate.

Global warming is the mother and father of environmental problems today. The degree of consensus among international scientists is remarkable: a 1.5°C to 4.5°C warming by 2050, with a possible rise in sea levels over the same period of up to 1.65 metres. Some scientists go much further in their predictions. Some, by contrast, believe there are still far too many variables involved (like not knowing whether cloud cover slows down or speeds up the process of global warming, or just how much carbon dioxide the oceans can absorb) to make any definitive interpretation of the data. A tiny minority are of the opinion that all this perceived warming is just so much irrelevant distraction as we move inexorably (from a geological point of view) into the next Ice Age.

It should be noted that it is the scientists who are driving the global warming agenda, not the environmental pressure groups. It was the Changing the Atmosphere Conference in Toronto in June 1988 which alerted the media to the

What is the Greenhouse Effect?

ONE OF THE REASONS that a greenhouse is warmer than its surroundings is because glass lets sunlight pass through it, trapping heat inside. This principle helps to explain why instead of a cold, dead planet we have an environment which is kindly to life. The Earth is a giant greenhouse in space, but instead of a glass roof we have a blanket of gases to keep us warm, that act in a similar way to glass.

These heat-retaining gases, including water vapour, carbon dioxide, methane, nitrous oxides and tropospheric ozone, have maintained a delicate balance of solar and heat radiation for thousands of years. In the last two centuries however, human activity has begun to alter this balance by dramatically increasing the levels of these gases, and by introducing new 'super-absorbent' greenhouse gases like the CFCs and halons.

The world has already warmed by 0.5 to 0.7°C since pre-industrial times. There is now overwhelming consensus among scientists that because of the increase in greenhouse gases there will be a further rise of 0.5 to 1°C over the next few decades whatever we do, and that greater increases are inevitable unless positive action is taken to reduce emissions to a safe level, quickly. These increases may not sound like much, but even a relatively minor change in temperature can alter the climate completely: global temperature during the last ice age was only 4°C colder than today.

It has been predicted that without emission reductions there will be an increase in global temperature of 1.5 to 4.5°C by the year 2050, with a consequent rise in sea level of 25 cms to 1.65 metres. It is likely that low-lying areas would be flooded, causing widespread ecosystem and crop failure, with an increase in health problems due to sewage system damage and the spread of pests. The UK could become either much drier or much wetter, depending on whether the Gulf Stream changes course as temperatures rise and on how wind patterns change. The weather may well become more extreme, with a greater frequency of major storms, intense rains and droughts.

© ASSOCIATION FOR THE CONSERVATION OF ENERGY/WORLD WIDE FUND FOR NATURE, **1989**

---

importance of the Greenhouse Effect by describing it as 'an unintended, uncontrolled, globally pervasive experiment whose ultimate consequences could be second only to global nuclear war'.

Climatologist Stephen Schneider has pointed out that even the most modest projection of global warming over the next century (entailing an increase of around 2 degrees centigrade in average temperatures) means that the world's climate will be changing at something like ten times its natural speed. 'And ten times is the best possible case,' he comments.

There are still some who fondly believe that the fast route out of the Greenhouse is through nuclear power. By contrast, there are others who believe that some politicians are deliberately hyping up the Greenhouse Effect in order to boost the rapidly declining prospects of the nuclear industry.

Few of us could resist just the tiniest twitch of satisfaction when the British Government had to withdraw all nuclear reactors from its 1989 privatisation legislation on the grounds that it had discovered the 'true cost' of nuclear power. City analysts had looked hard at the industry, and declared it utterly unfit for investors to sink their savings into. As far as this

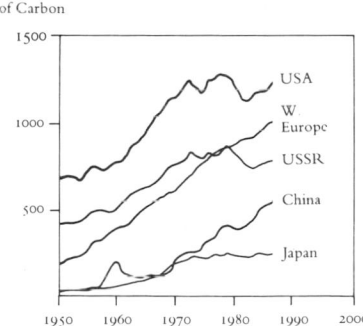

Million Tons of Carbon

CARBON EMISSIONS FROM FOSSIL FUELS, 1950–87

Government is concerned, what the City says goes, though we would have charged them far less for exactly the same advice.

Though the truth is now available even to government ministers, they continue to advocate the importance of nuclear power in order to reduce global warming. Yet a detailed study carried out by Dr Tim Jackson for Friends of the Earth in the autumn of 1989 revealed that nuclear power was one of the least cost-effective ways of achieving a reduction in carbon dioxide emissions. As Mrs Thatcher stressed in her address to the Royal Society in September 1988, 'no nation has unlimited funds, and it will have even less if it wastes them'. Hear hear! Given that investment in energy efficiency is at least five times more cost-effective as a way of reducing carbon dioxide emissions, it's truly remarkable that anyone could still be wittering on about nuclear power.

What's more, more nuclear power can do little to reduce the impact of the motor car on global warming. A significant proportion of the 5.5 billion tonnes of carbon dioxide released into the atmosphere every year from the burning of fossil fuels comes from the use of oil for transport. In the UK, for instance, we are responsible for about 540 million tonnes of carbon dioxide emissions every year (about 3 per cent of the

The prototype Fast Breeder Reactor at Dounreay in the north of Scotland.

28

global total). In 1987, road transport was responsible for 100 million tonnes of this total, with air and rail transport adding another 20 million tonnes. So, over 20 per cent of UK carbon dioxide emissions are transport-related, and the same sort of percentage can be found in most industrialised countries.

There are roughly 24 million vehicles in the UK, and more than 400 million across the world. Each car produces nearly four times its own weight in carbon dioxide every year. More than one-third of these cars are in the United States, but demand elsewhere is soaring. Between 1970 and 1985, the Soviet and Eastern European car fleets grew fivefold, and there is no doubt that the process of democratisation in Eastern Europe will guarantee a massive expansion in vehicle transport in those countries. Indeed, Western European economies are counting on it.

Though well below that of industrialised countries, car ownership in the Third World was also rising until the mid-eighties when the debt crisis really began to bite. Indeed, aid and trade programmes are often geared to promoting increased vehicle use, and many Third World governments make this a priority in order to enhance their own standing.

Both globally and in the United Kingdom, there's a complete contradiction between our awareness of global warming and the continuing promotion of the motor car as the favoured mode of transport. Although it is now almost universally accepted that new roads simply generate new demand, in 1989 the Department of Transport produced a report projecting increases in British vehicle numbers of between 80 per cent and 142 per cent by 2020. If the number of vehicles increases by 142 per cent, there will be 55.7 million vehicles in Britain – one vehicle per person, man, woman and baby. Transport consultant John Adams has pointed out that the extra vehicles involved would form a queue 124 000 miles long. If stationary, this could be accommodated on a brand new motorway stretching from London to Edinburgh – but only if it were 306 lanes wide!

Given current levels of congestion, let alone pollution, such an increase is an almost inconceivably stupid notion. But one must never underestimate the extent to which this Government is prepared to sacrifice intellectual credibility in order to serve the vested interests of the road lobby in this country: the oil industry, the motor manufacturers, the road engineers, the

Jam today and jam tomorrow.

mineral extraction industry and so on.

The simple but regrettable fact is that the UK has no coherent transport policy, and it is the road lobby that has most effectively and consistently exploited this policy vacuum. One administration after another has closed railways, undermined the financial base of public transport, provided huge hidden subsidies through the company car system, kept road spending immune from any cuts, and authorised road construction schemes.

As a consequence, Britain's rail system is desperately under-funded in comparison with most other EEC countries. The growth in road freight, the lack of public support for the railways and the insatiable demand for new roads have left our railways in a powerless state and highly vulnerable to the current anti-railway ideological assault.

The major difference is that our government believes all public transport systems should be profitable, whereas our European colleagues believe that they should primarily provide a public service. In January 1990, after six years as Chairman of British Rail during which he had remained silent in public on these matters, Sir Robert Reid ripped the government's approach to pieces in a powerful valedictory speech.

But if it's government policy not to have a transport policy, then the same is even more true of the Department of Energy. Given the many problems we now face with both fossil fuels and nuclear power, you might think there would be unstinting enthusiasm for energy efficiency and renewable energy.

You would be wrong on both counts! The budget of the Energy Efficiency Office has been gradually reduced from £24 million in 1986 to £12 million in 1989, and it will stick at around this level in the early nineties. Important demonstration schemes have had to be run on a shoestring; grants and other support to local authorities to encourage energy efficiency and insulation schemes have been slashed, and one bright idea after another has been 'permanently filed'.

And when it comes to the development of renewables, what do we actually find? Cohorts of well-drilled energy bureaucrats wrapping up their indifference in layers of technical gobbledygook; chastened environmentalists who dare not wax too enthusiastic about renewables for fear of being dismissed as 'unworldly' in this ever so pragmatic world of ours; and a whole generation of cynical politicians who can only bolster up their rapidly fading nuclear hopes by taking the mickey out of renewable energy. How many Conservative

Listen to Sir Robert

THE BATTLE for industrial survival in the barrier-free Europe of the mid 1990s may well be won or lost by the quality of infrastructure. But it may already have been lost for Britain. While France and Germany have been laying imaginative foundations for motorways, cross-city rail links and a continent-wide network of high speed trains, Britain has made a virtue of containing public spending and removing subsidies from BR.

The emerging map of new high-speed rail links planned or built across Europe is an impressive spaghetti of interlocking routes from the South of Spain to the North of France where it grinds to a halt at Calais. A small dotted line from Dover to London is Britain's contribution – if ever we get round to raising enough money privately.

If the criteria the Government has forced on BR was applied to high speed railways on the continent, it is quite possible none of them would be built. But they know over there the incalculable advantage of a high speed transport infrastructure in attracting international investment and lowering industry's costs when the real battle for Europe commences. Lyon has been galvanised by its fast link running from Paris down to the Mediterranean. Where is the vision in Britain?

No one, except a few regional lobbies, seems to have considered seriously a direct high speed train linking the North of England to the Channel Tunnel – without which the rest of Britain could well become the peripheralised backyard of the expanding Common Market. Every time the expansion of the railway system is raised the answer is the same. It will be too expensive, or it won't be profitable to BR. Tell that to the French whose economic growth, thanks in no small part to public sector investment, is starting to overtake ours. We have a decade to make up. If we are not careful we will end up with the most profitable backyard railway in the world.

© **THE GUARDIAN EDITORIAL, 10.1.90**

Proportion of public transport costs met by subsidy – 1988/89

City	Percentage
Turin	75
Rome	76
Rotterdam	83.5
Amsterdam	78
Genoa	60
Seattle	76
Bordeaux	65
Miami	69
Los Angeles	56
Antwerp	60
Stockholm	61
Milan	65
Paris	53
London	22

JANE'S URBAN TRANSPORT SYSTEMS, 1989

Party politicians have you heard on radio and television cataloguing the dire environmental hazards of wind power in terms of unaesthetic eyesores and severe noise pollution!

It's hard to think of a more grievous and potentially disastrous failure of the imagination than our continuing rejection of renewable energy as the answer to at least some of our prayers. What is it that gets young science and engineering graduates all steamed up about nuclear power, but leaves them stone cold when it comes to renewables? Spending literally billions of pounds on the pursuit of quarks and the elusive 'Higgs particle' in large electron-positron collectors and super-conducting super-colliders is considered eminently rational; spending a few millions on small-scale development projects to test the viability of wave energy conversion devices is still thought to be dangerously eccentric.

At precisely the time when we need far-sighted and creative thinking about an appropriate energy strategy for the UK in the next century, we keep drawing a complete blank from both the Department of Energy and the Department of Transport. As far as they're concerned, the Greenhouse Effect might as well be a new method of propagating tomatoes!

So, what *should* be happening? Indeed, what *is* happening?

GETTING MORE FROM LESS

There's no particular mystery about an alternative energy strategy. It's based on two central principles. Firstly, we need to get more from less, both at the *supply* end (in our choice of different technologies for providing energy), and at the *demand* end (in the way we use that energy). Secondly, we have to ensure that we meet as high a percentage as possible of our energy needs through *renewable* resources.

It's all about efficiency, good housekeeping, cost-effectiveness, elimination of waste, value for money, durability, flexibility, diversity, and plain, old-fashioned thrift. Given the prevailing political rhetoric of the last decade, one may well wonder why such a strategy has been consistently neglected by one Secretary of State for Energy after another.

The extraordinary thing is that Britain is blessed with a greater diversity of energy supplies than any other European country. We not only have our own very considerable reserves of coal, oil and gas, but are well provided for in terms of

hydro-power, estuaries for tidal power, coastlines for wave power, and almost unlimited amounts of wind.

Drax power station, the most modern in Britain and the only one, as yet, to be fitted with flue-gas desulphurisation equipment.

What changes will allow us first to reduce carbon dioxide emissions by 20 per cent before 2005 (the target of the 1988 Changing the Atmosphere Conference in Toronto) and, secondly, over a much longer period of time, to halve the overall amount of energy we use, as suggested by the Brundtland Report, 'Our Common Future', in 1987?

However rapidly we move towards renewable energy sources, we will remain dependent on our fossil fuels, particularly coal, for a good few decades to come. We must therefore find ways of burning them more cleanly and more efficiently. Unfortunately, however, those two things don't always go hand in hand. For instance, in order to reduce emissions of sulphur dioxide and nitrogen oxides (which are very significant contributors to the problem of acid rain), the UK Government eventually fell in line with an EEC directive to fit anti-pollution equipment, known as flue-gas desulphurisation (FGD) units, to our largest coal-fired power stations. This is an immensely costly business; the first FGD unit is currently being installed at Drax, and will cost somewhere around £700 million. The entire FGD programme will cost at least two billion pounds. There's no real choice about this; we would end up paying an even higher price without making that investment now, simply through the damage caused by air pollution to lakes, rivers, forests,

33

buildings and human health.

But it's not just a question of money; FGD also requires a lot of energy and raw materials. The Drax B plant will reduce the efficiency of the power station itself by around 2 per cent, thus adding significantly to the amount of carbon dioxide put into the atmosphere every year. Beyond that, each year it will gobble up 300 000 tonnes of limestone, which has to be mined and transported to Drax, and will produce 500 000 tonnes of gypsum as a by-product. Environmentally speaking, the whole process leaves a lot to be desired.

And in the end, the average conversion efficiency of the Drax B power station remains a paltry 35 per cent (meaning that only 35 per cent of the total energy available in the coal is converted into electricity; the rest disappears as waste heat up the global chimney). It's this chronic wastage which remains the most worrying aspect of our current coal-burning power stations, and already makes Drax B (completed in 1985) look like a technological dinosaur.

The coal generation technologies of the future will be much more specifically geared to raising conversion efficiencies. The first challenge is to reduce the emissions of sulphur dioxide and nitrogen oxides during the generation process itself, rather than having to strip them out later with an add-on unit. A technique known as 'fluidised bed combustion' operates at temperatures several hundred degrees lower than a normal boiler, which dramatically reduces the formation of nitrogen oxide. If limestone is added at the same time, 90 per cent of the sulphur in coal can be trapped *before* being released up the chimney. More than 300 such plants are already in operation in the Western world.

Even greater efficiencies (of around 50 per cent) can be achieved by 'combined cycle' technologies, where gas turbines and steam turbines are used in tandem. Gas-fired combined cycle plants and coal gasification plants are currently attracting a lot of attention, and will undoubtedly contribute very significantly to our energy needs in the next century.

By far the best way of raising conversion efficiencies is through using the waste heat which is otherwise rejected in the process of generating electricity: Combined Heat and Power (CHP). CHP schemes can either be very large or very small; they can use coal, gas, industrial or domestic waste as their basic fuel. They're flexible, reliable and cost-effective, and offer the single most important answer to getting us out of the Greenhouse. It really is one of the great scandals of UK energy policy that CHP is still relatively undeveloped in this country, despite endless worthy reports and more than 40 years of operating experience abroad.

Large CHP schemes (often known as District Heating schemes) can provide heat for a whole community. We visited a typical example of one of these, at Vasteras, one hundred miles west of Stockholm, where more than 100 000 people have their homes heated by the hot water from the power station. Literally hundreds of towns and cities in Europe are linked up to such schemes. Eighty per cent of homes in Helsinki (a city about the size of Portsmouth or Leicester) are heated in this way. But in the UK, only Sheffield has got to the point of introducing a scheme on this scale.

Smaller CHP schemes (mostly using gas-fired turbines, either for industrial or domestic purposes) are easy to introduce and much easier to finance. In Holland, there are an estimated

COMBINED HEAT AND POWER

IN BRITAIN over 90% of the electricity used is generated using steam turbines. These work just like a windmill contained in a barrel. Water is boiled in large boilers and the resulting high-temperature steam is forced through the barrel to turn the blades of the turbine. The turbine then turns a generator to make electricity.

But the trouble with this is that the laws of physics only allow at most 40% of the energy in the steam to be converted into electricity. The rest of the energy goes to waste. This is because the steam is cooled down and turned into water before being turned back into steam in the boilers and forced through the turbines again. This cooling process uses another lot of water; sometimes river water or sea water is used and discarded and sometimes the cooling water is reused, dispersing the waste heat to the atmosphere using giant cooling towers.

But Combined Heat and Power uses most of this waste heat. There is a small sacrifice in electricity production so that the steam that comes out of the end of the turbines is still hot enough to provide district heating, but in the end 80 per cent of the energy in the power station fuel can be used – twice as much as in conventional power stations!

So the power station cooling water becomes the district heating water, which is circulated under the streets of the neighbourhoods around the power station to provide the surrounding buildings with cheap central heating. And all that wasted energy is saved!

© POPULAR PLANNING UNIT, GLC, JANUARY 1986

800 mini-CHP schemes in operation; it has become standard practice for energy utilities to install and maintain such schemes in private buildings, then sell the heat direct to the owners. Such schemes are almost three times as efficient as conventional power stations, can produce power at about two-thirds of the cost, and can be installed in a fraction of the time. Invested capital is paid back in three to five years.

With the right kind of political backing, implementation could proceed much faster than people generally assume in the UK, and literally thousands of schools, hospitals, residential homes, barracks, prisons, leisure centres, high-rise flats, offices and factories could benefit as a result.

Underlying all this technological promise is the idea of getting more out of each unit of energy we feed into the system. And it's quite clear that this can best be done in much smaller plants than those we've depended on up until now. Such plants can be ordered, built and brought into service in three to four years. Large coal-fired plants can take up to ten years, and nuclear power stations even longer. Smaller plants are easier to site, and easier for people to accept as 'good neighbours', even in urban areas. They're more reliable, and more easily backed up in the event of failure.

This Government has always emphasised the importance both of 'security of supply' and of diversity. Ghosts of the miners' strike still stalk the corridors of the Department of Energy, and many people feel deeply uneasy at the notion of being 'held to ransom' by the power workers or miners. But how utterly bizarre to suppose that we would be any more 'secure' with ever larger amounts of our electricity being generated by nuclear power or in huge coal-fired power stations. Real security of supply will only come through the decentralisation of energy production systems, and the development of different generating technologies, using different fuels.

IN PURSUIT OF EFFICIENCY

So far, so good. By introducing these technologies, we will move some way towards achieving the goal of getting more from less, by converting far more of the available energy into usable energy in a clean and cost-effective way. But that's only half the problem: if we don't then use that delivered

energy as efficiently as possible, all the efforts of those
generating it on our behalf will be wasted. For example, heat
and electricity from the Vasteras power station we visited in
Sweden *could* go straight into poorly insulated, badly built
houses or flats, in which irresponsible, profligate wastrels left
the lights on and the windows open, used electric toothbrushes
and automatically turned up the thermostat instead of putting
on another layer of clothing.

Whole forests have been chopped down to produce books
and pamphlets extolling the benefits of energy efficiency. The
Department of Energy itself has produced more than its fair
share of these. But the reality is a little different: as we've seen,
the Energy Efficiency Office within the Department of Energy
has suffered death by a thousand cuts since the day it was
launched.

It's a lamentable state of affairs. In November 1989, I spent
a day at the Annual Conference of the Energy Systems Trade
Association. I was appalled at the banal and complacent
opening address by a government minister, but even more
appalled at the horror stories of reactionary, narrow-minded
companies with which the delegates regaled me during the
rest of the day. Even when presented with energy-saving
schemes that averaged 20 per cent savings in electrical energy
costs, with a pay-back on capital invested well within two
years, and sometimes within 12 months, many companies
have still preferred to stick in their energy-gobbling rut. It's
not the engineers employed by those companies who must
carry the can for this, but their senior management, who still
haven't got the basic intelligence to see that energy efficiency
is worthwhile both in the short term and as a strategic
objective.

Again, there's no magical mystery to achieving higher levels
of energy efficiency. It has been *proved* time after time that it
benefits not only the environment, but both industry and the
consumer. The market just needs a helping hand from
government to get things rolling. And if it can be done in the
United States, why can't it be done in the UK? The National
Appliances Conservation Act, signed into law by President
Reagan in March 1987, will outlaw by 1992 roughly 80 per
cent of the household appliances that were available in shops
in 1986. This one measure will save more than 70 million
tonnes of carbon dioxide emissions by 2010. Friends of the

37

Earth has proposed a similar measure for the United Kingdom, to force manufacturers to improve the energy efficiency of their products by an average of 30 per cent, setting minimum efficiency standards for the entire market. Such a measure would be accompanied by a comprehensive scheme for labelling all appliances to show their efficiency level.

Any talk of such intervention being 'contrary to the workings of the free market' is just so much claptrap. The market has always been regulated to ensure standards of safety, hygiene and fair competition. Carbon dioxide emissions are the single greatest threat to human wellbeing (let alone to the rest of life on Earth), and for Government not to intervene where it's fair, reasonable and cost-effective so to do is just an abdication of its responsibility to govern.

The same applies to UK Building Regulations. New regulations introduced in April 1990 will, in theory, improve energy performance by 20 per cent. The astonishing thing is that they will only bring the United Kingdom up to the standard achieved by Sweden back in 1930!

Until recently, even these small improvements were fought every inch of the way by the building trade. Roger Humber, erstwhile director of the House Builders Federation, will go down in history for one of the most revealing remarks of 1989: 'what's the point of bringing in regulations to keep the heat in, when it's heating up outside anyway?' (reported in *Building*, 27 January 1989).

Half the problem with energy efficiency in the UK is due to this sort of psychological blockage; too many people have linked it with ecological martyrdom or DIY fanaticism, even when the financial rewards are quite apparent. But, again, things are beginning to change. The pioneering work on energy-efficient housing done by Milton Keynes is at last being taken up by major housebuilders. In November 1989, both Barratt and Wimpey unveiled prototype energy-efficient homes which go well beyond the current Building Regulations. They've still not had the courage to incorporate design features based on passive solar energy, such as south-facing double-glazed windows and solar panels, but it's a start.

The National Energy foundation, based at Milton Keynes, is launching a new Energy Rating Scheme in 1990 to promote 'efficiency labelling' for houses, so that owners can have their homes rated on a scale of one to ten. If an EEC directive currently under consideration is eventually accepted by the UK, sellers will be obliged to show the report and the rating to prospective buyers.

But once we've overcome such psychological obstacles, the structure of the industry itself will pose a problem. Even when it's privatised, it still won't be possible for the Area Boards to invest properly in energy efficiency – their job will still be to sell as much electricity as they possibly can, because selling less will mean undermining their own profitability.

There's an easy way round this, and it's been practised in the United States for many years under the name of Contract Energy Management. Under the 1989 Electricity Act, the obligation to 'keep the lights on' will move to the Area Boards. As their licence to supply currently stands, they will have to do this by contracting for the most economic sources of electricity *supply* available. However, there are at least two different ways of 'keeping the lights on', and meeting customer demand for electrical services.

For example, if a customer wants the lighting output of a 60 watt incandescent light bulb, an Area Board can either: contract for 60 watts of supply from a generating company; or contract for 10 watts of supply and install a low-energy light bulb, that will, for 10 watts, provide the same quality of lighting as the standard 60 watt bulb. In both cases, customer demand for the lighting is met, but in the second instance there will be about 80 per cent less electricity needed, and therefore an 80 per cent reduction in associated pollution.

To meet customer demand, Area Boards could theoretically choose either contracts for electricity *supply* or contracts for electricity *savings*. The former would come from one of the two generating companies; the latter would come from a Contract Energy Management Company who would guarantee reductions in electricity demand through improved efficiency of electricity use

However, the Area Boards' licence currently prevents them from passing through any of the costs involved in such energy-saving contracts. The only costs that can be fed into their price formula relate to energy supply. Changing the licence so that the costs of energy saving can actually be 'passed through' in people's bills would obviously provide the Area Boards with an opportunity to operate in a more environmentally sensitive manner *without* compromising their commercial viability.

Please note, there is no element of compulsion or obligation here – just an opportunity. It is, in essence, a classic market mechanism: the consumer benefits (through reduced bills), the Area Boards benefit (through lower costs), and the environment benefits (through less pollution) – all done, without any green sleight of hand – according to traditional market economics. It may indeed sound odd, but under such a system it genuinely will pay the Area Boards to give away, for free, energy-efficient light bulbs, loft insulation, energy control systems and so on.

Nor is the usefulness of all these efficiency ideas confined to the developed world, as explained by Amory Lovins in one of his 1989 Newsletters from the Rocky Mountain Institute:

> 66 *Far from retarding development, energy efficiency may prove to be the biggest key to advancing progress in poor countries. If developing countries continue to squander much of their capital on supplying more energy to be inefficiently used, they won't have the money left to buy the things that were supposed to use the energy in the first place. Conversely, energy efficiency can free up enormous sums of money to finance development's essential tasks.*
>
> *Today, the average poor country is nearly three times less energy-efficient than the average rich country, which in turn can cost-effectively quadruple (or more) its efficiency. Therefore, if poor countries 'did it right the first time'– if they leapfrogged over the rich countries' mistakes, straight to the most resource-efficient infrastructure – they could, in principle, expand their economies by about tenfold with no increase in energy use.*
>
> *One caveat, however, must be noted: to abate global warming as quickly as possible, rich and poor nations alike must pursue the best buys first – what utility planners call a 'least-cost' investment strategy. Why? Because if we buy a costly remedy (little effect per dollar) before a cheap one (big effect per dollar), we get less remedy per dollar than if we did the cheaper thing first.* 99

THE CASE FOR RENEWABLE ENERGY

So, we know that we can burn our fossil fuels far more efficiently and cleanly than we currently do. But even at maximum efficiency, we will still be working our way through a strictly finite resource; and even at their cleanest, fossil fuels remain highly polluting, particularly in their contribution to global warming.

We also know that we can actually use the delivered energy from these sources far more efficiently than we do now. But even at maximum efficiency, we will still require an enormous amount of energy to provide us with the goods, services and quality of life that we demand.

As we will discover later in this book, it is perfectly possible to achieve a very high quality of life without becoming dependent on permanently expanding or replacing the goods we require. But even when we've tamed the monsters of built-in-obsolescence and compulsive consumerism, we will continue to require an extensive range of goods and services to meet our needs. In short, however green we may become, we're still going to need bags of energy. The *only* way to meet that demand, in a non-polluting and genuinely sustainable way, is through tapping into the many different varieties of renewable energy.

Jimmy Carter once referred to the energy crisis as the 'moral equivalent of war'. Any world leaders worth their salt (particularly if they happen to be scientists) would already be planning for a very different kind of future. Looking ahead to the year 2025, when the oil begins to run out and sea levels begin to rise, they would surely conclude that the greater the proportion of our energy needs that can be provided for by renewables, the better off we would be. They would then presumably decide, at a stroke, to do for renewables what the post-war politicians, for very different reasons, did for nuclear power: direct the necessary human and financial resources into research and development programmes with the best chance of coming up with the answers, not tomorrow or even the day after, but between now and that not so distant crunch point in the next century.

At the very worst, large sums of money would be wasted on technologies that simply couldn't be made to work or proved to be too expensive (like a re-run of our prolonged experiment with nuclear power!). But at least no one would be killed, and very little pollution would be caused. At the very best, internationally coordinated development programmes over the next 30 years would crack the outstanding technological problems, and provide humankind with unlimited, non-polluting sources of energy from then on.

41

We have only our pride and our little boys' delight in Earth-conquering technologies to lose; but, for some, that's clearly too high a price to pay.

Britain is of course singularly blessed by an enormous variety of potential sources of renewable energy: wind, wave, tidal and geothermal power are all particularly strong contenders. So let's just dream for a moment, and imagine that we are indeed ruled by wise and far-seeing politicians who decide, for environmental, economic and strategic reasons, that the UK should aim, just for starters, to meet 20 per cent of its primary energy needs in 2025 from renewable sources. (Such sources currently provide around 2 per cent of our energy, mostly from hydro-power schemes.) How might we set about achieving this target, in ten easy steps?

1   Set up a new Renewable Energy Authority and attract the best brains in the business from all over the world.

(At the moment, the development of renewable energy is in the hands of the Energy Technology Support Unit which is somewhat whimsically located within the Atomic Energy Authority. Critics have compared this to putting Count Dracula in charge of our blood banks!)

2   Totally reverse the balance of the existing research and development budgets between nuclear power (around £165 million) and renewables (around £12 million).

(Because these are wise and far-seeing politicians, they would still continue with a minimal research programme for nuclear power. No one has the right to slam the door permanently on a possible energy source for the future. And who's to say that in the twenty-second century our chastened nuclear boffins might not eventually come up with a reactor design that is fool-proof, bomb-proof, economically competitive, with no waste problems, and incapable of being abused for military purposes?)

3   Gradually phase in a pollution tax on all fossil fuels so as to ensure that the price of the energy generated from them properly reflects the environmental costs involved – in terms of acid rain, carbon dioxide and waste disposal.

(This classic market mechanism would greatly boost the development of renewables, allowing them to compete on what economists refer to as a 'level playing field'.)

What is Renewable Energy?

THE SUN'S energy maintains the temperature of the earth, enabling plants and animals to thrive. Without this continual input of energy, surface temperatures would plummet and the planet become a barren and inhospitable wasteland.

1 SUNLIGHT

The sun is a massive nuclear furnace radiating energy into space. One thousandth of a millionth of the sun's output of energy is intercepted by the earth. About 30 per cent of this energy is reflected back into space. The rest is absorbed by atmosphere, land, and oceans, or in evaporation, convection and precipitation of water.

2 WIND AND WAVES

The energy in wind and waves is also solar energy. Heating the earth's surface causes high and low air pressures and makes air move. The wind whips up the seas into waves. The energy that rustles leaves on trees – and occasionally blows them over – is solar energy. So too is the energy of ocean waves crashing on the shore and sending sea spray flying.

3 THE TIDES

The rise and fall of the tides follows a regular and entirely predictable pattern. The tidal range is relatively small in mid ocean, but a continental shelf, or the funnelling effect of bays, estuaries and straits that impede the tidal flow, amplifies its effects. Where the range is big enough, energy can be extracted using turbines mounted in a barrage.

4 BIOMASS

Material from living things, called 'biomass', stores solar energy. The sun's energy is used by trees and other green plants to manufacture simple sugars and convert these into more complex organic molecules like cellulose and lignin. When fuelwood is burnt for heat and light, the sun's energy is released. Likewise, food 'burnt' in our bodies is converted into heat and mechanical work. We too are powered by solar energy.

5 RUNNING WATER

The sun evaporates water from oceans, lakes and rivers and carries the vapour up and over the land. Cooling leads to condensation – rain and snow to feed mountain streams and replenish the earth.

The sun in effect 'lifts' the water from the sea and deposits it on higher ground. The energy it acquires is exploited by hydro-electric installations. As the water falls back to sea it can turn a turbine and generate electricity.

6 GEOTHERMAL HEAT

Geothermal heat comes from the earth's core and is enhanced in places by heat from the decay of naturally occurring radioactive elements which are present in the rock. It can be extracted either by drilling into natural aquifers and pumping out the geothermally heated water, or by forcing water under pressure through rock that has been deliberately fractured at depth.

THE CHALLENGE

The incoming solar energy absorbed by the earth in one year is equivalent to 15 to 20 times the energy stored in all of the world's reserves of recoverable fossil fuels. If just 0.005 per cent of this solar energy could be captured with fuel crops, specially designed buildings, wind and water turbines, solar collectors, wave energy converters and the like, it would supply more useful energy in a year than we get from burning coal, oil and gas. Unlike fossil fuels, renewable energy cannot be exhausted.

'ENERGY WITHOUT END',
© FRIENDS OF THE EARTH 1986

4 Initiate a massive wind energy programme, with a view to generating up to 20 per cent of our electricity from onshore wind generators by 2025. Simultaneously establish the first major UK offshore wind farm, in the North Sea, with a reasonable expectation of being able to generate more and more of our electricity in this way in the next century.

(Evidence from the Hinkley Point Enquiry and research by the British Wind Energy Research Association have established that this 20 per cent target is eminently achievable – and the wind generators wouldn't have to be sited in any of our most beautiful areas or on our highest

The winds of change

ON A wind-ravaged hill in north Cornwall, farmer Peter Edwards is laying plans to invest millions of pounds to take advantage of a government scheme to allow more renewable energy sources to contribute to the national grid.

Mr Edwards is hoping to put £3m into what will become England's largest private commercial wind farm. He would supply South West Electricity with power from 10 wind turbines in a contract which could earn him up to £600 000 a year.

The scheme is part of the Government's programme for reducing the emissions of greenhouse gases which contribute to global warming. The applications are being made to the electricity boards in England and Wales as part of their so-called Non-Fossil Fuel Obligation. Under this, the boards will have to buy 20 per cent of electricity from nuclear power or renewable sources. An estimated 18 per cent of the requirement will initially come from nuclear power, leaving only two per cent for the renewables.

However, the demise of nuclear and coal-fired power stations could boost the proportion of the UK's energy demand provided by renewables. The CEGB estimates that the alternative sources may provide eight per cent by 2005, rsing to 18 per cent by 2030.

© THE SUNDAY CORRESPONDENT 31.12.89

hills. But they would indeed be 'visually intrusive' for those who don't happen to find them rather beautiful, and they might well make a little bit of noise. Nor should we only concentrate on large-scale arrays of wind turbines. Small-scale, stand-alone generators could prove immensely useful.)

5 Commission a tidal barrage (with financial support from the Government) across the Mersey, to come onstream before the year 2000, and complete a detailed feasibility study on all the other potential sites in the UK for similar barrages: Morecambe Bay, the Solway Firth, the Wash, the Dee, the Humber and the Severn.

(*Some people might also be inclined to incur the terrible wrath of the Royal Society for the Protection of Birds, and Friends of the Earth, by commissioning the Severn barrage, which on its own would provide 8 per cent of our electricity. Sooner or later, environmentalists are going to have to make a straight choice between another nuclear reactor, an extra 11 million tonnes of carbon dioxide going up into the atmosphere every year from a new coal-fired power station, or the possible loss of a few wintering sites for wild fowl. I know which way I'll be voting!*)

6 Provide generous incentives to promote 'energy from waste' schemes, ensuring that we burn as much as possible of our domestic waste in state-of-the-art incinerators, either to generate electricity or to provide heat, and retrieve as much methane gas as possible from our landfill sites.

(*The Department of Energy estimates that up to 10 per cent of our current primary energy use could be met by converting our wastes into wealth in this way. Given the right technologies, it makes enormous sense, both economically and ecologically. In Sweden, half their domestic waste is burned in 25 large incinerators, operating under very strict emission standards.*)

7 Provide similar incentives to make maximum use of potential 'bio-fuels': agricultural wastes can be treated in specially designed digestors to generate gas that could be used for heat or electricity; straw and forestry wastes can be burned in specially designed furnaces, and 'surplus agricultural land' could be planted with fast-growing trees specifically for energy use.

(This may sound humdrum to our high-tech freaks hunting down their quarks, but it's worth bearing in mind that the United States already derives more energy from firewood (approximately 4 per cent) than it does from its entire nuclear programme. And there's nothing low-tech about this either; fulfilling the potential of bio-fuels will require the application of the highest possible engineering and scientific skills.)

8 Instantly restore funding to our wave power programme. Start investing immediately in small, shore-based wave energy stations such as the Oscillating Water Column, that has already been successfully developed in Norway. In the longer term, offshore deep-water wave energy is an immensely exciting prospect, and we should aim to have several large scale prototypes in operation within the course of the next decade.

(Britain's wave power programme led the world until the end of the seventies, when it was done for by a combination of government indifference and nuclear skullduggery. The potential of wave power is currently being re-examined by the Department of Energy.)

9 Increase funding for our geothermal research programme. Although it's unlikely that much will come of this until well into the next century, the potential for small geothermal schemes is considerable.

10 Aim to achieve a target of 5 million passive solar installations (involving roughly a quarter of current UK housing stock) and at least 5 million solar water heaters – bearing in mind that Japan already has more than $3\frac{1}{2}$ million of them. Set up a special team to conduct further research into the development and application of solar cells with a view to reducing their cost from $5 per watt to $1 per watt, at which point they will be in direct competition with electricity from the grid.

(Solar cells are already a highly economical electricity source for Third World villages, and a far higher proportion of their needs will certainly be met from this source in the next century. Indeed, it's clear that a large proportion of the energy needs in the Third World can only be met from this and other renewable sources.)

As an afterthought, I hope these wise and far-seeing politicians will also set up a special Renewable Energy Export

Agency, not only to recoup some of the considerable cost entailed in this kind of development programme, through massive export sales, but also to ensure that the benefits of these renewable technologies are shared as widely as possible with developing countries.

This is of particular importance when considering the future of photovoltaics, or solar cells. Huge progress has been made since the mid-seventies, with costs steadily falling and efficiency steadily improving. One major difficulty arises out of the need to store the electricity generated by the cells, and without some breakthrough on storage technologies (perhaps involving high-temperature superconductors?), photovoltaics are never likely to achieve their full potential. But I still believe this *has* to be the single most important technology of the future, simply because of its flexibility, its ease of maintenance and unparalleled environmental benefits.

These ten measures would *not* solve all our problems. All energy strategies entail considerable environmental and social costs, on top of their economic cost, and all we can do is to balance the relative costs of different options against their relative benefits. The longer the timescale over which one can make such comparisons, the more useful they will be. But they will ensure a far safer, more sustainable future than that which currently confronts us.

BEYOND THE MOTOR CAR

Bringing this kind of long-term outlook to bear on the short-

Lyckebo solar district heating plant near Uppsala, Sweden. High-efficiency flat plate solar collectors in a forest clearing supply heat to a rock cavern heat store, meeting part of the space- and water-heating requirements of a small community. Lyckebo is on roughly the same latitude as Lerwick in the Shetland Isles.

term perspectives of politicians, struggling to make sense of things on a day-to-day basis, has always been one of the biggest challenges for environmentalists. Expediency and electoral self-interest are incredibly powerful factors, and the temptation to put off decisions which are clearly necessary in the long term, but may be painful and unpopular in the short term, is overwhelming.

How many politicians have had the courage or the vision, for instance, to stand up and say that UK transport policy should now be geared quite specifically to making our city centres entirely car-free by 2010, and *halving* the number of cars on our roads by 2025? Yet something of that order will certainly be required, both socially and economically, if we're to make any kind of contribution to reducing our emissions of greenhouse gases and air pollution.

Given the crucial role which the car industry plays in our economy, it's perhaps hardly surprising that no one is seriously talking about life after the motor car. Our growing awareness of global warming has merely sharpened the debate on how to make the motor car more environment friendly. Using unleaded petrol is now seen as just the start of cleaning up our automotive act; from now on, more and more cars will be using catalytic converters, which will eliminate up to 90 per cent of pollutants such as hydrocarbons and nitrogen oxides.

But catalytic converters will still do nothing whatsoever to reduce carbon dioxide emissions. Indeed, they may marginally increase carbon dioxide if the fuel efficiency of the car is in any way impaired. So the next step is to increase fuel efficiency. Various prototypes currently being developed by Peugeot, Renault, Volkswagen, Toyota and Volvo are achieving anything between 75 to 120 mpg as opposed to current averages of around 20 mpg in the United States and not much better in Europe. So called 'lean-burn' engines (both petrol and diesel); the development of gas turbines; the introduction of ceramic components: all these will play an important part in engine design during the nineties.

Further improvements in efficiency can be achieved by increasing the average number of passengers carried in each car on regular journeys. But even if we succeed in doubling fuel efficiency over the next 15 years by these means, if we simultaneously double the number of cars, then the net

47

Electric cars 'may increase power station emissions'

WIDESPREAD use of electric cars could increase pollution from power stations, even if they reduce emissions on the roads, scientists have warned. They say it is misleading to dub battery-operated cars 'pollution-free'.

They say that, even if electric cars do not pour out the hydrocarbons and carbon monoxide of their petrol-burning counterparts, they will, in the UK at least, exacerbate the emissions of carbon and sulphur into the atmosphere. The problem is that frequent recharging of the batteries would increase demand on the national grid.

This week, General Motors unveiled a prototype battery-operated car which accelerates from 0 to 60 mph in eight seconds. But Roger Smith, president of the American firm, warned that a clean source of primary power was needed to realise its ecological advantages. 'If we try to do it all by using fossil fuels, we will be back at square one,' he said.

© THE INDEPENDENT 6.1.90

environmental benefit in terms of carbon dioxide reduction is absolutely zero.

Hence the increasingly enthusiastic search for alternatives to oil as the main automotive fuel. The main contenders here are the alcohol-based fuels, ethanol and methanol, from agricultural crops or wastes, and natural gas. By virtue of spending around $8 billion on a programme to produce methanol from sugar, Brazil succeeded in reducing oil imports by 60 per cent between 1979 and 1986. Despite considerable problems with the Brazilian scheme (not least a terrible shortage of methanol in 1989 and 1990, caused by sugar cane growers going back to producing sugar instead of alcohol because they could get more money for it!) many other countries are now introducing blends of alcohol and lead-free petrol, with much of the alcohol coming from surplus grain.

In March 1989, the South Coast Air Quality Management District (covering the Los Angeles area) published a three-phase plan to eliminate all vehicles using petrol or diesel by 2007. Free parking will be abolished, and a limit will be set on the number of cars per family. All business, rental and government car fleets will have to switch to methanol by 1992. It would seem that the Californian love affair with the car is coming to a sorry end; despite the strictest emission controls anywhere in the world (imposed way back in the early seventies), their smog-prone geography has done for them and their seven million vehicles. Smarting eyes and over-burdened lungs tell them that they've got no choice.

But there are several problems with alcohol-based alternatives. Vast amounts of land are required to substitute for any significant proportion of current petrol consumption. The World Watch Institute has calculated that up to 40 per cent of the entire United States corn harvest would have to be earmarked for ethanol production in order to meet just *10 per cent* of current fuel demand.

The next pipe dream down the road is to make all our vehicles battery-powered (see box). It takes a while to persuade enthusiasts that this makes no difference whatsoever if the electricity to recharge the batteries is generated from nuclear power or fossil fuels! Electric cars would therefore have to be powered by the sun (using photovoltaic cells), or by fuel cells (which convert the chemical energy in a fuel like methanol directly into electrical energy). A methanol-based fuel cell for

48

cars is currently being developed by General Motors.

Lastly, there's the hydrogen car. Hydrogen can be produced by passing an electric current through water (at present the cost makes this totally impractical), and when burned in a mixture of air (as with petrol), produces water vapour plus very small traces of oxides of nitrogen. Both BMW and Mercedes Benz have hydrogen-fuelled versions of some of their existing models, and both believe that it will be possible to solve the difficult problems of storage and safety. But they still reckon it will take another 40 years to develop the technology commercially.

Even if we let our technological dreams go all the way down that particular road (and some people do not restrict their dreams to the road, but are even now planning for their cars to take to the air!), the uncomfortable truth is that *no* car, however efficiently it uses the cleanest of fuels, can be described as environment-friendly, simply because of the energy and raw materials needed to produce it, the roads it requires, and the vast infrastructure of garages and depots necessary to keep it on the road. In January 1990, BMW announced that it was to build a 'car recycling plant' and, together with other manufacturers, is already researching the use of plastics suitable for recycling. Such an advance would clearly help, but it would *not* solve the basic problem.

The only solution over the next couple of decades is to build up our public transport systems, both within and between cities. We've all heard this a thousand times before, but one has to keep on saying it for the message still hasn't got through to the likes of Cecil Parkinson, who claimed at the end of 1989 that, 'public transport improvements are unlikely to achieve a major reduction in road traffic and congestion'.

Little wonder that Mr Parkinson continues to reduce the level of support for British Rail (from more than £1 billion in 1983 to well under £500 million by 1992), and little wonder that the UK will be left on the sidelines yet again as the rest of Europe signs up for the impending revolution in high-speed trains and in new rapid transit and light rail systems. Continental-style trams *are* being actively promoted in Bristol, Southampton, Sheffield, Leeds and Manchester to provide a high-quality commuter service, but in comparison to many other European countries, Britain's public transport services still look like museum exhibits.

49

Always jam tomorrow

IN COPENHAGEN there is a bicycle shop with an intriguing sign displayed in the window: 'We will accept your car as partial downpayment on your new bike.'

While it would be wrong to see the Copenhagen shop window as heralding a revolution in modern transport by persuading people to switch from car to bike, the sign illustrates how the Danes have been joining most other European nations in tackling the mounting transport problems before they cripple their capital cities.

Denmark is broadly typical of a European country seeking to improve the daily movement of people by restricting the use of private cars, encouraging the use of bicycles and turning over large numbers of roads to pedestrians.

Other nations are pouring growing sums into new railways and light railways, developing tramways, closing car parks and abandoning inner city road building schemes.

The contrast with Britain could not be starker, with roads reaching bursting point, the London Underground and British Rail commuter trains alarmingly congested, government money being drained out of the public transport system and huge sums being lined up for massive new road-building projects.

The key difference in approach is that most European nations have a clear national policy for transport which recognises the critical importance that it plays in the quality of life and economic well-being – and establishes priorities to meet those hopes. In addition to the national policy, major cities in Europe have their own transport authority to handle the demands of their major cities.

Britain is alone in Western Europe in not possessing a coherent national policy for transport and in not having an established authority with responsibility for the specific transport problems of its capital city. Britain, alone of the countries in Western Europe, relies on market forces to establish transport priorities.

By contrast, the major cities of Europe are planning on a larger scale than ever before. In Paris, for example, the Mayor, Jacques Chirac, has ordered the cancellation of more than 100 000 parking spaces in an attempt to curb the use of the private car. Chirac's plan is that 200 miles of road in the city centre will be declared a red zone where parking is forbidden.

The extra space will be used for public transport lanes and pedestrian areas, and those caught parking could lose their licences for a short period.

In Italy many older cities, such as Florence, have introduced restrictions on private cars, while Bologna, one of the first European cities to introduce free public transport, is continually restricting the movement of private cars and developing public transport, including trolley buses.

In Geneva, the authorities are increasing the pedestrianisation of the city and seeking to control cars by insisting that parking space should be prohibited at places of work in the city centre.

Stockholm is proposing a form of road pricing in which motorists pay a fee of around £10 for an electronic identification plate which progressively reduces in value like a phone card. An electronic cordon around the city, with 32 control points, would trigger the ID plate to begin deducting the cost of each journey into the controlled zone during the hours between 6 am and 6 pm, Monday to Friday.

A similar electronic cordon is being proposed for Oslo, which would operate 24 hours a day, seven days a week and is expected to 'tag' about 40 per cent of all city centre journeys.

Such measures seem a long way off as far as London's hardpressed commuters are concerned.

Cecil Parkinson, the seventh Transport Secretary in 10 years, may have to do a lot more than leave the chaos to be solved by market forces alone.

© MICK SMITH,
THE GUARDIAN 23.10.89

With massive public investment, there's little doubt that we could end up with the kind of integrated public transport system that all members of the travelling public dream of. But even that's not necessarily green. We must go one stage further and ask: are all those journeys necessary?

The greater the number of people who have to be conveyed on a regular basis from where they live to where they work, the greater the environmental damage. Even trains, buses and trams gobble up energy and raw materials. Our long-term goal (which is dealt with again in Chapter 4) must therefore be to ensure that as many people as possible live and work within walking or cycling distance, or at least within reach of a local public transport system. No more commuting!

ADJUSTING TO THE REAL WORLD

As yet, there isn't even the vaguest glimmering of this kind of approach among the manic motoring enthusiasts at the Department of Transport. But global warming may just provide the spur which even that Department cannot ignore. There seems to be little doubt that the Government's White Paper on the environment (due at the end of 1990) will recommend measures to increase the cost of energy supplies. Plans are being actively considered to impose VAT on gas and electricity prices, as already happens in most other EEC countries. (Typically, *we* only impose VAT on energy-saving equipment and insulation materials!) Beyond that, both Chris Patten and John Wakeham have already suggested that we may need an energy tax to generate new revenue to pay for anti-pollution measures, and that the price of energy must rise simply to reflect the true cost involved in its generation and use.

In the first few months of 1990, the Institute for Fiscal Studies, the Liberal Democrats (in a new policy paper), Mr Ripa di Meana (the EEC's Environment Commissioner) and even the International Energy Agency all expressed their support for steep taxes on fossil fuels. New proposals to use such a 'carbon tax' to raise funds for rainforest protection (i.e. northern countries agreeing to pay rainforest countries to 'import' their carbon dioxide emissions by keeping the forests intact) were also widely discussed.

51

The Institute of European Environmental Policy has mapped out some of the benefits that would result from high energy prices (by which they mean at least a tripling of existing prices):

1   Combined heat and power systems would be installed in virtually all cold and moderate climate cities.

2   Swedish standard heat insulation and heat exchange ventilation would be installed in nearly all homes and office buildings in cold and moderate climate areas.

3   Ninety per cent of long-distance cargo would be transported by rail; railways would develop a new generation of speedy freight terminals.

4   Seventy per cent of medium-distance passenger transport would be by rail; railways would have high-speed trains on all major routes.

5   Sixty per cent of daily commuters would use public transport systems, which would become more frequent and more comfortable.

6   There would be average energy efficiency increases of 50 per cent in machines, production processes and driving engines.

7   Products (including food) and services requiring high-energy inputs would virtually disappear from the market.

8   Aluminium, iron and a few other materials would reach a 90 per cent recycling rate; refuse releasing methane would be used to produce energy.

9   Windmills, hydro-power, bio-gas/heat pumps, passive solar, bio-fuel and geothermal energies would boom and reach 50 per cent of a shrunken energy market.

10   Energy efficiency and renewables would become favourite areas for research and development, both public and private.

Against these benefits (which would probably halve existing energy demand), one has to set major problems, not least for those industries whose business is dependent upon high energy consumption. Many jobs would almost certainly be lost but, equally, many new ones would be created.

The Age of the Tram

THE speed at which transport revolutions occur often baffles those caught up in them. The revolution brought by the steam engine and railways transformed the London of the 1840s and 50s. That of the electric tram, and the petrol engine and buses and cabs, rapidly replaced horse-drawn vehicles in inner London between 1901 and 1914. That of the car saw a quadrupling of ownership between 1949 and 1964.

We are now on the threshold of two major revolutions, the electronic revolution in control of vehicles and infrastructure, and the revolution in our appreciation of the use of space in the city.

The electronic revolution has been gathering pace for some time. Computer control of traffic lights has been with us since 1968, and has gradually become more sophisticated. It has just been announced that all London buses are now to be given priority when approaching traffic signals, by virtue of an electronic command. Automated railway lines are part of the Docklands Light Railway.

The other revolution is in the use of space. This is about to transform our cities. We have finally realised that people drive cars up to the point where their journey is as unattractive as the best alternative. For most people in the outer suburbs of London, most shorter journeys will continue to be more attractive by car, except perhaps to local centres. On the other hand, in central and inner London, individual automobiles do not and cannot use space efficiently.

A rapid transformation of our city streets will therefore happen by 2010, to remove the inefficient vehicles, cars, and replace them with the efficient: taxis (no parking problems), minibuses, buses and trams – yes, trams, the modern, smooth, comfortable trams seen all over Europe, are due to make a comeback. A number of cities in Britain are now in the process of re-introducing the tram: Manchester, Birmingham, Sheffield and Leeds among them. London will soon follow.

Moreover, the electronic revolution will make it easy to add on an electronic road-pricing system to increase the efficiency of the use of space, and generate extra money to pay for the changes.

Car users will be better off, because better public transport will improve the attractiveness of their journeys – only those who are prepared to pay for faster travel will pay: others will choose to travel by the better public transport and will still be better off than they were before. Freight movement will be faster, because the roads will be used more efficiently. Emergency services will be faster still, as they can use the lanes reserved for public transport. Walking will become a pleasure again, because roads in central London in key congested areas will be given over entirely to the pedestrian, with non-polluting trams the only public vehicles allowed; freight and emergency vehicles will be allowed on an access only basis.

With taxation switched from ownership to use, Londoners, in common with citizens of all the great world cities, will become more sparing with their personal automobiles. We won't recognise the London of 2010.

Amsterdam has one of the best integrated public transport networks anywhere in the world.

My main concern about these suggestions is that people would understandably feel pretty hostile about such a tax, as it would come on top of all our existing taxes. And that, in fact, is the clue to the most elegant, comprehensive and ecologically desirable solution of them all: the reform of the entire taxation system. This reform would mean gradually shifting the tax burden away from income tax, corporation tax, VAT and National Insurance, and on to the use of energy and raw materials. The aim would be to keep the tax burden more or less constant, both for individuals and industry.

This idea of a resource-based taxation system has hitherto been the exclusive preserve of one or two brave spirits, who have constantly seen it laughed out of court. The Odum brothers, Farel Bradbury and Professor Slesser (whose book, *Energy in the Economy*, is most helpful in this area) are just a few of those who remain utterly amazed at the way people so obstinately hang on to *money* as the main measure of all economic and social value. All consumption and economic activity is ultimately linked to energy, not money, and the measure which should matter to us above all others is the Primary Energy Content of any product or service. If sustainability really is the goal of our society in the future, then we have to find a way of viewing energy, not money, as the most significant indicator of economic activity.

Bradbury and Slesser advocate a single tax (UNITAX) to replace all other taxes. Primary energy would be taxed at the very few points where it enters the economy: oil companies, British Gas, British Coal, imported and domestically generated nuclear power, and independent generators (above a certain minimum size). The tax man would become all but redundant! Professor Slesser gives the following example of how it would work:

> 66 *Take 1984 as a typical year. From the Central Statistical Office we learn that the Government raised £123 billion in taxes with which to run the country. That's £2236 per capita average. To drive the economy, the UK used 6.64 billion Giga-joules (GJ) of primary energy, or 121 GJ per capita. (1 tonne of good coal has a heat content of about 28 GJ.)*
>
> *To raise the same revenue, the Government would have had to impose a UNITAX of £18.60 per GJ. It would make petrol (at present crude prices) £3.85 a gallon, and electricity 20 pence a unit.*

At first sight, one scarcely sees this tax being a popular measure! But consider what its effect would be:

– No income tax, no corporation tax, no VAT, no hydro-carbon duties, no national insurance payments.

– A reduction in the number of civil servants administering the tax, thus reducing government expenditure (it cost the government £1.4 billion to collect taxes in 1984).

– An incentive for energy conservation, making it an atractive investment both for the individual and the manufacturer.

– Pay As You Earn (PAYE) becomes Pay As You Use (PAYU).

The high tax on energy will substantially alter the emphasis from a society oriented towards careless consumption to one where resources are conserved and valued. It impinges most on the economically active section of the population. Those who consume contribute to the tax base; those who save or don't consume, do not. 🙾

I'm not mentioning this idea here because I see it as the answer to all our problems. Indeed, there are clearly difficulties with it. How would one protect the poor, who would suffer most under this tax? How would one favour renewables over carbon-based fuels? Wouldn't a government want to operate some taxes over and above UNITAX (for instance on tobacco, alcohol, pollution, etc)? How could one introduce such a tax on a European-wide basis?

But what interests me is why the debate about such an alternative is currently restricted to a few dozen academics. Quite simply, we've become so accustomed to the benefits of our wealth-creating juggernaut that we resent being asked to contemplate its costs. Until the end of the eighteenth century, when medical knowledge was able to demonstrate a clear link between alcohol consumption and gout, enthusiastic port-drinkers attributed their discomfort and pain to everything under the sun other than port! And, as we've seen with tobacco, even when people do know the likely consequences of a certain course of action, there's no guarantee that they will necessarily renounce it.

Ultimately, all these challenges boil down to what each and every individual expects of life. What is our unfettered entitlement? What constraints on our 'freedom of choice' are we prepared to accept? For all the optimism I feel when I look at what is technologically possible at this stage, let alone what will be possible in 20 years, it has to be said that this will count

What you can do

Check your loft has at least 6 inches of insulation and that hot water tanks and pipes are lagged.

Fit draught-proofing around door frames and badly fitting windows, and consider secondary glazing – as much as one quarter of a house's heat is lost through draughts.

Turn down central heating thermostats – a 1 per cent drop could lower your annual gas use by as much as 10 per cent.

Switch off lights when they are not needed. Buy energy-efficient light-bulbs – some use 80 per cent less energy.

Buying a new cooker, fridge or other electrical appliance? Ask about its energy efficiency.

Think about fitting a shower – they use half as much heated water than a bath.

When using the kettle, only boil the amount of water you actually need and save energy.

Walk, cycle or use public transport wherever you can.

Re-use and recycle items – the energy and resource savings can be high.

Write to your local MP supporting the move for a standard, easily understood label to indicate the energy efficiency of an appliance. This will allow you as the consumer to make informed choices.

© **Friends of the Earth, 1990**

for little unless prevailing attitudes and value systems undergo a profound transformation.

If we seriously believe that we have a basic right to go on consuming at current levels, albeit in a rather more environmentally sensitive way, then the long-threatened energy gap (where supply cannot meet demand) will become a reality – indeed, an inevitability. All pale green consumers (who have altered only the nature, but not the volume of their consumption) must then swallow hard and sign up with the likes of Walter Marshall and the Chairman of British Nuclear Fuels.

If we accept that we've been living off borrowed time and stolen resources, then we must accept the need for considerable changes in the way we measure wealth and set out to enjoy ourselves in life. Forget all those foreign holidays, the second car, the electric carving knives, and the complacent convenience of our unthinking, throw-away society. Some things *will* have to go.

But *not* our quality of life, our compassion for others, our responsibility for the Earth and for the future wellbeing of our children, or our ability to make the most of our full human potential. For the brave of heart, President Kennedy's message remains as relevant now as it was at the time: 'Some see the world as it is and ask "why?" I see the world as it could be, and ask "why not?"'

Chapter 3

THE FRUITS
OF THE
EARTH

THE LEGACY OF THE PAST

What's right for one generation can be very wrong for the
next. Farmers today confront an extraordinary dilemma: how
can it be that the work once held to be so urgent and valuable
(namely the business of producing more and more food) is
now condemned on all sides as wasteful and destructive? One
generation's hard-earned plenty has become another's
embarrassing folly – and the farmers feel they're now getting
it in the neck quite unfairly.

Farmers are of course renowned for their ability to talk up
a problem into a disaster, or a bad year into a permanent
catastrophe, but in this instance their warnings seem justified.
The level of farm debt has doubled in the last eight years, and
farm loans now exceed £6 billion. The labour force is
currently shrinking by about 9000 a year.

In 1964, there were 250 000 independently owned 'family
farms' of less than 40 hectares; there are now fewer than 120 000.
The average farm size in Britain is more than double

that of any other European country, and a smaller proportion of our workforce is involved in agriculture than anywhere else. There were roughly 750 000 farm workers after the Second World War; there are now around 110 000.

In an article in the *Observer*, Environment Correspondent Geoffrey Lean put these dramatic changes in context:

> 66 *Farmers have been the agents of these changes, but they are not primarily to blame for them. They have merely been responding to one of the most consistent and forceful of all government policies of the past four decades: to wrest as much food as possible from the limited terrain of the British Isles.*
>
> *The roots of the policy go deep, back to the darkest days of the Second World War, when U-boats threatened to cut off the country's food supply. The war followed more than half a century of agricultural depression, and a country that had once been virtually self-sufficient in wheat and flour now produced only a quarter of its needs. In all, Britain was importing two-thirds of its food.*
>
> *With peace came a justifiable determination never to be as vulnerable again. Money was poured into agriculture to boost production. Prices were guaranteed, and generous grants given.* 99

The turnaround has been astonishing. We are now self-sufficient in many areas of production, and the debate today is all about how much land is going to be 'surplus to requirements' over the next few years. Assuming that productivity continues to increase, and that demand for food rises steadily, up to 4 million hectares (nearly a quarter of our farming land) could come out of production between now and the end of the decade.

MORE AT ALL COSTS

Even if there is a substantial reduction in farming land, the future of the countryside will still depend primarily on farmers. They may no longer be the largest employers in rural areas, but farming is still the single largest contributor to economic vitality in those areas. Moreover, when environmentalists wax lyrical about 'the stewardship of the land', we would do well to remember that the vast majority of those stewards in the future will still be farmers. And if farmers are to continue to play that role, then they need to stay in business, and they need a reasonable, secure income.

That may sound self-evident. Yet current policy, whether explicitly or implicitly, seems to be geared to farming land coming *out* of production, and to more and more farmers going *out* of business. The reason for this is obvious: we're locked into a system which benefits a relatively small minority of farmers at the expense of the majority and at continuing cost to the land and the quality of our rural environment.

At its simplest, farmers have two fundamental responsibilities: firstly, to produce food; secondly, to protect and nurture the land. Before the Second World War they were pretty much one and the same thing, but in the headlong pursuit of agricultural self-sufficiency after the war the business of producing food increasingly came into conflict with the business of nurturing the land. Production inevitably took precedence over stewardship and short-term expediency triumphed over the interests of the future.

The Government's current approach formalises this divide in a 'dual-track strategy'. On the one hand, there is the 'fast track' with intensive modern farming, where the emphasis is on increased productivity, greater use of chemicals, larger average farm size, and more dependence on intensive livestock rearing. On the other hand, there is a much 'slower track', designed to compensate all those farmers who aren't 'economic' or 'competitive', those who've been progressively marginalised over the years.

From an environmental point of view, the fast track (which takes the lion's share of the £1.5 billion or so that goes into farming every year) is simply disastrous, leading to extremely serious habitat destruction, more and more farm pollution, and the growing problem of soil erosion – let alone horrors like bovine spongiform encephalopathy (BSE) or 'mad cow disease' as it's more commonly known.

BSE is a fatal brain disease in cows, which affects more than 3000 herds in Britain. In early 1990, about 150 cows a week were being destroyed. The disease was almost certainly transmitted from sheep (where it's known as 'scrapie'), via modern feeding methods which use the ground-up remains of other animals (including sheep) as a protein concentrate for cattle. The incubation period is about eight years.

In June 1989, the Minister of Agriculture banned the use of beef brains and offal in foodstuffs for humans but they are still being exported and used in feeds for pigs, poultry and pets.

59

ABOVE: BSE-infected cattle, slaughtered and burned.
OPPOSITE: In East Anglia, the fields are getting more like prairies each year.

The big question is whether BSE could be transmitted to humans from cows. The Southwood Committee described the risk as 'remote' in its report in February 1989, but the risk of the disease being transferred from sheep to cows was also dismissed as 'remote and theoretical' until 1986. Over the last decade, many farmers have felt deep misgivings about feeding the remains of other animals to herbivores, but the pressures of intensification (producing more at all costs as profitably as possible) are remorseless.

One of the most powerful intensifying tools in the future will be genetic engineering. Great things are promised with this new technology; terrible things are feared as a result of it. By 'splicing' combinations of genes that would never be found in nature, all sorts of things become possible. By the end of the decade, farmers will be bombarded with new hi-tech varieties of seeds with various special characteristics built in through the genetic engineering.

Many of these advances sound very benign, such as resistance to pests and boosters to increase soil fertility, but I remain deeply suspicious. The large chemical and oil companies which now dominate the field are unlikely to be motivated by altruism. One of their most important projects is to build in a resistance to pesticides (not to the pests themselves!) so that farmers can spray away to their heart's content knowing that the crop itself is genetically defended.

The destruction of the British countryside

IN THE past 40 years the English countryside has changed more than over the last 400. The change, as always, has come about at the hands of farmers.

The official statistics, intoned by such government bodies as the Countryside Commission and the Nature Conservancy Council, toll a mournful knell. Ninety-five per cent of Britain's traditional hay meadows, as immortalised by Constable, have been destroyed – half the remaining 5 per cent damaged. Ninety-nine per cent of the ecologically priceless lowland heaths have vanished, ploughed up or planted with conifers.

Since about 1940 Britain has lost four-fifths of its chalk downlands, once so studded with wild plants that 30 different species could easily be found in a single square yard. Four-fifths of the limestone grasslands, once typical of the North Country, have also been destroyed in the same period. So have more than half of Britain's fens and mires. Ninety per cent of lowland Britain's ponds, it seems, have been filled in.

Half the country's ancient lowland woods – descendants of the wildwood – have been cleared for farmland or replaced with conifers in the last 50 years; a greater destruction than throughout the previous 500.

At least 109 000 miles of hedges – enough to girdle the earth more than four times over – have been ripped up since 1947. Once encouraged in the name of productivity, hedgerow removal has been discouraged since the 1970s – but the rate of destruction has accelerated.

The Victims

AS our hedges and woods disappear, grasslands go under the plough or are poisoned by pesticides, marshes drained, waterways polluted and moorland overgrazed, our wildlife is perishing. Nineteen species of wildflower have vanished this century and at least 50 are in danger of extinction. As the plants go, insects are affected. Half of Britain's 55 butterfly species are declining, 10 are in danger. Four kinds of dragonfly have become extinct. In the last 30 years, more than 1800 insect species have become threatened; 500 are facing extinction. Three British birds – the corncrake, the red kite and the white-tailed sea eagle – are among the most endangered in the world. Fifty years ago, 2000 pairs of stone curlews nested here; now only 200 survive. About 25 pairs of bitterns are left, 10 pairs of marsh warblers, and just one pair of red-backed shrikes. The otter is now extinct over much of the country. Several of Britain's 15 bat species are in danger of extinction: the pipistrelle has declined by an estimated 64 per cent in the last decade, while the entire population of the mouse-eared bat is thought to consist of one 17-year-old male. Water voles and grass snakes are rare and the great crested newt is now officially an endangered species.

As with mad cow disease, Sod's Law tells me that something is bound to go wrong. We know so little about what will actually happen to these genetically engineered organisms once they've been released into the environment, and would be able to do nothing about it even when we did discover any problems. For instance, a genetically engineered bacterium may be quite harmless in itself, but could pass on the inserted gene to other bacteria, with potentially disastrous results.

PUBLIC MONEY, PRIVATE GAIN

It is hard to gauge the likely impact of all these changes on farmers but the chances are that a small number will benefit considerably (along with the agrochemical companies), while the majority will slip back even further on their less intensive 'slow track'. To limit some of the worst damage, the Government will probably continue with its scattergun approach in providing some minimal assistance: a few more Environmentally Sensitive Areas (ESAs), a bit of extra help for organic farmers, more emphasis on planting trees, new arrangements in the uplands, and so on.

However, this approach is doomed to failure because it does not even begin to reintegrate the business of food production with the need to nurture the land. Any suggestion of *redirecting* public monies out of intensive farming into environment-friendly farming is anathema to the Treasury gnomes; as far as they're concerned, redirection means redirection out of agriculture altogether.

If for no other reason, environmentalists and farmers should be coming together to oppose the threat of sweeping reductions in public spending in the agricultural sector. Coming from the National Farmers Union (NFU), that would, of course, sound like special pleading. After all, every other sector of the economy (except nuclear power) has been thinned down to fit these leaner, hungrier times. But a case can and must be made on the grounds that the farmer's dilemma is essentially of the government's making. The untold billions distributed over the years to encourage farmers to produce more and more, all but regardless of the social and environmental costs, means that they are now trapped on the production treadmill. *Not* to provide funds to ease farmers off that treadmill would be wantonly irresponsible.

What about those precious 'market forces' which are meant to be such efficient guardians of our interests? How can a government of this stamp possibly justify such substantial intervention by continuing to subsidise farming on such a scale? The common tendency to confuse 'the market' (an essential feature of *any* economy) with 'market forces' (a contemporary ideological abstraction) has obscured the rather obvious point that there are some things which are quite literally 'beyond price' because there is no market in which an appropriate price can be determined. Where is the 'market' for the British countryside? Where can countryside lovers go to express that particular preference in monetary terms, or even to outbid those who seek to despoil the countryside?

Of the two duties a farmer takes on, only food production is amenable to the workings of the market. There's no way the market can help in reinforcing attitudes of 'stewardship' among farmers; it is the clear responsibility of government to intervene on behalf of the entire population, and give substance to the collective desire (expressed so clearly in opinion polls) to see the countryside properly protected and enhanced.

I'm all in favour of farmers (and indeed the Ministry of Agriculture) having to respond more intelligently to consumer demand. But the market place must be properly regulated to protect the consumer, and the Ministry of Agriculture has unfortunately proved time after time that it is totally incapable of this.

WHOSE MINISTRY?

Consider the case of the pesticide Daminozide, or Alar, as it is better known. In January 1989, the Natural Resources Defence Council in the United States published a report forecasting that more than 5000 children in the US would get cancer from Alar residues in apples. In February, the Environmental Protection Agency (EPA) banned Alar, referring to the 'direct and inescapable link between the use of this chemical and the formation of life-threatening tumours'. In March 1989, the UK Ministry of Agriculture issued a list of chemicals it was planning to review, but Alar wasn't even on the list. 'An oversight,' claimed a Man from the Ministry.

In May, the Advisory Committee on Pesticides (ACP) declared that Alar 'did not pose a health risk to consumers'.

63

Feast of Poison

EVERY YEAR YOU EAT 12 LB OF ADDITIVES, A GALLON OF PESTICIDES, PLUS NITRATES, HORMONES AND ALUMINIUM

EVERY year we each munch our way through 12 lb of deadly food additives and guzzle a gallon of pesticides.

More than 6000 new chemicals have been concocted to add to our food over the last decade alone.

And the horrifying cocktail of preservatives, herbicides, nitrates, lead and hormones is putting our health at risk, warns a new guide to Greener eating. Up to 3000 people are taken ill and one person dies from pesticide poisoning a year, it claims.

© TODAY 30.12.89

No explanation was offered, and no data was made public. But between July and October 1989, Uniroyal (the manufacturers of Alar) received further reports on the effect of this product on mice and rats. The results must have made grim reading because in October Uniroyal ordered an immediate halt to worldwide sales of Alar on the grounds that it could no longer provide 'a totally clean data package'. Despite the best efforts of the ACP, Alar is therefore no longer on sale in the UK. There has been no comment from the ACP, let alone any apology for their appalling complacency.

In a speech in September 1989 John Selwyn Gummer, the Minister of Agriculture, stated that his job was 'to stamp on those who try to create anxiety without need'. In February 1990, he lashed out at 'food fascists' for stirring up opposition to new food processes. He apparently includes in that number all those currently opposed to the irradiation of food, despite the fact that this opposition is worldwide and based on highly authoritative scientific information. Indeed, in the UK, the decision to proceed with the introduction of irradiation has been made despite the findings of the Ministry's own Advisory Committee, which stated that although irradiation kills up to 90 per cent of poisonous organisms, 'it can also produce mutant micro-organisms which could be more carcinogenic than native forms'. They might be 'difficult to detect, and might also be more radiation-resistant'.

Beyond that, Professor Richard Lacey has pointed out the real danger that we might be lulled into supposing that irradiated food is pure:

> 66 *the 10 per cent of listeria unaffected by irradiation can grow during the prolonged shelf life, even under refrigeration. When the food is sold, it could contain more listeria than before irradiation, because the process removes most of the competing bacteria. Irradiation can be counter-productive.* 99

In nutritional terms alone, the Ministry's decision is absolutely unjustifiable. *Food Irradiation*, Tim Lang and Tony Webb's excellent book on this controversial subject, details the true extent of the damage to vitamins in the irradiation process: the loss of vitamin C in fruits is between 20 per cent and 70 per cent; of vitamin B1 in meat, between 42 per cent and 93 per cent; of vitamin B1 in fish, up to 90 per cent; of vitamin A in chicken, between 53 per cent and 95 per cent etc.

Crop spraying.

Valuable time and resources have to be expended trying to hold the line on issues like pesticide contamination and irradiation. However, there is a real danger that the most important scandal will go unnoticed amid the inevitable fuss surrounding such single-issue campaigning. This scandal is, of course, the Government's continuing refusal to develop a coherent food policy for the UK, as laid down within the framework of two major reports released in the eighties by the National Advisory Committee on Nutrition Education (NACNE) and the Committee on the Medical Aspects of Food.

It is both sobering and astonishing to be reminded that the basic arguments on diet and nutrition were won ten years ago. These days very few people (even within the food industry) dissent from the broad guidelines of the NACNE report, and many now find its recommendations excessively modest. Despite years of paying lip-service to the notion of prevention, almost nothing is done about the preventable diet-related diseases which now place such a burden on our health services. Preventive medicine is interpreted largely in terms of

65

Danger pesticide found in chocolate

LINDANE, a highly toxic pesticide linked with cancer, has been found in chocolate.

A Mail on Sunday analysis discovered residues of the powerful insecticide in four different popular chocolate bars.

It comes from the cocoa beans produced in West Africa where the pods are regularly sprayed with Lindane to kill bugs.

The results of the laboratory tests, carried out last week, have concerned scientists who fear the chemical may have long-term effects.

We put the test results to manufacturers who said yesterday they did not present any health risks to consumers as the levels were well below the maximum recommended limits for Lindane in chocolate.

But some scientists believe that although the residues are small, it is further proof that pesticides are building up slowly in our bodies through diet.

© THE MAIL ON SUNDAY 21.1.90

---

early diagnosis and extensive screening programmes, rather than by reference to the promotion of basic health care and dietary guidance.

The Ministry of Agriculture sees its prime responsibility as the defence of the producers' interests, yet surprisingly most farmers feel completely left in the lurch by the Ministry. The sheer incoherence with which the Government rummages around for new policies, shuffling back and forth between Whitehall and Brussels, is both confusing and depressing for those involved in agriculture. For instance, though the media have made little of this, farmers positively hate the policy of set-aside, in which they are paid £80 an acre to take land out of production altogether for up to five years, in order to cut surplus grain production.

There is no environmental benefit in this whatsoever. While being paid for doing literally nothing on one part of the farm, it quite naturally makes sense for the farmer to intensify production elsewhere to make up for any loss of income. As a result, there is little reduction in the application of chemicals, and no lessening of pollution from slurry, silage and nitrate run-offs.

Set-aside can in fact be likened to a very overweight person going on a rigorous and painful diet during the day, while night after night creeping down to the larder and enthusiastically tucking into all those chemical goodies that made them fat in the first place.

In partial recognition of this, a new Countryside Premium Scheme has been established which will allow a tiny number of farmers to manage their set-aside land specifically for conservation purposes such as the creation of wildflower meadows, encouraging wildlife and public access. However, many farmers deeply resent the notion that their only value to the community is as glorified park-keepers, without any responsibilities for food production.

LACK OF VISION

It's infinitely more profitable for farmers to get into a completely new crop – houses. The Department of the Environment is intent on permitting more housing development on surplus agricultural land, while relaxing the controls on the re-use and conversion of rural buildings,

The world's rainforests are disappearing at an astonishing rate: 1.8
per cent of the remaining area is destroyed every year. With the
exception of Western Amazonia, Zaire and Papua New Guinea,
there will be little left in 20 years' time.

i

ABOVE: After 40 years of uncontrolled and hopelessly inefficient industrialisation, Eastern European countries now face a fearsome legacy of air pollution problems. Poland is particularly badly affected.

RIGHT: Industrial pollution in the Blackstone River, Massachusetts.

ABOVE: Late summer wild flowers on the chalk soils of the South Downs.

LEFT: Tractors work the land near Worthing in Sussex. Arable production on the South Downs is inefficient and highly damaging to the environment.

ABOVE: 'Spoilt for choice' in a modern supermarket – but what about genuine variety, taste and nutritional quality?

LEFT: A typical French market stall in Dieppe.

ABOVE: As global warming takes effect, the ice sheets of Antarctica will almost certainly begin to melt. The resulting worldwide rise in sea levels could have disastrous results for parts of Britain and other low-lying countries.

LEFT: An impressive array of wind generators in the Gorgonio Pass, California.

ABOVE: A typical Dutch *woonerf* in
the town of Goor. Cars are permitted
but people are given priority.

RIGHT: Ashram Acres is a pioneering
city garden scheme in inner-city
Birmingham. It makes use of wasted
land and wasted skills in the
community, which benefits not only
from the fruit and vegetables grown,
but also in terms of health,
opportunities for rewarding work,
learning, playing and socialising.

The Dorset heathland has been
particularly badly affected by new
housing development. The fact that
much of the area is a Site of Special
Scientific Interest has made no
difference whatsoever.

ABOVE: Small-scale farming in Kenya, mixing crops, livestock and forestry in a highly productive and sustainable combination.

RIGHT: A pineapple plantation in Thailand.

including those currently in agricultural use: 'The Government's aim is to encourage growth and diversification in the rural economy, whilst achieving this in ways that will enhance the quality of life in rural communities and conserve our country heritage.'

I would be the first to agree that this balancing act isn't easy to achieve. I have become increasingly critical of the 'urban romanticism' of those who seem to suffer from a surfeit of undigested Wordsworth. Many of these people can barely be brought to accept that the countryside is actually shaped by human hands, and that, without extensive and sustained intervention, there will be far fewer of those five-star views that they have become accustomed to seeing on their motorised excursions into the countryside.

We have to accept that the rural economy can only be regenerated by providing opportunities for good work and living conditions in rural areas. Some farmers need to be able to diversify out of their existing enterprises, and people who live and work locally need housing at prices they can afford.

The development debate seems to have suffered enormously from an apparent obsession with quantity rather than quality. All the talk about numbers has inevitably obscured the question of quality. A mere handful of planning authorities have introduced quality guidelines for architects and developers to ensure that regional diversity and vernacular styles can be naturally maintained. Central government is rightly suspicious of trying to impose uniform quality criteria, recognising that they simply wouldn't work. However, it must also accept that the Not In My Back Yard reaction is a quite natural and rational response if what is being dumped in one's back yard is built first and foremost to accommodate sheer numbers of people in standardised and utterly depersonalised 'dwelling units'. The Government could at least oblige planning authorities to develop their own regional quality criteria to guard against the worst instances. There are some who argue that this approach would make all our rural towns and villages into museums. But to refer to well-designed, well-built, properly landscaped houses, in harmony with the rest of the community, as 'museum pieces' strikes me as inverse snobbery of the worst kind.

How wise is it anyway to be taking large amounts of fertile land *permanently* out of production? The surpluses that were

67

causing such acute embarrassment two or three years ago have now largely disappeared, sold off cheap to the Soviet Union, given away, or destroyed. It's clear that the EEC still has the capacity to keep agricultural supply well in excess of demand, but it would surely be advisable to take account of the uncertainties of global warming, including the possibility of extended drought in the breadbasket of America, famine in Africa, and chronic climatic disruption elsewhere in the world. If land is just set aside, it can be brought back into production quite quickly; if it's covered in bungalows, it's done for.

This is the least of the challenges which global warming poses to the viability of modern farming, simply because modern farming is utterly unsustainable. The dramatic increases in yields over the last 20 years have been achieved largely by increasing the amounts of fertilisers and pesticides used, and by expanding the size of the average field in order to allow for larger machines, which in turn need more fuel. We've had to dig very deep into our fossil fuel reserves to supplement the energy that comes directly from the sun.

In one respect, farming is no different from any other business. There are inputs (chemicals, transport costs, seeds, machinery, etc) and outputs (measured in yield per hectare). In money terms, it still makes sense to farm as intensively as possible in order to get the best returns through the highest yields. In energy terms, it's often a total nonsense, as farmers may well be putting more energy in than they're actually getting out! Any farming system that is dependent on strictly finite energy sources *cannot,* by definition, be described as sustainable.

Worse still, modern farming treats the soil itself as some kind of mineral reserve, to be mined as intensively as possible. Soil erosion is not just a problem for exposed soils in Third World countries; more than 2 million hectares in the UK are at risk today, particularly on sandy and chalk soils. The Ministry of Agriculture gradually withdrew its support for the work of the Soil Survey during the eighties, and has refused to publish important findings gathered from soil-monitoring programmes in the mid-eighties.

Although soil *is* a renewable resource, it is only renewable so long as the rate of soil loss does not exceed the rate at which the soil is naturally building up. Any farming system that takes out more on a regular basis than it puts in is only as 'sustainable'

Educational tours are an increasingly popular method of 'diversifying' beyond the business of straight food production.

as the soil is deep. One day, it will be gone. Farmers are well aware of this but, driven as they are to produce more in order to placate the bank manager or simply to stay in business, they just hope that 'one day' is far enough away to worry someone else and not them.

OF MUCK AND MAGIC

For a farmer to talk of the future having to look after itself would have been heresy before the advent of chemical farming. As far as Britain's 1500 organic farmers are concerned it's still heresy. Over the last few years, public attitudes towards organic farming have changed dramatically: Pat and Tony Archer (of Radio 4's *The Archers*) have become organic celebrities in their own right; Prince Charles has given his unstinting support from the early eighties onwards; government ministers have gradually realised that snide jokes about 'the muck and magic brigade' are really a bit passé; and, above all, consumer demand for organic produce has burgeoned.

Surprisingly, organic farmers and environmentalists have only recently realised that they share a common cause. Until then, for perfectly understandable reasons, the emphasis was mainly on the health and nutritional benefits of organic food, particularly in terms of concern about pesticide residues. Many

69

conservationists have been too narrowly concerned with the protection of specially designated sites, often neglecting the wider countryside in their keen desire to guard the 'jewels in the crown'. By the same token, some representatives of the Organic Movement have been blinkered and intolerant in their approach to environmentalists.

The Soil Association's adoption of some important conservation guidelines has made a huge difference. Some of the environmental benefits of organic farming are obvious: pesticides and fertilisers are not permitted, and a mixed farming approach forms the basis of most successful organic enterprises. But the guidelines go further in terms of ruling against intensive livestock systems, and encouraging the maintenance of hedgerows, wetland areas, wildflower meadows and other 'marginal habitats' which make more sense on an organic farm (where species diversity is beneficial) than on a conventional chemical farm.

Again, if we revert to that all-important definition of sustainability (namely, 'the ability to go on doing something *indefinitely*'), only organic farming comes close to meeting the requirements. By the use of sunshine, animal and crop manures, and the rotation of different crops, organic farming requires no imported nutrients; it recycles the natural wealth available on a farm, and constantly regenerates the soil.

But organic farming is still very small beer in the UK. It accounts for around 1 per cent of total food production, and out of a staggering total of £33 billion that Britons spend on food every year, organic produce accounts for less than £50 million. Even pot noodles have a bigger share of the market! Last year, demand greatly exceeded supply; 95 per cent of organic produce sold in the UK was imported.

The very sizeable premium on many organic lines (between 30 per cent and 75 per cent) remains a big problem, placing organic food beyond the reach of many people's budgets. But until organic producers are able to gear up to a far higher level of operation, with much more efficient distribution networks and marketing operations, this premium is unlikely to decrease significantly. At the moment, there are only two packers in the whole of the UK for organic produce, so wherever an organic swede or carrot is grown, it first has to take a trip either to West Wales or to the Geest depot in Lincolnshire.

The Soil Association believes that it will be possible to boost production from 1 per cent to around 20 per cent by the end of the decade. Consumer demand may indeed be that strong by then, but the real question is whether or not enough farmers will have the flexibility to get into organic production. It can take up to five years to wean a farm off its regular diet of chemicals, during which time the reduced yield would bankrupt many farmers.

In this respect, UK farmers are in more or less the same position as many Third World countries. Both borrowed a lot of money in the seventies and early eighties, when money was relatively cheap and bankers relatively friendly; both wanted that money to expand their productive enterprise by increasing their output. In the eighties, both have seen interest rates rise and rise, the value of their produce fall or remain constant, and an ever greater share of their income disappear on servicing their debts. Both now find that bank managers are very much fair-weather friends. Both are trapped.

For UK farmers, the obvious answer is to set up some kind of system for a 'transitional grant' to be made available to any farmer wishing to convert to organic, thus covering the temporary loss of income. Such a system would be no different

Barry Wookey's 1700 acres of rolling Wiltshire downland is a modern, commercially successful arable farm. It has been farmed organically since the early seventies and has encouraged many other farmers to find ways of coming off 'the chemical treadmill'.

in principle from the compensation the Government pays under the Wildlife and Countryside Act for 'the profits foregone' by farmers in not developing or 'improving' a Site of Special Scientific Interest. A transitional grant for conversion to organic farming methods would at least bring some temporary relief.

In January 1990, John Selwyn Gummer announced a new initiative to provide such grants under the EEC's 'extensification rules'. Though this is obviously welcome, it is in reality little more than gesture politics. The amount of money involved is pitiful: less than one third of one per cent of total spending on agriculture!

The long-term solution has less to do with agriculture *per se* than with our understanding of wealth, energy and sustainability. In Chapter 2, we looked at the feasibility of both a carbon tax (added to the existing tax base, specifically to promote energy efficiency and penalise pollution), and a completely new system based on taxing energy use rather than labour or added value. It's a pretty sure bet that the former will be with us before the middle of the decade; the latter may take a little longer.

Either way, our modern, super-efficient farmers will certainly have to pay the *real* price for the oil-based inputs they currently take for granted. At the moment, conventional farmers are able to externalise (or offload) many of their costs: on to the environment (in terms of farm pollution), on to the consumer (in terms of pesticide residues and excessive water content), on to the entire community (in terms of the contribution that farmers make to global warming), and on to future generations (in terms of their wasteful depletion of finite fossil fuels). Only when all these costs are properly internalised will the organic producer be able to compete on an equal footing.

COMING OFF THE TREADMILL

Most commentators cannot see how organic producers are going to be able to satisfy more than around 5 per cent of demand by the end of the decade. That just leaves 95 per cent to go! We could continue on the dual-track route, which I explained before, with a minority of farmers taking an ever greater share of the market, through increased intensification on their larger prairie farms, while the majority become increasingly dependent on ad-hoc add-on schemes to keep the bank manager at bay. Alternatively, they will simply sell off as much of their land as they can for new leisure centres or housing estates.

We could, on the other hand, change the entire thrust of modern agricultural policy, just as they did – in very different circumstances – after the Second World War. Instead of hanging on to the idea of *maximising* output, whatever the cost, we could learn to *optimise* output. The same amount of food would be provided at more or less the same price by keeping all our land in production and farming it in an environmentally friendly way.

There's even a mechanism available to us to make this possible: the Environmentally Sensitive Areas Scheme. This was set up in 1986 to encourage farmers in 19 different areas (covering a total of around 738 000 hectares) to use fewer chemicals, reduce stocking densities, maintain local features (such as stone walls or hedges), restore wildlife habitats, and to put machinery on the land less often. Participation is completely voluntary, and farmers are able to enter a part of their farm rather than the whole of it. (In certain circumstances, this has led to the same unfortunate consequences as the Set-Aside Scheme, in that there's nothing to stop the farmer from intensifying production on the rest of the farm.)

For the BBC series that this book accompanies, we looked in some detail at the South Downs Environmentally Sensitive Area. This is a strange and very beautiful area, shaped over many thousands of years by the grazing of sheep and cattle. It boasts an astonishing variety of different flowers. But since the Second World War, farmers have adopted conventional intensive arable techniques, which have led to the inexorable loss of 90 per cent of the original chalk downland and to very serious soil erosion.

The South Downs was declared an ESA in 1987, with one very special feature: farmers were to be paid an additional £64 an acre if they undertook to convert the arable land *back* to pasture for grazing sheep, thereby encouraging the return of the local flora and fauna. It's fair to say that the jury is still out on this and all other ESAs. There are undoubtedly problems: the scheme is bureaucratic and relatively expensive to monitor (it works out at around £1 million per ESA), and

73

many farmers remain sceptical, worried about the short-term nature of the scheme, and 'only in it for the money'. But the idea of reducing inputs in such a way will become increasingly attractive as the cost of those inputs rises. The present rise in oil prices will in time be reflected in the cost of inorganic fertilisers. The problem here is that such a price rise hits the smaller farmer much more seriously than the large farmer. A far fairer method would be to impose a nitrogen quota.

The justification for this is simple: nitrogen inputs are the single most influential factor in increasing cereal yields. Cereal production in this country has by no means reached saturation level (when yields no longer respond to any further increase in the application of fertiliser), and further massive increases in productivity are inevitable. In order not to discriminate against small farmers, a nitrogen quota would have to be set at around 100 kilograms per hectare. This would represent an average 50 per cent cut. Moreover, these quotas would not be transferable from one part of the country to another, for otherwise there would be an inexorable drifting of the quotas towards East Anglia.

In one fell swoop, such a proposal would achieve a reduction in surpluses (without land coming out of production), an improvement in water quality (and with more than one million people still exposed to nitrate levels in excess of the EEC limit of 50 milligrams per litre, this would be no bad thing in itself), and a major step towards de-intensifying modern agriculture.

Without this kind of nitrogen quota, applied universally across the EEC, the ESA Scheme is inevitably inadequate. At the moment, we have a series of 'green ghettoes' isolated within an intensively farmed factory floor. And what really struck me on the South Downs was the utterly arbitrary distinction between one field which fell within the ESA, and the neighbouring field which fell just beyond it. One environmentally sensitive field, one environmentally insensitive field – though they looked absolutely identical to my untutored eye.

The obvious solution is 'extensification' – though never can so important a notion have had to go forth into the world under such a desperately ugly title! Extensification is the umbrella term used to cover all those policy initiatives which run counter to the movement towards further intensification

74

and further surpluses. Farmers need to know exactly what is expected of them on a long-term basis, and cannot be expected to respond to one new initiative after another, especially when they often seem to be pulling in different directions. There's nothing wrong with lots of different options being on offer, just so long as the over-riding policy thrust behind them is explicit and internally consistent.

From all the opinion polls, it's clear that extensification would be overwhelmingly supported by taxpayers, who are clearly not prepared to see huge sums of money pumped into the farming community on an utterly unaccountable basis. Above all, it would allow for a considerable expansion of the ESA Scheme, including the idea of *organic* ESAs, so that more and more of our countryside could be farmed with fewer and fewer pesticides and chemicals being used.

'But what about all those pests?' I hear you say. 'Won't they run riot if they're not regularly and liberally doused with the latest and most lethal chemical?' Robin Page's *Farmer's Diary* (page 76) may provide part of the answer to this mystery.

The halfway house between conventional and organic (or totally pesticide-free) farming is Integrated Pest Management (IPM), which depends on the use of biological and other non-chemical approaches to pest control, reserving the use of chemicals for particularly difficult or special circumstances.

One of the major problems with pesticides is that they not only kill the so-called pests, they often kill the predator insects (or 'beneficials', as they're known in the trade!) which were going about their normal business of killing the pests in the first place. Worse still, the pests are often able to develop an immunity to chemicals. In a 1989 paper from the World Watch Institute, Sandra Postel comments that before the Second World War scientists were aware of just a handful of pests that had developed resistance to chemicals; by 1985, that number had grown to 447.

Modern farming makes things as easy as possible for pests. In all its ignorance and arrogance, it insists on planting the same crop in the same field year after year. Farmers are now re-discovering that one of the most effective IPM techniques, apart from using the pest's natural enemies, is crop rotation. For this and other reasons, the agro-chemical companies don't like IPM one little bit. As farmers become less dependent on chemicals, these companies' profits are increasingly affected, which probably explains why billions of dollars are still being pumped into the development of new pesticides, while IPM has to struggle to get any kind of research and development support.

With or without such support, IPM is booming in the United States, where the Environmental Protection Agency (EPA) has been extremely tough in taking pesticides off the market if there is any suggestion of toxicity to human beings. The huge demand for 'beneficials' has led to the growth of companies providing literally billions of bugs every year in special 'insectaries'. Once released, these bugs do not harm the crop itself – they simply devour the pests.

Pestilential practices

A PLAGUE ON ALL YOUR PRAIRIES, CRIES ROBIN PAGE TO THE AGRI-BUSINESSMEN

I AM puzzled. Earlier in the year, John MacGregor, the then Minister of Agriculture, referred to farmers as 'guardians of the countryside'. Since then, from the farming lobby, I have heard how British agriculture is becoming more 'green'. With diversification, extensification, set-aside and faultless husbandry, England is again becoming a green and pleasant land – or so it is said.

Sadly, this message does not seem to have reached my part of Cambridgeshire. Yes, it is true that there are areas of set-aside but elsewhere some 'guardians of the countryside' have become even more intensive. Incredibly, over the last two or three years, still more hedges have disappeared, fields have become huge and real 'prairies' have been created.

The farming lobby does not like the word 'prairie' to describe the destruction some farmers have caused. But prairie farming exists. And proof of its ill effects came this Summer. It started with warnings from ADAS, the Ministry of Agriculture's advisory arm, about aphid infestation in cereals. Panic set in – aphid spray was sold out in days and those farmers who were unlucky then bought various other insecticides which wiped out not only aphids but every other bug, beetle and insect.

On our small farm, we found this amazing. We are rarely troubled with aphids and have not sprayed against them for years. This year we did not spray either and had absolutely no problems. The reason why we did not have to spray is simple: this year, our fields held thousands of ladybirds – all good aphid-eaters. At the same time, all our arable fields are surrounded by large hedges – ideal hibernating and breeding areas for ladybirds and ground-beetles, also vigorous aphid-killers. So our form of pest control is attractive to look at; it enhances the landscape; and it encourages wildlife.

This raises a number of interesting questions. If the farming lobby is convinced that prairie farming does not take place in Britain, why did so many big farmers have an aphid problem this year? Also, aphids can be controlled naturally without the use of sprays, simply by having sensibly and attractively sized fields. So why has the Ministry of Agriculture and ADAS not circulated the farming community, advising smaller fields with hedgerows?

I have a simple remedy for all this nonsense: It would reduce the use of sprays and, without huge grants, it would transform the British countryside almost overnight.

I believe that the time has come for the extravagances of the Prairie Farmer to be stopped. An environmental tax of £10 per acre should be charged in areas of cereal growing for every field over 25 acres in size. We would not, of course, pay £250 a year on our large field – we would simply divide it in two with another hedge and have some more ladybirds.

© THE DAILY TELEGRAPH 14.10.89

INTENSIFICATION	EXTENSIFICATION
FARMERS	
Considerable wealth for a few, bankruptcy looming for many. Thousands leaving farming every year; family farms in dire straits. Low public esteem.	Secure income, without being made to feel 'park-keepers'. Fairer distribution between different sectors of farming community. High public esteem.
COUNTRYSIDE	
Factory-floor approach to farming. Narrow specialisation and loss of diversity. Habitat loss. Major ecological problems: nitrates, pesticides, farm pollution.	Mixed farms; food production and land stewardship reintegrated; species diversity; attractive countryside encouraging greater access.
SOIL	
An exercise in 'mining' the soil. Steady erosion. Chemical abuse, coupled with steady loss of fertility.	Soil maintenance and sustainable farming techniques. Farmers far better placed for post-oil era.
ANIMALS	
Battery farming; institutionalised cruelty; poor hygiene and totally inadequate regulation by MAFF.	Extensive rearing techniques; free range. No battery systems, and far stricter welfare standards.
CONSUMERS	
Convenience, processed foods. Low nutritional standards. Endless food scares. Inadequate notions of quality, with consumers often being ripped off.	High quality food, including organic. Emphasis on taste, nutrition, variety. Good value for money, but not necessarily cheap.

The principle of extensification isn't restricted to arable crops. It would also allow for a massive expansion of the Government's Farm Woodlands Scheme launched in 1988. This is another good idea that hasn't been properly developed. The scheme aims to encourage the planting of broadleaf woodlands on 10 000 hectares of farmland every year, though the NFU has calculated that three times that area could be absorbed with the right kind of incentives. And while encouraging new planting on surplus farmland, the Government has done nothing to prevent the felling of our remaining semi-natural woodlands or of hedgerow trees.

One of the more dynamic ideas to come out of the Countryside Commission over the last few years is the proposal for a new National Forest in the Midlands. Amounting to 240 square kilometres, it would be a 'multi-purpose, broadleaf forest' (i.e. one that combines a variety of uses other than forestry, involving some agriculture, housing, tourism and recreation). Such a proposal will obviously require the withdrawal of a significant amount of marginal farmland from production. The details have yet to be worked out, but it's an exciting development, and may well encourage the Government to think about the possibility of recreating other threatened habitats in different parts of the country, such as wetlands, or herb-rich and wildflower meadows.

ANIMAL WELFARE

And what of the millions of animals that are slaughtered every year to keep our butchers and supermarkets well stocked? Are there any benefits for them in these extensification proposals? It really does seem absurd to be talking of thousands of hectares of land coming out of production, while in the same breath condoning or further promoting perversely cruel factory farming methods, which in themselves have significantly reduced the demand for farming land.

The cruelty involved in intensive pig rearing, for instance, is considerable. Sows are confined in stalls (sometimes tethered to the concrete floor by chains) for their 14-week pregnancy; they are unable to turn around, and have no contact with other pigs. Once they've given birth, they're moved into farrowing crates and have their piglets with them for around three weeks. After that they're mated again and put back into the stall,

where they rapidly get bored and neurotic. John Douglas of the Royal Society for the Prevention of Cruelty to Animals sums it up: 'My own opinion is that it is morally obscene to keep a pregnant animal in such conditions. Pigs are very bright animals. They like to know what's going on.' The Farm Animal Welfare Council (which advises the Government on animal welfare issues) would like to see the dry sow stall phased out as soon as possible, but, as usual, the Ministry of Agriculture is deaf to such advice.

Intensive pig units are a breeding ground for disease, and growth-boosting antibiotics are a regular component in the pigs' feed. Despite 'a minimum withdrawal period', residues of drugs like Sulphadimine (an anti-bacterial drug which has been linked to thyroid cancer in the United States) keep turning up in the pork people buy.

It's always argued that it is 'uneconomic' to rear livestock in any other way, but this really isn't the case. A Meat and Livestock Commission study compared the performance of 35 outdoor-housed herds of pigs with that of intensively reared, indoor herds. The net margin of profit per sow was identical. Outdoor pigs consumed more feed, and the number of piglets weaned per sow was lower. But the cost of building maintenance, heating and housing were much higher indoors. Make no mistake: it is with an eye fixed as much on profit as on animal welfare that companies like Baxter Parker Ltd specialise in outdoor pig rearing. After five years in the business, they concluded: 'Extensive breeding can be profitable, provided the soil type is right, and the level of stockmanship is of high calibre.'

Exactly the same holds true for chickens. Most battery houses (for birds producing eggs) have four birds to a cage which

At Sam Olive's farm at Kings Somborne in Hampshire he has developed his own unique breed of pigs by crossing wild boar with blue sows. This produces a much higher-quality meat, with much more flavour, and attracts a high premium of around 40 pence in the pound. His Wild Blues are reared in the field, and given additive-free feed. It's a well-run, successful small business, producing a high-quality specialist product. As Sam Olive says: 'People are eating less, but better meat. This is why my pig meat will appeal; it costs more, but it has more flavour than ordinary pork.'

measures 45 cm by 50 cm. The birds are allowed none of the five freedoms which the influential Brambell Report stated that every farm animal should have: freedom to move, to turn around, to groom, to get up and to lie and stretch. The birds cannot spread their wings or dust themselves, and cannibalism is not uncommon.

As we all know, after the traumas of 1988 and 1989, the industry is in a state of crisis as a result of over-production, high feed prices and falling consumption. It does indeed cost slightly more to produce free-range eggs than battery eggs, but as the average person in this country eats just over three eggs a week, this represents no more than a few pence each. It's clear that the public is prepared to pay slightly more for free-range eggs – witness the increasing number of farmers producing eggs under free-range, aviary and deep-litter systems – though there are worrying indications that the market for free-range has reached a plateau of around 20 per cent.

I'm not sentimental about animals, and I do not actually believe that there is anything inherently immoral about eating meat. However, I do believe that it is immoral to inflict utterly unnecessary suffering on any animal, including a farm animal, either in rearing or slaughtering it. As the final beneficiaries of the process, we meat-eaters share in that fundamental immorality. For that reason, I believe we have an obligation to find out how the meat we eat has been reared and slaughtered, and to buy free-range or organically reared meat wherever possible. This isn't easy (in many parts of the country it's impossible), which is why more and more people are giving up eating meat altogether.

At present there is very little the consumer can do about the way in which animals are slaughtered. By all reports, what happens in UK abattoirs is utterly inhumane, often unhygienic and quite inadequately controlled. Out of 852 abattoirs in the UK, 779 do not conform to EEC standards – yet more evidence of the Ministry of Agriculture's grotesque complacency and indifference to animal welfare. As is so often the case, we should expect very little from our politicians and civil servants, let alone the Meat and Livestock Commission itself (which is currently persuaded that 'voluntary guidelines' alone will be enough to sort out the carnage going on in our abattoirs). A combination of strict EEC regulation, proper enforcement and consumer pressure will be necessary to bring our abattoirs up to a far higher standard of humane and hygienic operation.

Successful extensive rearing is invariably more labour-intensive. But is it really such a fearful heresy to suggest that support should be used to encourage farmers to take on more stockmen rather than to build yet more intensive units? Such an approach would stem the loss of agricultural workers, while simultaneously bringing about enormous environmental benefits, particularly the reduction of increasingly serious pollution caused by slurry from intensive rearing units.

FOOD QUALITY

The *ethical* issues of animal welfare make up one of the most important dimensions of food quality. Bearing in mind *environmental* concerns, *nutritional* concerns (to achieve the kind of balanced diet recommended by the NACNE Report), *natural* concerns (to minimise the amount of food processing and adulteration) and *sensual* concerns (to ensure that food appeals as powerfully as possible to our senses), it's possible to move towards a rather different definition of food quality than that which has held sway over the last couple of decades.

Since the sixties, quality has been all about convenience, standardisation, ease of packaging, blemish-free appearance, shelf life, and all those other features which supermarkets tell us the punters were crying out for. But who can say whether the changes in our diet during that time were not driven primarily by the needs and operating procedures of the supermarkets, rather than by genuine market-led pressures?

Supermarkets have, of course, brought us enormous benefits: huge variety (of a kind), relatively high standards, and the undoubted convenience of occasional, big shopping expeditions for those who are lucky enough to have a car. I also suspect that it's become easier for critics to take it out on the supermarkets and the farmers, rather than accept that many of the problems of poor food quality are really down to us, the consumers. We get the food, as well as the government, we deserve.

The sad truth may just be that people in this country simply care less about food than they seem to do elsewhere in Europe. I keep wondering why there's no British equivalent of those astonishing local markets in France and Italy, where one stall after another is weighed down with the highest-quality fruit, vegetables and other delicious goodies, all conspiring to excite the imagination and get one back into the kitchen to do justice to such beautiful produce.

Such romanticism cuts very little ice in the hard, hassle-free world of quick-chill, home-freezing, and microwave convenience. But it is interesting that more and more consumers are now putting greater emphasis on the notion of quality in one form or another, whether it's organic, natural, wholefood or locally grown. It has to be said that farmers have been very slow to respond to these trends; why, for example, is it still practically impossible for people to buy extensively reared, organic or 'real meat', despite the very sizeable market niche out there consisting of 'conscientious meat-eaters'?

And why is there no equivalent in the UK of the admirable Japanese Seikatsu Club, which we featured at some length in the television series? This consumer cooperative has 170 000 family members, and combines formidable business and professional skills with strict social and ecological principles. The club members have a vision of a community-centred economy, which provides a radical alternative to both socialist and capitalist industrialism. In their own words:

> 66 *what started as a strategy to save money gradually developed over the next 20 years into a philosophy encompassing the whole of life. In addition to cost-effective collective purchase, the club is committed to a host of social concerns, including the environment, the empowerment of women, and workers' conditions.* 99

The 170 000 families involved are tightly organised into about 27 000 'hans' (the local group unit, averaging eight members). The hans elect a representative to their branch, which in turn sends representatives to a 'general assembly' to make policy and elect the board of directors. Eighty per cent of the board's members are women.

The business revolves around the distribution of around 400 different products to these hans. It's carried out through a unique computer-operated advance-ordering system, to enable producers to plan in advance and guarantee product freshness. The Club will not handle products which are detrimental to members' health or to the environment. When it cannot find products of adequate quality, or ones which meet its ecological and social criteria, the Club will consider producing them

The Selkatsu Club gets better produce by co-operating with local farmers and participating in the life of the farm.

itself; it currently owns two organic milk factories for precisely that reason.

The Club also places great emphasis on direct producer/consumer links in order to bring people back into contact with the food which they're eating. (Consumers regularly visit farmers to inform themselves about and help them with their work.)

Through all their campaigning against synthetic detergents and other causes of environmental problems, Club members quickly realised the importance of the political process, and began to form independent networks to contest local elections. In 1979, the first member was elected to the Tokyo city government, and there are now 33 women councillors in Tokyo, Yokohama and Chiba. Their manifesto reads very much like that of a European Green Party: very environmental, peace-oriented and anti-nuclear, with an emphasis on local participatory democracy, and equal status for women.

Anyone who comes into contact with the Seikatsu Club is profoundly impressed with the way in which they have put

83

OPPOSITE: Bill Mollison, founder and leading light of the Permaculture Movement.

consumers back into direct contact with the producers of the food they eat. We are just beginning to see the stirrings of similar moves in the UK. There's a growing number of consumer cooperatives that are endeavouring to provide a much more accountable service to their customers; we're seeing an upsurge of farm shops, or local shops selling only local produce; some organic producers have established direct contacts with customers, cutting out the middle men altogether; one or two enterprising apple growers have leased out individual trees to apple enthusiasts, who are notified of when they should come and pick them in the autumn.

But, in truth, it remains hard to break the stranglehold of centralised production and distribution systems, let alone to counter the continuing thrust of modern farming to increase productivity at all costs. The ideas outlined in this chapter would almost certainly require a new Act to replace the 1947 Agriculture Act, and it's difficult to say at this stage whether such an approach is compatible with our continued membership of the EEC.

My own feeling is that we will (and should) move towards the increasing 'repatriation' of agricultural policy, reclaiming the authority to make more decisions for ourselves, particularly as regards the use of public subsidy. It is simply impossible to see how 12 very different countries, with totally different agricultural systems, are going to agree upon any standard method for integrating food production and land stewardship.

And I wonder if farmers have really looked hard at the *logic* behind the Common Agricultural Policy (CAP). First and foremost, it is driven by an obsessive technological determinism: i.e. if something can be done, then it should and must be done. For example, if the hormone bovine somatotrophin (BST) can increase milk yields by up to 40 per cent, then it must be a good thing. Don't worry too much about those unfortunate dairy farmers who'll go out of business, let alone the welfare of the animals, or the fact that the consumer will still end up paying exactly the same price for the milk. We're getting more out of the same unit of production, and that's progress. BST is just a shadow of the sort of genetically engineered increases in production which are looming on the horizon, a mere puff of wind before the tornado.

More importantly, one of the central principles of the CAP

Just let nature do all the work

THE MOST fertile and down-to-earth Green idea started life in Tasmania as a humble scheme for growing vegetables: let nature do most of the work.

Bill Mollison called it permaculture, which means permanent agriculture: lots of mulching but no digging, little weeding and no artificial inputs.

Now, 15 years later, Mollison has developed permaculture into a design for Green living with 4000 active disciples around the world who believe they have the answer to the planet's food, energy, pollution, population and financial problems.

Permaculture works in Malayan paddy fields, Nepalese hillsides, Ohio ranches, New York city farms and market gardens in Shropshire. The technique is taught at 21 institutes around the world. Britain's Permaculture Association has 200 members including farmers and businessmen.

Mollison's idea is indeed simple. Take a piece of land. Identify what grows, lives or simply exists: soils, weeds, insects, worms, slugs, birds, butterflies, rocks, water sources. That's your eco-system.

Get rid of anything poisonous or wasteful like machines that cost more in energy than they earn. Add plants, animals, people, houses, workshops – whatever fits into the system and keeps it self-sustaining.

The result can look messy, with plants growing all over each other and little or no space for a lawn. No vast fields. Everything on a human scale, within easy reach. Your herb garden will be right outside the back door.

Mollison concedes that intensive agriculture has much higher yields per acre under a single crop, but he insists that permaculture grows many different things on the same acre at a fraction of the cost in energy, without poisoning the earth. The better it works the more people and animals it can support, hence his claim that food and population are no problem once we abolish mass agriculture.

'Most large cities can grow most of their own food and even an excess,' he claims. 'Not cities like Los Angeles or Sao Paulo because there isn't any open space. But New York as a whole city – easily. Plenty of space out towards the outskirts. You can't just bulldoze 400 000 acres.

In its first phase, permaculture was designed for self-reliance in single households and small communities. Now his massive Designers Manual covers the theory and practice of managed eco-systems, and is full of homely drawings and detailed instructions on financial and legal implications.

One picture shows contrasting ways of producing an egg. On the left: the industrial egg which requires iron, coal, steel, oil, fish feeds, chemicals, plastics, fertilisers, deadly biocides, grain, and unhygienic hens diseased by unnatural stress.

On the right: the permaculture egg drops from a free-range chicken eating perennial hard seeds dropping from a tree, surrounded by high-protein fruit trees, a fruiting hedge and perennial greens. Only the henhouse drainpipe requires iron and steel for its manufacture. A vine clings to the henhouse.

Mollison finds his message easier to propagate in the Third World, Australia and the New World, where 'people accept alternative ways as feasible. In Europe people feel stifled, they tend to lose heart before they start.'

Meanwhile in Shropshire, permaculture seeps discreetly through farms and nursery gardens. Helen Woodley says, 'It's a lot of common sense really: what the organic movement leaves out.'

Bruce Marshall makes his own breakthrough in the Scottish Borders. Trying to restore lost fertility on the hillsides and plant native broadleaves to replace conifers, he found that clover germinates better after it has passed through the gut of a worm. A discovery worthy of the master.

is 'comparative advantage', which encourages each country to specialise in whatever area of production it is best at, so as to maximise output across the whole EEC. As further quotas are introduced, to reduce surpluses, there will be increasing specialisation. So, Denmark gets the bacon, Spain gets the olives, Holland gets the vegetables, France gets the sheep, Italy gets the sunflowers, and East Anglia gets the wheat. And just wait until Eastern European countries, with their massive, as yet untapped agricultural potential, decide to join the club!

I exaggerate, of course. But comparative advantage and increased specialisation pull us in exactly the opposite direction to the principles of mixed farming and increased self-reliance for each country, not just for the EEC as a bloc. It makes the integration of food production and land stewardship all but impossible.

Such a high-tech 'vision' for the future is the polar opposite of the ideas of the Green Movement today, let alone of Bill Mollison who has pioneered the idea of permaculture (or permanent agriculture):

'Just let nature do all the work.' The very idea is utterly subversive, precisely because it challenges the unconscious assumption that so many people carry with them, that food is primarily man-made. Our problems today are made much worse by most people's alienation from the Earth and the bounty it offers.

The adulteration of food has a long history in the UK, coming into its own in the nineteenth century as new food techniques were developed. The systematic exploitation of the soil, and the life-support systems which produce our food, came rather later in the day. But, if anything, it is this pattern of exploitation which has had an even more profound impact on the ways in which people interpret their relationship with the living Earth.

Until we learn not just to respect but also to revere the Earth, and not just to enjoy but also to celebrate the food we eat, it is highly unlikely that we will heal the wounds we have already inflicted, let alone learn to use the Earth's natural wealth to meet our human needs on a sustainable basis.

Chapter 4

BUILDING
A NEW
SOCIETY

ONE OF THE most important distinctions between green politics and socialism is the emphasis placed on the role of the individual. Most Greens have become deeply suspicious of all those bourgeois individuals on the Left who devote their entire lives to criticising the phenomenon of bourgeois individualism.

Personal responsibility, rooted in a recognition of both one's rights *and* one's obligations as an individual, is the starting point of green politics. Without that recognition, the spectre of 'green fascism' looms very large; whether that fascism be inspired by the Right or by the Left is immaterial. The fact is that we face very troubled times ahead as we come hard up against the limits of the Earth, and inevitably there will be a succession of voices calling for the kind of authoritarian short cuts and 'we-know-best' collective solutions that time after time have brought down democracy in one country after another.

Part of the Left today (but perhaps no longer the larger part?) is still wedded to a centrally planned, state-dominated, inflexibly centralised concept of government. At its best, this results in well-meaning but hopelessly inefficient paternalism; at its dictatorial worst, there is much about Eastern Europe before 1990 that shouldn't be too easily forgotten.

There is individualism and individualism. A determination to make the most of one's own potential; a readiness to use one's talents and skills to benefit others (in addition to one's immediate family); a willingness constantly to explore ways of improving the quality of life for all people; a recognition of one's duties as a citizen of planet Earth; tempering any sense of our own uniqueness with an acute awareness of the extent to which we are all dependent on each other and on an infinitely complex web of relationships with the living world: to me, these are the hallmarks of green individualism.

They are somewhat different from the imprint of individualism stamped so ruthlessly on the eighties, during which the very concept of 'society' was undermined and even denied. This was a decade when individuals were given licence unapologetically to pursue their own material interest at the expense of the 'common wealth'. To them that had, more was given; as for them that hadn't, it was their own fault anyway. Phrases like 'get rich quick', 'loads of money', and 'greed is good' (the most memorable of many such statements from the highly successful film, *Wall Street*) defined the character of the decade with depressing accuracy. Leading representatives of 'One Nation Conservatism' (who emphasise the Conservative Party's responsibility to defend the interests of all people with equal rigour, rather than promote a 'survival of the fittest' approach) were either driven out of the Cabinet or effectively silenced.

The upshot of all this has been to call into question what was surely a legitimate aim of the Government at the start of the decade: to encourage greater self-reliance and reduce excessive dependence on a score of paternalistic agencies. By the end of the decade, self-reliance had come to mean narrow-minded isolationism; reduced dependency has entailed unacceptable hardship and loneliness for many thousands of people.

But it's entirely meaningless to blame every social evil and human failure on the Government. The automatic response of the opposition parties to any bad news on the social front (be it another rise in crimes of violence or worries about our dirty streets being more copiously covered in dog mess) is to attribute it exclusively to the failure of the Government's economic policy. Such ritualised political point-scoring masks a range of far more serious and deep-seated social problems that have little to do with one government or another.

It's hard not to get depressed at the catalogue of ecological woes that flashes up on our TV screens week after week. But it's even harder not to get even more depressed at the catalogue of wrongs inflicted by human beings (mostly by men, it should be said) on themselves or on other humans. Day after day, details of the latest horrors involving child abuse, rape, assault, drug addiction or alcohol abuse are scattered through the newspapers or TV and radio bulletins. Behind those peaks of inhumanity, there looms an entire range of statistical information about the less newsworthy varieties of suffering and unhappiness: mental illness, homelessness, runaway children, bullying at school, abject poverty, family breakdown, and loneliness. There is considerable controversy about whether or not these things are on the increase. Since they've always been with us, some might ask, why should we get more worked up about them now than we did before?

What worries me is the ease with which we take all this for granted. Isn't it time to ask some rather more fundamental questions? Given that we have failed to reduce residual levels of violence, unhappiness and alienation, despite all our wealth-creating powers and industrial might, shouldn't we consider the possibility that there is something inherently flawed in the vision of progress which has goaded one generation after another since the start of the Industrial Revolution? Furthermore, are things ever going to improve without a different vision to fire and inspire us, or are we content to tolerate an inequitable and violent society for the foreseeable future?

The fact that you are reading this paragraph, and may have been one of those who watched the series on television, probably indicates that you're comfortably ensconced among the 'haves' (relatively speaking) and may very well retain a lingering confidence in the notion that social problems can only be resolved through the redistribution and 'trickling down' of the wealth created as our economy continues to grow. The prevailing 'wisdom' has it that quality of life is a by-product of a permanently expanding economy. As long as we've got enough money to throw at the social services, at the National Health Service, at schools and at our dirty, decaying old cities, then all will be hunky-dory.

But what if the actual process of generating that growth simultaneously engenders social problems at least as great as the capacity of that new wealth to deal with them? And what if the kind of value system necessary to ensure success in a competitive, growth-oriented economy (one which reinforces narrow self-interest, acquisitiveness, indifference to others, and devil-take-the-hindmost consumerism) is progressively undermining society in so profound and damaging a way that no amount of money can ever compensate for the human cost involved?

I believe the evidence of this surrounds us at every turn, but we just don't want to confront it. It's much easier to turn the proverbial blind eye to the irreparable damage done to people's sense of community, identity and mutuality as we oscillate back and forth between vicious individualism and disempowering collectivism. It's easier by far to imagine that a different government would magically close the gap between rich and poor and equally magically produce the extra billions required to sort out the National Health Service and the educational system. But these are futile pipe dreams.

You may remember Mark Twain's famous comment: 'If your only tool is a hammer, then all problems look like nails.' As regards the National Health Service, the only tool which governments seem to have at their disposal is the promise of more money; yet there are so many loose nails that the whole edifice is slowly collapsing. Strange though it seems today, the founders of the National Health Service anticipated sharp increases in expenditure for the first few years, followed by a steady *decline* in expenditure as free maternity services, free immunisation programmes, and free advice on prevention and diet ensured that fewer people fell ill. In fact, real spending has increased year by year, and there are now more doctors per head of population than ever before.

I therefore continue to listen in astonishment when politicians compete amongst themselves to prove that their care and concern for the National Health Service is greater than that of their opponents. The one absolutely guaranteed way of proving just how much you care is to demonstrate that during your time of office more patients had more operations, more outpatients had more treatments, and more GPs issued more prescriptions. Everybody cheers and raves about these statistics, as if they genuinely constituted a significant measure of progress in society. The truth is that if people continue to see health in terms of the provision and consumption of illness services, and an exponential increase in those illness services year after year, then there is *no* solution to the problems of the National Health Service.

The underlying argument runs something like this: people fall ill because they are feckless, ignorant or unlucky. The answer is to provide health services, and the money to pay for these services must be raised from the proceeds of a successful and permanently expanding industrial economy. Health services can only be improved if the economic activities within that economy are increased, regardless of the resulting environmental and social costs. When you begin to realise that much of the ill-health in our society is a direct consequence of inappropriate economic activity, then the vicious circularity of that argument is fully revealed.

It is exactly the same argument with the environment: the environment needs to be protected and enhanced; therefore we need more environmental services and more expenditure on the environment. To achieve this we need to speed up the process of economic growth, even if that process is precisely what caused the problems in the first place. Both approaches are equivalent to suggesting that one might deal with food poisoning by prescribing a course of botulism-ridden hazelnut yoghurt.

Conventional economic theory has always assumed that the creation of wealth and the creation of health are two totally separate things, and that the effort of improving health has to be regarded as an economic cost. Though good health is regarded by most people as something of inestimable and unquantifiable value, it is treated by economists as a costly extra. Worse still, our economists and politicians do not seem to have looked at the whole question of public health from an historical perspective. Public health has indeed improved dramatically at different times in the history of industrial society. However, these improvements were not achieved through better health services *per se* (which actually made a fairly minor contribution relatively late in the day), but rather through better housing, improved diet, safe drinking water and decent sewage systems. Improved health in the nineteenth century was almost entirely due to better environmental and economic policies.

As we all know, substantial inequalities in health still exist, and these inequalities are directly related to people's socio-economic class. Healthier diets, for example, tend to be more expensive diets. The continuing relationship between the distribution of ill-health and the distribution of wealth in our society exposes the debate about increased funding for the National Health Service for the dishonest nonsense it really is.

No doubt there are many important things that *could* be done if the NHS received extra funds. However, if funding is seen as the *only* problem, we shall find ourselves in precisely the same position this time next year, and the year after, until the end of time. Until we achieve a much more fundamental redistribution of the funds available, away from high-technology treatment facilities and reactive, curative approaches, towards genuine health education and health promotion programmes, then it seems that we will be stuck indefinitely in this trap. And it is worth recalling, as an example of the imbalance in public expenditure, that Community Health Councils receive 0.006 per cent of the total NHS budget today. So much for preventive health care.

One might suppose, looking at the inherent absurdity of trying to run a Health Service within such a context, that our politicians are either criminals or fools. But they are neither: they are victims of an economic system that almost inevitably ends up promoting poor health through poor diets in order to prosper.

Let us test that rather dramatic assertion by assessing the contribution of the food industry to Gross National Product (GNP) – which, as we'll see in the next chapter, is the *only* respected indicator of progress and wealth in an advanced industrial economy.

When they emerge from the Earth, or are plucked from the tree, raw, natural foods do indeed have a value in the market place. That value is determined by an immensely complex set of variables, such as soil quality, organic or inorganic inputs, farmers' incomes, distribution and retailing costs, etc. But beyond all these variables, that *basic* value can be powerfully enhanced (with proportionately beneficial impacts on GNP) by adding *extra* value through additional processing. My staple diet as a child (when left to my own devices at lunchtime)

Only one Heartbeat away from being fit

DOCTORS and health authorities as far away as New Zealand and the Soviet Union are keeping close tabs on Heartbeat Wales, the ambitious fitness campaign which aims to reduce heart-attack deaths in the principality by 15% by the end of the century.

The aim is to involve the whole 3 m Welsh population in a drive for better eating habits, less smoking and improved all-round lifestyle.

Professor John Catford, the Heartbeat Wales' director, says: 'We are quietly optimistic that this can be achieved, because our recent interim survey reveals that the message is getting across: 40% of those questioned have changed to a healthier diet and sought to lose weight; 32% are fitter and taking more exercise, while 12.5% of smokers claim to have given up for more than three months.

'Wales is Britain's largest consumer of skimmed milk, while farmers and butchers are responding to our campaign for leaner meat. Restaurants compete for Heartbeat awards which acknowledge the serving of nutritious dishes. And chips-with-everything school dinners and works canteen lunches are being replaced with healthier alternatives.'

IOLA SMITH, © THE SUNDAY TIMES 11.12.1988

was the ubiquitous fish finger, liberally adorned with lashings of tomato sauce! The autumn 1989 issue of the *Food Magazine* caused me to question, a little belatedly, the wisdom of such a diet:

> **❝** *Shoppers in the UK bought some £300 million worth of fish fingers last year. They offer a relatively inexpensive and attractive way of encouraging reluctant fish eaters to eat highly nutritious food. But for the amount of fish you find in some fish fingers, you might get a better bargain buying fresh salmon.*
>
> *Our analyses showed that, for the purchase price, shoppers appeared to be getting poor value in terms of fish for their money. Products appeared to be between 40 per cent and 50 per cent fish, and buying fish in this form could cost over £6 per lb weight.*
>
> *These figures suggest that fresh salmon would cost little more than the average fish finger, on a fish per penny basis. Products such as tinned sardines or mackerel represent better value, and so does much fresh or frozen white fish such as cod or coley.* **❞**

In all such instances, from exotic-flavoured crisps to squashed-fly biscuits, adding value through processing makes excellent economic sense. Having found a way of adding value to the product, you then have to persuade people that their lives will

93

be totally impoverished without it, thereby generating lashings of GNP-enhancing wealth through advertising, public relations, promotions and so on.

That the product may subsequently cause enormous health problems is *entirely irrelevant* to the process of generating economic growth. That cost is externalised on to the population at large (through taxation to support the NHS), rather than internalised in the cost of the processed item.

By the same token, crime has a peculiarly beneficial effect on the economy. Take burglary: from the moment the illegal entry is effected, GNP begins to benefit, through the manufacture of the new goods needed to replace those which have been stolen, the insurance company staff needed to check out the claim, the investment in burglar alarms and other security devices to deter further break-ins, the increased investment in the police to investigate the crime, new courts of law and more judicial officers, more prisons and more prison officers to staff them, and more social workers to ensure that the criminal is properly rehabilitated into society after making this astonishing contribution to our economic wellbeing! At the end of 1989, the total cost of crime in the United Kingdom, including the police force, was £100 million a week.

It would pay us hand over fist to invest *real* sums of money, particularly in inner-city areas, to reduce that burden on the economy and on society. And a burden it is, whether or not it increases GNP. But the mechanisms available to us for assessing real costs and real benefits are extraordinarily primitive.

EDUCATION FOR LIFE ON EARTH

The gradual breakdown of so many of our inner cities has exacerbated cycles of poverty, oppression and poor health in a way that defies the powers of the different agencies charged with the task of alleviating or removing these burdens to do very much more than keep the lid on the whole boiling lot. From personal experience, I know only too well what that actually means for teachers in inner-city areas, many of whom consider themselves quite lucky if they spend more than 50 per cent of their time actually teaching. Standing in as surrogate parents, social workers, child-minders, councillors, entertainers, and the butt of everyone's complaints keeps them pretty well occupied the rest of the time.

Just as I was finishing off this chapter in December 1989, a report from Manchester University revealed that 5 per cent of secondary school teachers were leaving the profession every year – five times the Government's official estimate of 1 per cent. That amounts to more than 20 000 highly qualified people leaving a profession which they probably entered with more than the average share of dedication and commitment.

The report, involving 417 secondary schools in England and Wales, identified low pay, a loss of professional status, and the enormous pressures caused by the introduction of the GCSE and the National Curriculum, as the major reasons for teachers moving on. Those extra pressures would almost certainly have been absorbed if teachers today didn't feel devalued, even humiliated, by Mrs Thatcher's Government.

There are many things that commentators will regret about the eighties, but none will weigh more heavily upon the UK's future prospects than the sustained and utterly scandalous assault on the teaching profession by one Secretary of State for Education after another. John MacGregor, the present incumbent, seems at long last to be reversing this trend, but given the barrage of critical, censorious, belittling and patronising comments made about teachers over the last ten years, is it any surprise that it's now impossible to recruit enough graduates, let alone the best graduates?

Even if we aspired, as a nation, to be more successful in conventional economic and technological terms than we are now, the wasted decade of the eighties has all but guaranteed our progressive decline. The chances of equipping people with the skills and attitudes they will need for the different challenges that now confront us are in some ways even more remote.

I was lucky: I left teaching in 1984 to become Director of Friends of the Earth, thus missing out on the ensuing collapse of morale. Yet I loved every minute of the nine years I spent as a teacher of English and Drama at a comprehensive in West London, and remain utterly committed to the state system. To some, that has always seemed rather eccentric, given that I myself was fortunate enough to be educated at Eton College, a place that has become synonymous with privilege, power and wealth.

Yet it was precisely because I enjoyed my own education so much, and felt it had given me such enormous benefits, that I wanted to be a teacher. Having now seen the best and the worst of both the private and the state systems of education, I feel the deepest frustration at the way in which the educational debate in this country revolves for ever around those two fixed points. I very much sympathise with those who believe that the best should be available to *all* children and should never be determined by one's ability to pay. However, for reasons both good and bad, a growing number of people have come to believe that the state system, particularly in inner-city areas, cannot provide the best. In many cases (though nothing like as many as the press would have you believe) this is sadly true.

Committed though I may be to the state system, I am *not* committed to the vast, alienating comprehensives which for so many represent the only option. The loss of human scale, the detachment of such schools from the community (indeed, what can 'community' mean when a school's catchment area embraces hundreds of thousands of people?), the near impossibility of allowing the children themselves to participate in the running of such schools, the inevitable standardisation of teaching style and organisational inflexibility – these things all but guarantee that large comprehensives will fail a great many of the children that pass through them.

As ever, it won't surprise you to hear that it doesn't have to be like this. There are many different models, but none conforms more closely to the green ideal than the Danish education system. Their state schools are far more diverse than ours, though many of them are still very large, and function on the principle of encouraging maximum participation from both children and parents. The 1975 Danish Education Act states:

> 66 *Schools should prepare pupils for participation and co-determination in our democratic society in order that they can assume co-responsibility for seeking solutions to common problems. Freedom of expression, intellectual liberty and democracy must therefore be the foundations upon which the school's existence is built.* 99

A subsequent paragraph would no doubt have made Kenneth Baker's hair stand on end:

> 66 *The planning and detailed arrangements relating to all educational matters, including the choice of curricula content, teaching methods and organisational structure, must be decided jointly by the teachers and the pupils.* 99

96

Their state schools provide a very reasonable education for the majority of people, but the Danish system goes a great deal further. Acknowledging that there will always be some parents for whom such a system is inadequate, the Danish government subsidises 85 per cent of the cost of all *independent* schools, in effect providing the same amount of money for each child regardless of the school in which they're educated.

Denmark's independent schools are quite different from ours. They're no Etons or Harrows; nor are they the breathtakingly awful private schools for which so many British parents still sacrifice so much. The reason for that is simple: the parents set up the schools themselves, and are essentially able to determine the style of teaching, the curriculum content (over and above the basic National Curriculum) and even the appointment of teachers. A school must have 12 pupils in its first year, 20 in the second, and a minimum of 27 from then on in order to qualify for the basic per capita subsidy. Roughly 10 per cent of children between seven and 16 attend a private school, and that percentage is not 'class-based'. The 15 per cent contribution from parents (around £500) is considerably reduced for those who are unemployed or on social security.

Don't for a moment imagine that this means that all Danish schools are bright green in their approach to education. The principle is that the 'consumer in the education market' (i.e. parents) should have a genuine choice. As it happens, the largest number of independent schools are actually very exam-oriented, and many of them are really quite 'ungreen'. Others are specifically set up as Christian schools, or as 'progressive' schools. Around 50 fall into the category of 'small schools', with an average of about 60 pupils.

The two schools we visited in Denmark for the TV series may well have been within a few miles of each other, but they were like chalk and cheese. The first (Morks School) was founded in 1895 as one of the earliest independent schools in Denmark. Its ethos is very traditional, with great emphasis on discipline, politeness and factual knowledge. The second (Hillerod School) was set up in 1965 by a group of parents with the specific aim of encouraging creativity, 'learning by doing', and an active democracy within the school. The children are genuinely involved in day-to-day decision making, as are the parents, who seem to mix quite naturally in many of the school's activities.

97

This diversity is precisely what I like about the Danish system. It trusts its people, unlike our system, which tells us that we can like it or lump it. Only a minority of children in Denmark are getting what I would call 'a green education', but the potential is there, as awareness grows, for that rapidly to become the majority. There's no such potential in the UK.

And that's why the endless stream of rhetoric from government ministers about extending freedom of choice is so infuriating; if they'd had the stomach for some genuinely radical reforms, the 1988 Education Act would have looked very different. What's the big deal, after all, about 'opting out'? What about new, independent, parent-led, state-funded schools opting *in*? On previous occasions, the Government has also rejected the idea of educational vouchers as being too radical. So too has the equally reactionary Labour Party, whose recent policy review had nothing new to offer on education, preferring nostalgia for the top-down, paternalistic model of the seventies to any serious review of genuinely empowering alternatives.

In fact, a voucher scheme (in which parents receive an entitlement for each child, and the funding for schools comes via the allocation of these vouchers rather than directly from government) might well provide the Labour Party with something a little more radical if it were operated on a discriminatory basis. Quite simply, the less well off a family, the greater would be the value of its vouchers, thus providing an incentive for schools to raise their per capita allocation and use the increased resources to supply more teachers and better facilities. The attitude seems to be that parents are basically ignorant, and wouldn't be able to handle a voucher system, so it's best to leave it to the professionals to make decisions on their behalf.

In the face of such patronising paralysis, the best we can do is work within our wretchedly monolithic system to sew as many green seeds as possible. And here the prospects are really quite encouraging.

Environmental education is to be one of the five cross-curricular themes within the National Curriculum, together with health, economic awareness, careers and personal development. This will mostly affect the teaching of geography, science and design and technology, although it needn't end there. As an ex-English and Drama teacher, I remember how easy it was to choose class readers and suitable projects which had some bearing on the environment!

The success of this cross-curricular approach over the next few years will depend on the provision by government of properly funded programmes of in-service training.

There's already a lively debate about exactly what is meant by environmental education. Teaching about acid rain, nuclear power and whales is relatively easy for a teacher, especially when you've got hold of some good audio-visual aids to keep the 'little beasts' quiet on yet another interminable Friday afternoon! But looking beyond the *issues* themselves, to the relationships between them and to the power structures and value systems that provide their context, is altogether different. It is now generally accepted that environmental education needs to give children the confidence to make reasoned personal responses to environmental matters, must be based on child-centred participation in the learning process, and should emphasise our relationship with all aspects of the living world, to give a sense of the whole picture rather than a few of its individual parts. As Peter Martin, Education Officer of the World Wide Fund for Nature (WWF), says:

66 *To achieve such a fundamental effect, environmental education cannot be limited by being included in the curriculum as just another 'subject'. It must be seen as something that is delivered by the whole curriculum – and is of such importance that it should be seen as a prime function of education in total.*99

Fortunately, there's bags of good material on the market to assist the worried teacher or parent. Some of the best of this has been produced by the Centre for Global Education at York University, in cooperation with WWF. *Earthrights – Education As If The Planet Really Mattered*, first published in 1987, remains both an essential primer and a definitive text in its own right. Teachers who take to this kind of 'holistic approach' will certainly want to lap up the Centre's later books, *Green Prints For Changing Schools* and *Global Teacher, Global Learner*.

Other pioneers include the Institute for Earth Education (who have some of the best hands-on, eyes-open, ears-flapping ideas in the business!), the International Centre for Conservation Education (whose range of tapes/slides sets is second to none), the Council for Environmental Education

99

Children at Norton School, Stockton-on-Tees, at work in their own wildflower garden.

(who can answer all your questions about what kind of materials are available) and the Royal Society for Nature Conservation's Junior Section, Watch.

But I can save you a lot of time, and myself a lot of words, simply by referring you to the recently published *Teaching Green* by Damian Randle, founder and editor of the magazine *Green Teacher,* extracts from which make up the body of the book. This is a most useful contribution to the debate, bringing inspirational hope and practical ideas even to those teaching in the most parched and sterile of cultural wildernesses.

There are many schools in the UK that are already intent on 'greening' themselves as rapidly as possible. We visited Norton School in Stockton-on-Tees, not least because of the harsh industrial backdrop of the huge ICI complex against which the school buildings are silhouetted. With that on one side, a prison under construction on another, and the main road at the front, Norton School does not exactly conform to any stereotyped notions you might have of a 'green school'!

But there is a vast amount going on within the school that has already brought it national recognition. They have their own herb garden, have planted scores of trees and helped design and construct a pond and wildlife area. Children are encouraged to find out as much as possible about the local environment; as part of a project run by Living Earth, they have been twinned with a school in Kenya, and are preparing for an exchange of students with a view to learning directly about the starkly contrasting environments in which they live. Some of the Third World children run a kindergarten group for parents and toddlers, other link up with various Employment Training schemes.

None of this may sound particularly dramatic, but it is the stuff of which environmentally aware education is made. The teachers at Norton would be the first to agree that they have still got a long way to go before they can claim to be putting into practice all the green ideas they might aspire to.

I know only too well how hard such a process of change can be. As someone who spent ten years in a West London comprehensive, branded as a muesli-munching weirdo for preferring a bike to a car, suffering all the while as innumerable plants or beautiful objects disappeared down Vandals' Alley, or courting disaster by organising school trips with the hardened horrors of 3B to 'experience poetry' in abandoned graveyards, I am not insensible of the demands that such an approach puts on the individual teacher. A lot depends on other members of one's department and, ultimately, on the quality of one's Headteacher. In both these respects, I was singularly blessed.

The environmental challenge is so daunting, and the scale of the problems so enormous, that it is only natural for people to feel powerless when confronting them. To pitch the whole thing at too gloomy a level is more likely to induce despair than anything else; to pitch it neutrally, as a fascinating scientific experiment with us looking on in detached wonder, is a dangerous and deceitful escape from the pressing reality of what is actually happening. As Keats wrote:

> **66** *Philosophy will clip an Angel's wing,*
> *Conquer all mysteries by rule and line,*
> *Empty the haunted air and gnomed mine,*
> *Unweave a rainbow.* **99**

What emerges from any rigorous analysis of the ecological problems we now face is the overwhelming need for a synthesis of scientific enquiry into the workings of life on Earth, and reverence for the residual mystery of that life force. Bill Devall and George Sessions, co-authors of a fascinating book called *On Deep Ecology*, explain it as follows:

" One might go so far as to say that a manager without a sense of the enchantment of the world is without any real understanding of the land. A manager who is not in the 'sacred circle' (in the American Indian sense), who is not participating, who is not in turn being healed by the land, cannot really help heal or protect the land. Such ecological consciousness is tuning to the land, to the spirit of the place, and is not merely manipulating the land to serve some abstract economy."

Education for life on Earth therefore poses a new challenge for teachers – to add to all those already heaped upon them! Getting children down to earth, with their hands literally on the marvel and mystery of creation, must be seen as a prerequisite for any kind of ecological sanity among today's young people. Hence the very real tragedy of millions of city kids alienated from the Earth by impenetrable concrete and tarmac and all the detritus of life-condemning industrialism.

LIVING CITIES

If the Green Movement has anything to offer, it must therefore be able to offer it to people in our concrete jungles as well as to those living in rural areas or in distant rainforests. It is in the cities that expectations are still at their lowest; many people take it for granted that a lousy environment is an inevitable consequence of having to live in an urban area. Planners and politicians rapidly lose any sense of wider purpose in the day-to-day business of holding the whole lot together.

The problem is that cities have never been planned with social and environmental concerns, or even quality of life, uppermost in the planners' minds. Post-war urban planning has been dominated by the need to accommodate the motor car and by a series of disastrous housing policies (starting with high-rise flats) which have all but destroyed the sense of community in many UK cities.

Any 'greenprint' for the city must therefore start with the business of *reclaiming* the street for children (so they have somewhere to play without being packed off to some sterilised play area), for old people (so they don't feel they have to take their lives in their hands merely to get down to the local shops) and for all residents (so they can simply enjoy the interactions and relationships that bind a community together).

Once 'reclaiming the street' becomes the overriding

priority, planning is not so difficult. The Department of Transport's sole spasm of enlightenment over the last few years has been to allow local authorities to install 'sleeping policemen' much more widely than was previously permitted, and they're now beginning to pop up all over the place. That's just one of a variety of engineering features which can be used to 'calm the traffic'. The next step is to give priority to pedestrians at road intersections in residential areas, to achieve a continuous pedestrian network. Suburban residents in the United States and Canada have an automatic right to demand speed limits of 10 mph on their patch if they so wish.

The most highly developed variation of this approach is the Dutch 'woonerf,' where traffic calming is combined with tree planting and other features to create a far more congenial environment. The more that pedestrians and cyclists are specifically planned for, the more attractive walking and cycling become as ways of getting around. The Dutch have experienced some difficulty with the woonerf, largely because motorists automatically assume that they have priority over everyone else (wherever they happen to be driving), but they've established some vital principles which traffic planners elsewhere in Europe are now beginning to adapt to their own particular circumstances.

The degree of enthusiasm for schemes of this kind is partly dependent on the compactness of the community involved. In suburban areas, people tend to favour their cars, and walking is a minority pastime; in densely packed inner-city areas, the car can more easily be relegated to the bottom of the pile. Unfortunately, many new residential developments have progressively reduced housing densities in a highly inefficient way.

From an ecological and social perspective, high concentrations of people in cities are actually very desirable – but let me say at once that high density is a very different thing from high rise. High density allows for the most efficient use of energy; it makes it far easier and more economical to plan for proper public transport; and it encourages mixed use, in that the local shops, pub, post office, doctor's surgery and school can be kept in the community, instead of people having to go elsewhere for those services. Lower densities encourage far greater car use, and a corresponding dispersal of shopping and other services without which a community rapidly loses its heart and soul.

Professor Hugh Freeman in *Mental Health and the Environment* has called for the reversal of the 'overwhelming preoccupation that planners, architects and local governments have had for many years with the reduction of high urban density'. Then he goes on to say:

> 66 *High density is actually essential for the positive qualities of towns and cities, such as cultural life and specialised professional services; the low densities of these suburbs make these facilities difficult to provide without imposing a degree of car travel which is both environmentally damaging and unjust to the more disadvantaged sections of society.*99

Reversing that preoccupation would be a real breakthrough. So too would be a change in the planning guidelines to encourage mixed use, bringing together residential, retail, office and recreational uses which our obsession with 'separate zoning' currently makes impossible. City areas that suddenly become semi-deserted at half past five, because they're all offices or shops, are dangerous and unfriendly places; by contrast, nothing enhances a city's reputation more than lively, lived-in streets where there's plenty going on.

The separation of home and workplace serves to weaken people's sense of identification with either, and it is that degree of identification which makes the difference between a community and a name on the map. As can be seen in many Dutch and German cities, living, working, trading, shopping and playing all gain from being linked in a much more vibrant and diverse set of relationships. It's interesting that the Duchy of Cornwall's proposal for a new town outside Dorchester is being master-minded by Leon Krier, a keen advocate of mixed-use, high-density settlements. In his words:

> 66 *The zoning of uses which has become a planning orthodoxy and ruined our towns, is also the single most important factor behind pollution and the waste of energy everyone is for ever on the move. At least 80 per cent of productive activities could be sited within towns – integrate them into the urban fabric and you contain them.*99

But Dorchester is surrounded by beautiful countryside, which is not the case for the majority of city dwellers. High-density communities need to be balanced by designated 'green spaces' of every description: parks, public gardens, city farms, allotments, playing fields, adventure playgrounds, copses and

New, high-density housing in Clerkenwell Green, near the City of London, designed to make the most of inner-city space.

woods, meadows, overgrown wild areas, green rooftops and so on.

Our predecessors did their level best to keep the natural world *out* of our cities. The city was, after all, a city; if you want greenery, get thee to the countryside! This has encouraged city dwellers to believe that we *can* live totally cut off from nature, and that the natural cycles and life support systems on which we all depend are really none of their business.

Bit by bit, cajoled and inspired by people like David Goode (the erstwhile GLC ecology supremo) and Chris Baines (one of the founders of the urban conservation movement, and still its most articulate exponent), people have been encouraged to defend what green spaces are left and to think far more creatively about new opportunities on disused railway lines, derelict land and hole-in-the-corner 'pocket parks'. Many of these ideas were first pioneered in Holland through a wide variety of experimental landscapes designed to be played in, walked through, touched and smelled, to provide freedom and excitement. At Utrecht, a reed-fringed wetland was laid out round an office block. At Delft, the courtyards of high-rise flats became woodland glades. In inner areas, old buildings were knocked down to make way for parks. Fresh types of green space were invented: cuddle gardens for children, and 'heemparks' where native flowers grew in their natural Dutch habitat of dyke, dune and polder.

At a fraction of the cost of establishing conventional parks,

COMMUNITY FORESTS:
Proposed programme

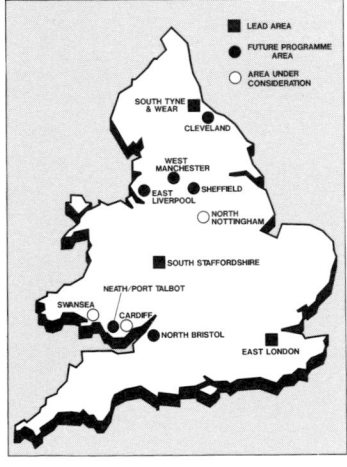

Proposed sites for the Countryside Commission and Forestry Commission's 'community forests', which, with the help and support of the local communities involved, will be flourishing on derelict land outside 12 urban areas in Britain by the middle of the next century. Planting has now begun in south Staffordshire and south Tyne and Wear.

it's possible to evolve a mosaic of living green spaces. And the more involved and active the residents most immediately affected, the more durable and vandal-proof the scheme will be. In Edinburgh, for instance, the Environmental Resource Centre has pioneered environmental education schemes that have been highly successful in preventing vandalism. Leicester now has all sorts of schemes on the boil, including the cropping of grasslands for hay in the middle of the city. In 1986, Tower Hamlets established a limited scheme to plant 10 derelict sites with fast-growing trees so as to provide wood for local timber companies and craft industries. Bristol appointed its first Woodlands Officer back in 1980, and has gradually developed an impressive and highly successful working plan for woodlands within the city.

A proper woodlands strategy for all cities can be a real boon. Not only do trees look attractive and offer genuine contact with the natural world, they also help to filter air pollution and provide a buffer against noise pollution. We should therefore be thinking of much larger schemes, as well as the small, irregular woodland areas that are beginning to be planted. Complementing excellent initiatives such as the Forest of Cardiff, the Countryside Commission and the Forestry Commission have been promoting the development of much larger 'community forests' on urban fringes, for both community and recreational use, and a special Urban Forestry Unit is being set up in the Black Country.

We just need to be a little bit more courageous and visionary in our approach to all this. As David Goode says:

> 66 *If woodlands, why not wetlands? Derelict docks and sewage farms offer possibilities for wetland wildlife which could be very popular in urban areas. Future plans for the vast acreage of Beddington Sewage Farm near Croydon include an extensive nature reserve with lakes, reed beds and lagoons for marshlands birds. It will be a most attractive landscape for people as well as water fowl.* 99

Once we've sorted out our air pollution problems (by reducing the number of vehicles in our cities as rapidly as possible), why should we not encourage more market gardening, allotments and small farms within our cities? We are, after all, a nation of gardeners, and could easily turn some of that enthusiasm into productive enterprise. The National Federation of City Farms launched their newsletter in May

1989 by giving details of city farms and community gardens throughout the United Kingdom, each one providing children with limited but crucially important contact with nature and with the business of food production. Instead of selling off their playing fields, one longs to hear of more enterprising schools establishing their own orchards or gardens.

But it's no good expecting all these initiatives to thrive and prosper unless we change our entire approach to planning in our cities. Instead of viewing conservation and ecology as constraints on the process of inner-city regeneration, they must be seen as preconditions for its long-term success. The GLC, Manchester and West Midlands all deveoped conservation strategies prior to the abolition of the Metropolitan County Councils. These are extremely useful documents, which have since been taken up by many local authorities, but the concern for green spaces and conservation needs to be integrated with local plans to encourage energy efficiency, promote public transport, and introduce extensive traffic calming measures.

One place to which none of these ideas would come as a surprise is the town of Davis in California. This is one of the most astonishing places I've ever come across: it has a population of 40 000 (which they're keen to restrict to no more than 50 000), with 40 000 bicycles and just 9000 cars. There are 70 kilometres of bike lanes. Energy saving is given the highest priority; strict building standards are enforced; thousands of trees have been planted to discourage people from installing air conditioning, and they even hang out their washing in their back yards, which for America is quite unique. They are aiming to derive half their energy sources from the sun by the end of the century. As much domestic waste as possible is recycled, with a separate collection made by specially designed dust carts – *and* it makes the town a healthy profit.

It all started back in the sixties when three students at the University of California's Agricultural Faculty got elected on to the Local Council – and one of those students is now the Mayor. A flow of local legislation began to affect every aspect of life in Davis: bylaws restrict houses to two storeys and business premises to four; average housing densities are much higher than in similar towns elsewhere in the States; allotments are made available to all flat owners without a garden, and

RIGHT: Typical housing in Davis, California – solar panels are taken for granted.

BELOW: The local market in Davis, with fresh produce grown in the surrounding area – quite a rarity for the United States.

organic vegetable and fruit growing is enthusiastically encouraged; there is a twice weekly market, provided for mainly by local farmers – 'Local Supply Stimulates Local Growth' is their favourite slogan.

And it does all seem to have worked. There are no slums, no ghettoes, very little unemployment and the lowest crime rate in the United States. Planning experts come from far and wide to see how it's done. The changes have had the support of the vast majority of the inhabitants of Davis, who have discovered for themselves that thinking and living ecologically does not mean donning a hair shirt and renouncing the world. Real quality of life comes in many different shapes and sizes.

One of the most striking features for me (over and above

all this green theory actually working in practice!) is the emphasis placed on public participation. The local council actively encourages the involvement of interested parties at their meetings, and there is an incredibly strong sense of community.

Participation is an essential element in any urban regeneration strategy; people have to feel that they have a stake in the changes made, and a partial responsibility for their success or failure. It is only possible to improve the urban environment by empowering the people who live in it, and this has to be undertaken consciously and explicitly. Empowerment is one of those things that simply doesn't trickle down from on high.

One of the best examples of this approach in the UK is the Priority Estates Project (PEP), an independent non-profit organisation that links up with local authorities and housing organisations to establish locally based management teams on difficult housing estates. The essential elements of the PEP approach are a full-time local office on the estate itself, resident caretakers, a local repair team on site, a budget coming under the direct control of the estate manager and the fullest possible involvement and participation of the estate residents.

Regeneration and urban greening imply a great deal more than bricks and mortar or trees and potplants. The success of such strategies depends on elusive, nebulous concepts like identification, familiarity, a sense of place, community, feeling safe, home territory, and so on. That intricate web of relationships with people and places that binds a community

Kentish Town City Farm.

together – providing continuity and security – is almost impossible for planners and politicians to deal with, precisely because it's unquantifiable. And that's why politicians and planners should always live among the people they aspire to serve.

An urban community works well when it integrates all the different facets of our lives, and allows each of us to work well as a whole person, not just a bit of a person who happens to be passing through. And that wholeness *has* to include the natural world, contact with other species, changing seasons, a view of the sunset, the cycle of things growing and dying – even if it's only in one's own window box. Without that, a city has no soul, and people will continue to leave it in pursuit of that elusive quality of life in the countryside or the suburbs.

GREENING THE HEALTH SERVICE

Green cities are also healthy cities. A substantial amount of sickness and ill-health in cities is wholly preventable, in that it stems from high levels of stress in dirty and often dangerous environments. As far as city dwellers are concerned, these factors are additional to all the other preventable causes of ill-health, such as poor diet, lack of exercise, smoking, excessive drinking and so on.

There's no hidden magic in the green approach to health. It boils down to four basic principles:

1 Prevention is better than cure – in practice as well as in theory.

2 It's important to deal with the whole person, not just an isolated symptom.

3 It's important to work with, not against, people's own energies.

4 We must invest in giving people *time,* not just another prescription.

We keep coming back to the principle of prevention, in this and other chapters, because it's the cornerstone of a healthy society. But it requires real investment – money up front over a prolonged period of time. At the moment, all those on the preventive front line find their budgets being cut or even axed altogether. Health visitors, Community Health Councils, the Health Education Authority, school nurses: these are precisely the people whose work today is so seriously undervalued. But with the entire NHS operating on a basis of crisis management, the business of looking after people's *future* wellbeing is permanently subordinated to the task of holding things together in the here and now. Excellent initiatives like 'Heartbeat Wales' remain the exception rather than the rule.

What is so frustrating is that this of all governments, with its obsessive interest in cost-effectiveness and value for money, might just have taken up this challenge of the preventive approach. But prevention entails getting out there and talking to people wherever and whenever they're most likely to be listening, and that sounds like nasty old paternalism as far as this Government is concerned. I'm sure you've heard it a hundred times on the radio: 'I'm a government minister, not a nanny. Who am I to tell people what they should eat, or suggest that they should stop smoking?' It's as if such people have never heard of the huge success of the preventive programme in the United States to reduce coronary heart disease, or of similar programmes in many EEC countries.

Sadly, of course, it goes a great deal further than that. The Government's extremely cosy relationship with the pharmaceutical companies ensures that drug-based curative medicine will remain paramount in our society until there's a genuine medical revolution. Joe Collier's excellent book, *The Health Conspiracy*, takes the lid off the way in which the pharmaceutical companies retain and extend their influence with both government officials and GPs.

It's the GPs on whom we must count to bring about any lasting transformation. At the moment, most GPs are *not* on the front line of preventive medicine. Far from it. If anything, the majority are in the business of perpetuating patterns of dependency and helplessness among their patients. Many are indeed very hard-pressed, and do their best in almost impossible circumstances, but many simply don't know how to talk to their patients and are only too happy to go on dishing out the prescriptions. If all else fails – particularly tolerance, patience and compassion – there's always a pill.

A green approach to health quite simply means making healthy choices easier choices. In this respect, our physicians must examine themselves very closely indeed. So too must those charged with administering the NHS itself. As the largest employer in the whole of Western Europe (involving more than a million employees), with vast purchasing power and unparalleled opportunities to influence people at just the time when they're thinking most acutely about health, the NHS should be enthusiastically enlisted in the battle for the planet. On issues like transport (encouraging cycling or walking), energy efficiency (God knows how much energy our hot-house hospitals are responsible for squandering!), food (nutritional expertise still seems a little thin on the ground in hospitals), pollution prevention (from CFCs and aerosols through to rigorous controls on their own incinerators), recycling, building materials, avoidance of tropical hardwoods and many other points, the greening of the NHS has to be a major priority for the nineties.

HOLISTIC HEALTH

Millions of people in this country have already made up their own minds about conventional medicine. The Research Council for Complementary Medicine estimates that 10 per cent of all medical consultations in Britain take place with alternative practitioners. Others have put the figure as high as 30 per cent. There are now more than 30 000 alternative or complementary therapists, offering people a more holistic approach to health, in which they are treated as people rather than as a collection of arbitrary and unconnected symptoms.

The connection between this kind of approach to health and the concern that so many people feel for the environment is explained by Dr Patrick Pietroni, Chairman of the British Holistic Medical Association:

> 66 *As we sow, so shall we reap, and many of the concerns, distresses and epidemics affecting us at this stage of our progress are the direct result of the influence of the environment on us. Just as we need to increase our awareness of the interconnectedness between body, mind and spirit, so we need to understand how each of our actions, from smoking a cigarette to throwing a can of beer away, affects our fellow human beings, some of them many thousands of miles away, others neighbours in our streets. Looking after your own environment will help make you aware of the interconnections and encourage the balance and harmony necessary to your individual health.* 99

When making the television series, we visited Dr George Lewith at the Centre for the Study of Complementary Medicine in Southampton. The services at the Centre include acupuncture, osteopathy, chiropractic, homeopathy, clinical ecology, psychotherapy, the Alexander Technique and hypnosis. A study they carried out in 1985 showed that most of their patients first came to them because of the failure of conventional medicine, but that they had not entirely lost confidence in their own GPs, despite what they saw as their narrow approach.

Complementary medicine remains a peculiarly controversial issue in this country, largely because the medical establishment feels threatened by something they cannot understand and over which they have no control. The British Medical Association's 1986 report on alternative therapies was a mind-bending exercise in prejudice and partial evidence, and exhibited a degree of hostility that simply isn't felt by most GPs and practising doctors. One survey of 200 GPs in Avon found that 59 per cent of them referred patients to alternative practitioners, 16 per cent practised a form of alternative medicine themselves and 42 per cent wanted further training in alternative techniques. An earlier study found that 86 out of 100 young trainee general practitioners had a positive attitude to alternative medicine.

Complementary therapists know that they must now get their house in order, with proper accreditation schemes and more demanding qualifications. For there are indeed a minority of quacks and inadequately trained lay practitioners among their number, and the sooner they are discredited, the better it will be for everyone.

For me, the most interesting thing about the work George Lewith and his colleagues are doing is the way in which it integrates orthodox and complementary approaches. At the moment, complementary therapies are very rarely available on the NHS, but their goal is to see far more practices where conventional doctors and complementary therapists are working side by side, and learning from each other. It's already possible for so-called 'ancillary staff' to be brought into NHS practices, and Lewith is suggesting that this should be extended to include not just psychotherapists and counsellors, but osteopaths, acupuncturists, and homeopaths.

He also believes that the GP's new contract will actually

make things somewhat easier; practices will have to become more 'consumer-oriented' (more patient-led) and the programmes of individual health maintenance will be better balanced if they embrace complementary therapies and preventive principles as well as orthodox responses. Doctors will also be encouraged to undertake additional in-service training, and many will opt to extend their range of skills within the complementary area. This will further erode an already artificial dividing line between two approaches which could so easily be mutually reinforcing rather than mutually exclusive.

Within a decade, such integrated practices (of which only a very few exist at the moment) could become the norm. But a lot will depend on proper resourcing. Complementary therapies are very cheap on medication, but demand a lot more time from the staff involved; conventional medicine saves a lot on time, but costs an arm and a leg for medication (£1.5 billion in 1988, with 300 million prescriptions). There will clearly have to be some juggling to redirect resources away from drugs into human beings. Such a reallocation of time is currently judged to be 'uneconomic'.

This is very reminiscent of the different attitudes embodied in chemical and organic farming: we want less of the artificial, synthetic inputs (in terms of chemicals on the land and drugs in the human body) and more of the human input (by way of better and more labour-intensive husbandry in farming, and face-to-face counselling in medicine).

Just as organic farming is coming out of its ghetto, so too are the complementary therapists. Looking ahead, 1992 and the single market will accelerate that trend, as large homeopathic interests in Germany and France begin to take an interest in the UK. If the nineties are indeed to be the decade when the self-reliance and individualism of the eighties are tempered and softened by greater compassion and less materialistic attitudes, then complementary medicine will clearly be well placed to meet that new demand. For its aim is to make people more independent of health practitioners precisely by giving them a better understanding of the workings of their own bodies. It's as much about *real* quality of life as it is about freedom from disease and illness.

Chapter 5

A WORD ON ECONOMICS

Aɴ Aᴍᴇʀɪᴄᴀɴ economist once described economics as 'a severe form of brain death'. In its current form, I'd go along with that judgement, as I imagine would millions of people around the world who remain completely baffled by the way in which economics and common sense have become almost mutually exclusive.

We're just halfway through this book, and yet there have already been dozens of instances where conventional economics seems to compel people to act against their own long-term interests by sacrificing the environment, and where sound, practical alternatives have had to be ruled out because they're judged to be 'uneconomic'. As we will see in the second half, this happens even more frequently when it comes to international issues.

This has become a matter of particular anxiety for the Green Movement, in that real economics is actually what we're all about. The concept of 'economics' has two Greek roots: *oikos* ('our house, or home', and therefore by extension 'our planet') and *nomos* (meaning 'to manage'). Economics is just a fancy word for housekeeping.

No one can deny that, in ecological terms, human beings are absolutely hopeless when it comes to planetary housekeeping. We have befouled and begrimed our home with all the manic enthusiasm of a visiting vandal, as if we were under the impression that our residency here on Earth is only temporary and, that once we've made the most of its natural wealth, we'll all be 'beamed up' to some extra-terrestrial space station to continue our pillagers' progress through the Milky Way.

Western-style economics now dominates practically every corner of the Earth, with the odd exception like Albania, which has little to offer the rest of the world by way of an alternative. Eastern Europe is going West as fast as it possibly can, and even the most remote Third World country has long since been drawn into the toils and snares of today's world economic order. But what is startling is the conceptual bankruptcy at the heart of this all-conquering economic order, and the frailty of the foundations on which it is built.

So accustomed have we become to today's prevailing orthodoxy, and so successfully has it colonised every other facet of our lives, that one hears scarcely a peep of protest at its inherent idiocy from within the system. Even when the whole pack of cards looks as if it's about to come tumbling down (another crash on the Stock Market; threats of a major debtor country defaulting on its loans; dire predictions of the world economy going into recession), it's the inadequate skills of those building the house of cards that are criticised, not the terrible weaknesses in the process itself. Speaking personally, I hate that sense of vulnerability, of my economic security resting in the hands of jaded City yuppies, dehumanised bankers, or weary, ill-informed politicians. And, of course, it's an illusion to suppose that even they are in control.

Manipulation on the money markets, a run on sterling, or a collapse of confidence on Wall Street or in Tokyo, and years of patient policy development by any one country or government can be laid low in a moment. Such dependence on powerful, utterly unaccountable forces makes a mockery of any aspirations to determine our own future as a nation.

Breaking that dependence, and building an alternative, sustainable economic system will no doubt be the work of several generations. However, we need to consider some of the rudiments of that alternative now, for the long-term value and significance of the Green Movement clearly depends on its ability to challenge today's economic orthodoxy, and to find something better to put in its place. Economic growth, sustainability, self-reliance and debt: if we could just get to grips with 'the big four' we'd be halfway there.

GROWTH GROWS UP

Few words can have caused more confusion or consternation in the development of green politics than 'growth'. Some utter this simple word with unconcealed distaste, as if the foulest imprecation had just passed their lips. Others invest it with magical, indeed holy powers, as if the mere repetition of the word might be sufficient to ward off all political mishaps. Since the mid-sixties, some have seen the pursuit of economic growth as the root of all evil; others as an automatic passport to heaven on Earth.

The reality, as ever, is rather more prosaic. The concept of growth is a useful economic tool that has been profoundly abused by politicians and by economists, who have never properly defined its usefulness. For it is useful in two ways: as one of a number of mechanisms by which human aspirations can be met, and as one of a number of yardsticks by which we measure our success in meeting these aspirations.

In an unpublished article, the economist Michael Jacobs has some interesting thoughts on this:

The Japanese Stock Market.

66 *The extent to which any given rise in GNP [Gross National Product] is damaging to the environment depends therefore on what it is that is growing. GNP simply records the overall total. It is quite possible for GNP to go up with fewer resources being used, and less pollution being generated, if the content of growth tends away from environmentally degrading activities.*

In the use of some resources, this has indeed been happening. For most of this century, technological progress (which raises the productivity of material and energy inputs) and the trend away from manufacturing towards services, have combined to reduce the 'materials intensity' of GNP. That is, there has been a reduction in the quantity of resources needed to produce each unit of GNP.

Of course, this is not happening with all the resources and pollutants; the statement that current patterns of economic growth are causing major ecological problems remains valid. But the point is that it need not be true. 99

117

But rather than acknowledging the limitations of the concept and pursuit of economic growth, almost all politicians since the Second World War have progressively built up its conceptual significance so that, instead of it being merely one of the means by which we achieve our ends, it has become the single most important end of human society.

The process is somewhat akin to obsessive obesity: instead of simply assuaging hunger, providing energy, ensuring convivial company or pleasant aesthetic experiences, the business of eating becomes the only activity which provides any kind of meaning or satisfaction or fulfilment, and eating itself becomes the only goal of existence. All industrial economies are now terminally confused between means and ends, between eating for living and eating for eating's sake.

Economic growth is simply not an adequate measure of economic welfare. It gives no indication of the sustainability of growth; as regards North Sea oil reserves, for instance, the more oil we export in any one year, the better it is for the economy. The future can look after itself.

Economic growth cannot measure the genuine efficiency of growth; as we've seen, modern farming is in fact one of the least efficient systems in the world when measured in terms of the energy used to produce a given output of calories.

Furthermore, it cannot indicate just *who* is benefiting from the growth; it is perfectly possible that an increase in luxury consumption will lead to a growth in GNP, while poor people actually become worse off. It cannot discriminate between the genuine benefits of industrial production and the costs, and it is incapable of acknowledging the value arising from the work done in the so-called 'informal' sectors of the economy, including both cash transactions within the black economy and all the unpaid work done in households, communities and voluntary organisations.

Though it is unfashionable, it would be a bracing experience for politicians to have to lay out their actual *goals*, and only in the light of having completed that process, to assess the best means of achieving them. Ever one to practise what I preach, here goes:

1   To satisfy the basic material needs (food, water, shelter, clothing) and fundamental social needs (such as health care and education) of all human beings.

2   To protect the life-support systems of planet Earth to
    ensure that we can meet those needs *sustainably* (i.e. on an
    indefinite basis).

3   To achieve the highest quality of life via the minimum
    throughput of energy and raw materials in the economy.

Satisfying our subsistence needs must obviously come first,
and basic human justice demands that these needs be universally
met. To avoid terrible suffering in the future, those needs must
clearly be met today in such a way that does not rule out their
being met tomorrow.

Over and above those subsistence and basic social needs,
there is a range of less quantifiable, less definable human
aspirations which contribute to the real quality of our lives:
good friends, supportive neighbourhoods, security, cultural
and recreational pursuits, clean air, pure water, access to nature,
peace of mind, etc – the list of these 'quality of life' factors is
a long one, and differently balanced in different cultures.

If these goals were to be agreed upon as the most useful for
humankind, then the usefulness of economic growth could be
assessed *exclusively* in terms of its ability to attain those goals.
In that context, merely generating higher levels of GNP, of
production and consumption, would be seen as totally
irrelevant: *some* of that increased GNP might work towards
our goals (especially in Third World countries), but much of
it would not.

It is now four decades since the Dag Hammarskjöld
Foundation coined the term 'Another Development', when
it put forward a radically different approach. The five
principles of Another Development, which are at last beginning
to make something of an impact, emphasise that development
should be:

1   Needs-oriented, meeting both material and non-material
    needs.

2   Self-reliant, with each society relying primarily on its own
    strengths and resources to meet its needs.

3   Ecologically sound, recognising and working within the
    'outer limits' of a finite biosphere.

4   Diverse, with a variety of development patterns respecting
    the diversity of different cultures and values.

5   Participatory, with a return to the human scale, self-management and appropriate technology.

The principle is clear: the key to successful development lies not in maximising the flow of energy and raw materials through the economy, but, on the contrary, in delivering the culturally demanded standards of living with minimum use of mineral, energy and environmental resources.

SUSTAINABILITY

The notion of 'sustainability', in an environmental context, has been with us for a very long time. One of the earliest controversies between environmentalists was fought out in the United States around the turn of the century. In the dark green corner were the likes of John Muir (founder of the Sierra Club), out and out *preservationists* who believed that America's vast expanses of wilderness should be preserved from all but recreational use. In the light green corner was Gifford Pinchot, adviser to Theodore Roosevelt, who advocated a *conservationist* approach to wilderness areas, arguing that their natural resources should be properly managed and exploited on a rational and sustainable basis.

'Sustainable exploitation' has been widely referred to since then – though very rarely put into practice anywhere in the world. But over the last few years, talk of sustainability has become all the rage among environmentalists and politicians alike: sustainable development; sustainable growth; sustainable progress; sustainable agriculture; sustainable markets; sustainable yields – about the only thing that isn't sustainable is the level of dishonesty with which such an important word is being abused!

The Brundtland Report of the World Commission on Environment and Development, *Our Common Future,* defined sustainable development as follows:

> 66 *Meeting the needs of the present without compromising the ability of future generations to meet their own needs [...] The process of change in which the expectation of resources, the direction of investments, the orientation of technological development, and institutional change are all in harmony and enhance both current and future potential to meet human needs and aspirations.* 99

You wouldn't know it from that kind of jargon, but 'sustainable' has quite a simple meaning: something capable of being kept going on an indefinite basis – not till the end of the week, or the end of the decade, or even the end of the next century, but *indefinitely*. To refer therefore to 'sustainable extraction techniques of our North Sea oil reserves' is an utter nonsense. Or to suppose that modern farming is even remotely sustainable, as the National Farmers Union persists in doing, is wilfully misleading. As we've seen, modern farming depends on a massive input of incontrovertibly *finite* fossil fuels, and a process of mining the soil which will last only as long as the soil is deep.

The concept of 'sustainable growth' is in fact a contradiction in terms: exponential growth (in either human numbers or volumes of production and consumption) *cannot* be sustained indefinitely on a finite resource base. A 3 per cent growth rate implies a doubling of production and consumption every 25 years. Nobody actually disagrees with this, not even the most manic 'growthist'. But, professional Micawbers that they all are, they just go on hoping that something will turn up before their bluff is finally called.

The difference between growth and sustainable growth (or so-called 'green growth') can be likened to the difference between an ordinary car and one fitted with a catalytic converter. The latter is indisputably less polluting than the former, but it is still a petrol-guzzling, environment bashing vehicle. Green growth *may* turn out to be less polluting, less wasteful and more efficient in terms of energy and resources (all of which are highly desirable goals, enthusiastically to be campaigned for), but its adherents still seem to subscribe to one, all-powerful item of economic dogma: that it is only through the continuous expansion of production and consumption that it will be possible to meet human needs, improve material standards of living and ensure that wealth trickles down to the unfortunate billions who haven't yet had 'their share of the cake'. And we saw in Chapter 1 just how grave an illusion that is.

But sustainable development *is* possible. Production of timber from forests can be sustained indefinitely, cycle after cycle. The production of food through organic agriculture can be sustained indefinitely. Unlimited energy supplies can be sustained indefinitely from renewable sources, such as sun, wind, wave and tidal power. And though it is technically inaccurate to say that even the most commonly occurring raw materials can be mined or extracted on a sustainable basis (in that eventually, however far in the future, they will run out), a combination of re-use, repair and recycling could slow down the rate of depletion so as to make their supply all but indefinite.

When one looks at it more carefully, what we're really talking about is putting the world economy on to a *less unsustainable* path than it's on currently, rather than seeking to achieve absolute sustainability. But, as with all these things, there is a distinct tide in the affairs of man, and endlessly pointing out the linguistic errors of our ways serves little purpose. Just as it is infinitely preferable that we should aspire to become green consumers rather than old-fashioned Earth-bashing consumers, so it is better that world leaders should at least (and at last) be grappling with the notion of sustainable development, even if it is a rather anaemic version of the full-blooded original.

ALTERNATIVE INDICATORS

If sustainability is to be *the* key economic concept of the future, then the use of GNP as the exclusive measure of economic success has obviously had its day. It's a bit like trying to assess one's enjoyment of a piece of music by measuring the number of notes in it.

It's tempting for people to dismiss the idea of finding alternative indicators as being of secondary concern, which is why politicians to date have simply gone along with the system, confining their disagreements to policies on inflation, unemployment and so on. However, it looks as if the next British general election will at long last open up the political debate about economic indicators, as both the Labour Party and the Democrats have begun to develop an alternative approach over the last two years. There are essentially three options here:

1   Get rid of GNP altogether and replace it with a new catch-all measure.

2   Adjust GNP in such a way that it reflects some of the environmental and social concerns which are otherwise neglected.

A new teak plantation in Java,
Indonesia. This is where our tropical
hardwoods will come from in future.

3 Devise a whole set of comprehensive economic and social
indicators, of which GNP is just one.

Various proposals have been made (and even experimented
with) as regards some comprehensive replacement for GNP.
These include the Physical Quality of Life Indicator (which
gives much greater weight to factors like housing, health and
education, as a counter-balance to increases in flows of money)
and the Basic Human Needs Indicator devised by the United
Nations. By and large, these have not been judged a great
success. They have raised as many problems as they have
solved. Not surprisingly, the notion of an Adjusted National
Product (ANP), or Net National Welfare, as it has been called
in Japan, has proved rather more attractive to economists,
though there is considerable debate as to the nature of the
adjustments needed to get the kind of information required.

Some things may need to be added, such as the value of
work done in the household in terms of cooking, cleaning
and childcare. It is, after all, a bit odd that when we go out
for a meal, all the preparation and cooking is included in
GNP, but whenever we do exactly the same amount of work
at home, it counts for nothing. Paying a child-minder or a
nanny is good for GNP; looking after one's own child, as far
as GNP is concerned, is worth nothing.

Other things might be subtracted. One obvious category
would be any expenditure on those activities which damage
the environment or are necessary to prevent damage being
done to the environment. Beyond that, various proposals have

been made for deducting from GNP a figure for any 'environmental or resource depreciation'. This simply means extending the notion of capital goods to cover our 'natural capital' provided by the environment – the water, soil, forests and atmospheric services on which we all depend.

In 1989, the World Resources Institute (WRI) carried out a fascinating analysis of the Indonesian economy between 1971 and 1984. The official figures showed an average 7 per cent growth rate, which no doubt made everybody feel pretty pleased with themselves. But when deductions were made for the 'loss of natural capital', particularly in terms of the soil erosion caused by more intensive farming systems, that figure came down to 3.6 per cent. The WRI Report commented that the increased agricultural yields were 'almost wholly at the expense of potential *future* output', providing a fine example of robbing Peter (future generations) to pay Paul (those benefiting temporarily – but unsustainably – today).

Exactly the same kind of analysis could be carried out for the United Kingdom or any other country. In this crazy world, the faster we deplete our resources and the more damagingly we pollute our environment, the better off we *appear* to be. We get rich by causing pollution, and even richer by cleaning it up. As Senator Albert Gore has said: 'It's simply amazing to me that we have allowed this bizarre system of accounts to remain in place. It makes black, white; up, down; and inside, outside'.

ANP would therefore provide a much more realistic picture. But as Victor Anderson has argued in his interesting book, *Alternative Economic Indicators*, the more changes you make, the less sure you can be of what ANP is really measuring. What's more, ANP is not so very different from GNP in one crucial respect: everything still has to be calculated in terms of some *monetary* value. All those things so damagingly left out by GNP, in terms of human welfare and quality of life, are still left out, even after adjustment.

Victor Anderson suggests that the only solution to this is to develop an expanded framework of economic indicators, covering three separate areas: financial indicators, natural indicators (reflecting the state of the planet) and human indicators. We need to find yardsticks to measure 'success' and 'progress' that go far beyond the purely financial and monetary. A predictably long list emerges:

1   The secondary school enrolment ratio for girls

2   The secondary school enrolment ratio for boys

3   Average hours worked per week

4   The rate of unemployment

5   Average calorie supply as a percentage of requirements

6   Percentage of the population with access to safe drinking water

7   Percentage of the population below absolute poverty income level

8   Household income received by the top 20 per cent of households divided by that received by the bottom 20 per cent

9   Marketable wealth owned by the top 20 per cent of households divided by that owned by the bottom 20 per cent

10 Infant mortality rate

11 Deforestation in hectares per year

12 Species loss per year

13 Carbon dioxide emissions in millions of tonnes per year

14 Soil loss in tonnes per hectare (of the whole area) per year

15 Number of years taken for the population to double

16 Hectares of forest lost per million dollars of GDP

17 Species lost per million dollars of GDP

18 Millions of tonnes of carbon dioxide emitted per million dollars of GDP

19 Tonnes of soil per hectare lost per million dollars of GDP

20 Energy consumption (in tonnes of oil equivalent) per million dollars of GDP.

The principle of measuring not just the simple rates of deforestation, species loss, carbon dioxide build-up and soil erosion, but measuring them in terms of their relation to GNP

125

allows us to begin to assess *quality* of growth, as well as *quantity* of growth. Levels of progress and success are totally dependent on that notion of quality for, as we've seen, the increases themselves mean very little. To quote Victor Anderson:

> 66 *For example, if GNP is to grow by 4 per cent a year, then the number of tonnes of carbon dioxide per million dollars of output needs to fall by 4 per cent each year merely to maintain existing rates of carbon dioxide emission.*
>
> *The management of the economy on this basis would include two key areas – one of them, the centrepiece of existing economic management, being to influence the quantity of output as measured by GNP, and the other one being to influence the quality of output. Instead of 'quality of output' being a mere vague rhetorical phrase (as 'quality of life' is in danger of becoming), the quality of output could be measured and monitored.* 99

SELF-RELIANCE

Further essentials of a 'green economy' need only be touched on at this stage, as they're discussed in greater detail in the remaining chapters. But it's worth pointing out, yet again, that the green alternative is not just about 'the environment', preventing pollution, protecting cuddly animals or recycling our domestic waste: it is about an alternative *economic* strategy that is based on managing our natural wealth to meet human needs on a sustainable basis.

One of the basic assumptions of conventional politicians and economists is that the position of Third World countries can only be improved if they can increase the volume of trade they are engaged in. Peruse the manifestos of all the major parties and you will find an astonishing degree of unanimity about the idea of the Third World trading its way out of economic decline. If it was possible for South Korea, Taiwan and Hong Kong, they argue, then it must surely be possible for Peru, Bangladesh and Botswana. All development organisations still dedicate themselves to improving access for goods from the developing world to the developed world, and to ensuring that they get a better price for them. It is therefore deeply unfashionable to question the value of trade, let alone to identify it as one of the main engines of destruction in the world today. Yet from a green perspective, that's how it looks.

The conventional theory is a simple one: the more a country can export, the greater its ability to import the goods and services it needs, and the more easily it will attract new investment. This will increase economic growth, which will in turn raise per capita income as (some of) the resulting wealth trickles down to the poorest and neediest.

It would be wrong to assert that this never happens. Increased trade has indeed brought many benefits to *some* developing countries at *certain* times. Per capita income levels have been raised, though never at the same speed as in the developed world, with which the vast majority of the trade actually takes place.

Ted Trainer's powerful book, *Developed to Death*, gets behind the figures to explain the reality of 'development' for many millions of people:

> **66** *If we take the average 1965–1984 increase in GNP per capita, the rich Western countries (with only one-seventh of the world's people) were increasing their annual per capita incomes by about $270 p.a. in the mid-1980s, while the Low Income Countries (with half the world's people) were increasing theirs by $7 p.a. ...*
>
> *It has been estimated that 200 years ago the rich countries had an average income only 1.5 times that of the poor countries. [...] in 1960 the ratio between the rich Western countries and the Fourth World was 20 to 1, and by 1980 it had risen to about 46 to 1.*
>
> *The world seems to be polarising. About one-fifth of its people are increasing their wealth fairly rapidly, while the poorest fifth did little more than stagnate during the long boom, and are now probably becoming poorer in absolute terms.* **99**

The unquestioning assumption that more trade is necessarily 'a good thing' has underpinned classical development economics right from the start. In different ways, both the World Bank and the International Monetary Fund (IMF) have devoted themselves to promoting export-led growth in the Third World. Indeed, they've promoted little else! Whatever their individual circumstances, all countries get the same message: export or perish.

The inevitable result is that much of the Third World's productive capacity is now geared to the 'needs' or demands of the developed world. In several countries, more than 50 per cent of the most productive land is given over to producing export goods. At first glance, you might think that this would

127

Out shopping, North and South. Lucky
for some.

be good for Third World economies, but the prices they
receive for their commodities have been progressively eroded
as more and more produce in one sector after another comes
on to the market. And the relative decline in the value of their
produce is exacerbated by continuing protectionism in the
developed world.

We must, as James Robertson says, face the reality of what
the system actually entails:

66 *We shall start by recognising that the world has never had a
genuinely fair and free trading system. Ever since people argued*

whether trade follows the flag or the flag follows trade, trade has been based on domination and on dependency and has been an instrument of them. The ideology of free trade has been used, as ideologies often are, to justify the strong in taking advantage of the weak and to persuade the weak that it is neither conceptually respectable nor in their own best long-term interests to protect themselves.

Some people (especially within the 'development business') suppose that this situation could be sorted out with the right mix of enlightened self-interest on our part (the old Brandt Report line that the more prosperous people are in the Third World, the better off we will be as a consequence), and entrepreneurial acumen on their part (in terms of spotting new market opportunities, improving production techniques, etc). To go on supposing this, in the face of all the evidence, is wilfully foolish.

Even if all this increase in trade *was* bringing in a better return, so that one could at least claim that the conventional policy of development through trade was bringing the Third World some economic benefit, the price to be paid is already being counted in terms of ecological devastation. By and large, the more intensive the agricultural system adopted, the higher the yields will appear to be. But, as we've seen, this is just a sleight of the accountant's hand, for such yields depend on the progressive depletion of the ecological capital and life-support systems on which the future of those countries depends.

The green approach to these problems is direct and dramatic: firstly, devote the productive resources of *all* countries primarily to meeting the needs of their own people, trading only in products and services which do not divert ecological or financial capital from that fundamental task.

Secondly, ensure that as much of that trade as possible is regional rather than international. Aid from the developed world should be geared to promoting self-reliant development rather than increasing the dependence of Third World countries through increased trade.

This approach is widely misunderstood. It does *not* mean striving for total self-sufficiency, or seeking isolation from the rest of the world. It simply recognises that, in a finite and fundamentally unequal world, trading one's way into a state of sustainable equality is an impossible dream. And it's worth

129

thinking back to Chapter 2 as regards energy use. Though transport costs now make up a relatively small part of the cost of most goods, any kind of internationally agreed carbon tax will be devastating to those countries dependent on the export of cash crops. The whole system is only viable on such a large scale today because the *real* energy costs have not been incorporated into the price of the exported goods.

Adopting such an approach is not easy. Even when political leaders have tried (as President Nyerere did in Tanzania), the external pressures for the world economy are huge. Moreover, many Third World leaders wouldn't dream of following such a course of action, simply because their political careers and (sadly) their own personal fortunes would be at stake. Though many well-meaning liberals in the developed world feel uncomfortable about this the corruption, greed and sheer incompetence of many Third World governments constitute as serious an impediment to bringing justice and sustainable livelihoods to the world's poor as does the selfishness, greed and short-sightedness of our own governments.

We should be honest about the advocacy of self-reliance. It does indeed mean renouncing the goal of Western-style affluence for the Third World. But if we are not prepared to moderate our unbridled expansionist tendencies, what chance is there of persuading those currently deprived of the basic necessities that there are better ways of achieving progress? One of the first products to penetrate even the poorest of poor communities is the television, opening up a Pandora's box of unattainable material aspirations through its Western programmes and aggressive advertising.

DEBT

Lastly, even if a handful of courageous and honest Third World leaders lasted long enough to persuade their people that sustainable self-reliance offered better long-term prospects than fighting it out in an inherently inequitable world economy, would our bankers and leaders actually let them? Many countries are *driven* to expand their export base simply to go on paying off the interest on the debt they owe to the West. When 50 per cent of the value of your exports instantly disappears in debt repayments, you have to grow twice as much, or mine twice as deep, to derive the same benefits.

In 1987, total Third World debt was in excess of $1000

Television: part of the poor man's burden?

billion, and servicing that debt was costing Third World countries in excess of $135 billion every year. The *net* flow of resources from South to North in 1989 was $52 billion! 'To them that have...' The story of how this human tragedy occurred has been told many times, but nowhere more powerfully than in Susan George's *A Fate Worse Than Debt*. However one shares out the responsibility (to greedy Western banks with a surfeit of petrodollars on their hands in the seventies, to Western financiers for keeping interest rates so high for so long, or to gullible and often corrupt governments in the Third World), the simple reality is that a significant proportion of these debts will never be repaid. Western banks have grudgingly acknowledged this over the last two or three years by making provision for inevitable default in their accounts, while continuing to extract as much interest as they can, even from those debts which they have written off.

It's not easy to remain dispassionate and rational when one sees the terrible suffering inflicted on millions of people and the irreparable damage done to the environment as countries struggle to convert their natural resources into another monthly repayment to keep the bankers at bay. We shouldn't mince our words on this: our friendly High Street banks, along with their equivalents in Europe, Japan and the United States, are little more than thieves and ecological vandals.

The much-discussed Brady Plan offers no real solution to this intolerable burden, although one or two countries (as we shall see with Costa Rica in Chapter 7) will indeed benefit.

131

Food riots in Venezuela

Rescheduling of the loans, or arranging new loans, makes little difference, especially if it's done as part of a restructuring package organised by the IMF. This medicine of restructuring is often far more deadly than the economic malaise it is supposed to cure: cuts in public spending on welfare are ruthlessly enforced, further damaging the already less well off; the currency is devalued; food prices raised; and terrible sacrifices imposed to increase export earnings – which is, as we've seen, the only way the banks can ensure that 'their nice little earners in the Third World' are kept alive. Third World countries have no option but to accept being restructured in this way, because it's the IMF and the World Bank that determine their credit rating.

The continuing folly of all this is inconceivable. Must we really wait until the entire system collapses, or large-scale public protest (in the shape of violent food riots, like those in Venezuela in 1989) destablises one country after another? The only answer is an internationally agreed, government-backed plan to write off the debts progressively in return for specific commitments from Third World governments to implement agreed environmental programmes.

Genuine efforts, by governments and industry alike, to create wealth and meet people's needs on a sustainable basis are doomed to failure unless the world economy is fundamentally restructured. Of that, there is as yet little sign, but much more encouraging signals can now be seen among many of the world's leading companies.

Chapter 6

INDUSTRIAL
FUTURES

Wᴴᴱɴ ᴄᴏɴꜰʀᴏɴᴛᴇᴅ with our appalling environmental
record, many industrialists have a way of looking deeply hurt
and aggrieved, as if such accusations were totally unjustified.
Given half a chance, they will patiently explain that protecting
the environment cannot be their primary responsibility: they
are answerable to the customer (in providing the goods and
services for which there is a genuine demand); to the
shareholder (in ensuring as substantial a dividend as possible);
and to government (in complying with whatever regulations
apply in any given area of production). The implication is
simple: if the environment is to be protected, then government
must legislate for it in parliament, and the consumer must opt
for it in the market place. Industry can therefore be seen as the
neutral provider, an innocent party that only needs guidance
as to how best to perform its function.

That analysis is deviously simplistic. Fifteen years in the
Green Movement have taught me that industry is *never*
neutral, and in many instances individual companies have lied,
cheated, broken the law, conspired, lobbied, manipulated and
forcefully campaigned to maintain profitability at the *known*

expense of the environment. The current 'greening of industry' is therefore to be taken with the usual bucketful of salt. Though their PR agencies may be expensive, industrial 'greenspeak' comes pretty cheap. Too often, industry is full of words rather than deeds. Sadly, this is particularly true of British industry. In comparison with many of their competitors in Europe or Japan, British companies have often fought longest and hardest against environmental improvements. The combined campaign of the motor manufacturers and the oil companies against the introduction of unleaded petrol in the seventies and early eighties is a case in point, which should not be forgotten now that they've all 'gone green'.

And it's not just the manufacturers. In January 1990, the Institute of Directors magazine conducted a survey of 500 service-based companies which showed that most of them were unashamedly in the business of green lip-service. Eighty per cent had no one in charge of environmental issues; less than 30 per cent were using recycled paper or cared about energy efficiency. The survey concluded: 'time and again they express a keenness to carry out such policies, but feel that their hands are tied by the need to justify the added costs'.

In all too many British boardrooms, it's still business as usual: if canned fruit-juice can best be supplied by cutting down a chunk of tropical rainforest and turning it into an orange grove, that will be done. If a company's waste products can be disposed of most cheaply by pouring them into the River Tees, that will be done. If a company can 'grow' by purchasing another company, some bank or finance house will lend the money, and that will be done.

Businesses aim to maximise their profits; banks endeavour to invest their clients' money where it will earn the greatest returns; governments set out to achieve the highest possible rate of economic growth. And all too many ordinary people see it as their sole purpose in life to earn as much money as they can.

I do not put the onus entirely on industry. We, as consumers, go on purchasing their products. As shareholders, we hope to get rich on their profits. As voters, we go on tolerating one environment-insensitive government after another. Even when the will is there to change our ways, progress may be blocked by outmoded laws. In today's economy, if you are a manager of a pension fund (or any other kind of fund), you are obliged *by law* (through what is known as 'fiduciary trust') to seek the highest rate of financial return on your investment. If that means investing in companies which get their profits from felling part of the Amazon rainforest to build an aluminium smelter plant, then so be it. That is how our economy 'works'.

Many companies have also dug themselves into a very deep pit. In the United States, the aggregate debt of all US corporations amounts to $3.2 trillion – no less than one-third of their total corporate value! To pay off such a sum requires a vast increase in profits through an equally vast increase in turnover and consumption. And that just can't be done on a sustainable basis.

Through past mistakes and present complacency, our economy inflicts many other ills on us: boring and degrading factory and office work; dangerous working conditions; inflexible working practices; personal lives subjugated to working too hard or to not being able to work at all.

We have made gods of personal selfishness and material greed, placing them at the heart of our social order, enshrining them in our systems of business, banking, investment, law and government. Not so long ago, the word 'wealth' meant 'the condition of being happy and prosperous', or simply 'wellbeing'. Today, it means only one thing: money. As long as we make increased profit, growth and consumption more important than any other goals, we will inevitably end up in this kind of mess. 'The Earth provides enough for everyone's needs,' Gandhi said, 'but not for everyone's greed.'

But here, as elsewhere, things are changing. Some companies are starting to pay more attention to their impact on the environment. Some banks are seeking to lend in a more socially responsible way. Some investment funds are beginning to place their money where it will cause less damage to the world, and even perhaps help protect it. Some consumers are refusing to purchase goods which harm the environment. At long last, we can begin to look beyond the industrial horizons which have constrained our vision over the last 200 years.

GREEN CONSUMERISM

On 28 September 1989, people woke up to a barrage of stories about Green Shopping Day. The airwaves rang with exhortations to buy unleaded petrol, recycled paper, organic food, and a host of handy tips on how to be green when you're out shopping. This was but the latest manifestation of one of the most significant shifts in consumer behaviour since the Second World War. Green consumerism is now all the rage. People still want the good things of life, but they want them to be environment-friendly. It's no good smelling all sweet and fragrant if the chemical concoction in the aerosol which helps you achieve this olfactory miracle is simultaneously punching holes in the ozone layer.

Supermarkets have been falling over themselves to be seen as clean, green and ever so keen to save the world. Tesco's advertising slogan, 'The Greener Grocer', was instantly topped by Sainsbury's as 'The Greenest Grocer'. The environment is currently being touted as the biggest 'marketing opportunity' of the nineties.

But such claims are now being subjected to far more rigorous scrutiny. Having spent millions 'greening its image', British Petroleum must have been mortified to see the company taken to pieces in *The Sunday Times* for the devastation one of its subsidiaries had caused in the Brazilian rainforest. They were also soundly castigated by the Advertising Standards Authority for claiming that their supergreen petrol caused 'no pollution of the environment' simply because it was lead-free.

Even more telling, Heinz (winner of the Green Manufacturer of the Year Award in June 1989) was on the point of signing a £75 000 sponsorship deal to support Green Shopping Day when it suddenly pulled out. The management had apparently discovered that Friends of the Earth and others were planning to alert green consumers to the slaughter of dolphins by Starkist (a Heinz subsidiary) in their pursuit of the lucrative yellowfin tuna.

As well as helping to change the behaviour of millions of people, green consumerism has therefore provided organisations like Friends of the Earth with a new range of campaigning tools. The message for multinational companies is a simple one: 'If you want to be green these days, cleaning up your image is not enough. If the changes you make aren't genuine and substantial, you and every one of your subsidiaries can now be publicly held to account.'

Many companies are quite genuinely keen to carry out their environmental obligations without being exposed to such

pressure. A good example of this is Varta, a German company and the biggest battery manufacturer in Europe. Until recently, Varta was not exactly a 'household name' in the UK, but during the last two years it has skilfully marketed itself as the most environment-friendly battery manufacturer.

Batteries are not, of course, good news for the environment. They are a classic throwaway product, and most of them contain cadmium and mercury, two extremely dangerous heavy metals. Varta was one of the first companies to market batteries that were free of cadmium and mercury, simultaneously adopting a 'green philosophy' within the company: unleaded petrol in all company cars; recycled paper; energy-saving measures; no-smoking offices. Other manufacturers soon followed in their wake, obliging them to go one step further by introducing a postage-paid recycling scheme for their rechargeable batteries. Rechargeable batteries are infinitely preferable from an environmental point of view (in the course of its working life, a rechargeable battery can replace up to 300 normal batteries, and can be recharged up to 1000 times), but they cannot currently be made without the use of cadmium. Recycling is the only answer.

Such an approach has certainly worked for Varta. Their annual share of the multi-million pound battery market went up from 9 per cent to 15 per cent in 18 months. They have also been very conscientious about their labelling, replacing an earlier slogan of 'environmentally-friendly' with the clumsier but much more honest 'environmentally-friendlier'.

Friends of the Earth and the Consumers' Association have both become extremely anxious about the misuse of 'eco-

Rejecting the throwaways

IN the nineties, consumers will reject the throwaway society as environmentally and economically irresponsible, according to a report published by the business consultancy Marketing Improvements. Shoppers are expected to return to a philosophy of durability and quality.

Disposability, says the report's author, Tim Pollard, is about to be rejected and will be replaced with a new sense of ecological and moral responsibility when purchasing products.

Although green consumerism is still in its infancy in Britain, it is going to grow up into a buying force to be reckoned with, he adds. Our throwaway society, so used to tossing out razor blades, plastic cups or ballpoint pens after using them only once or twice, is likely to be regarded with distaste by the next generation.

Pollard's findings are echoed in the Henley Centre's recent study which concluded that cut-price consumerism was giving way to the new 'connoisseur' consumer. Pollard says that those companies which believe the only concession they need to make to comply with the green revolution is an expensive redesign of their environmentally-unfriendly packaging, are in for a rude awakening.

138

labelling', and the very strong likelihood that consumers are being taken in by the use of terms like 'environmentally-friendly' or 'green'. For instance, it is technically accurate to describe an aerosol as 'ozone-friendly' if it does not use any of the chemicals that deplete the ozone layer. But that most emphatically does not make it environment-friendly. Just as with batteries or nappies, aerosols in any shape or form are hostile to the environment. They still use dangerous chemicals, take a lot of energy to manufacture, and disposing of 850 million of them every year in the UK alone requires a very large hole in the ground.

Accurate labelling is therefore the key to the success of the Green Consumer Movement. In Germany, the Blue Angel labelling scheme has been running since 1978, and more than 3000 products now carry the distinctive logo. The scheme was set up by the German Government, and before the logo is awarded the criteria are agreed, on a product by product basis, in consultation with representatives of both industry and consumer and environmental groups. Similar schemes have been set up more recently in Canada and Japan.

The UK Government produced some labelling guidelines for consultation in August 1989, but they were roundly criticised by environmentalists as not allowing for a product to be assessed on a 'cradle-to-grave' basis (i.e. from manufacturing through to final disposal). The Government also looks likely to wait for an EEC scheme rather than pursuing its own, which could take years. But, on the positive side, it has now agreed to amend the Trade Descriptions Act in order to outlaw misleading green claims. Until those amendments are in place, Friends of the Earth has launched its own Green Con of the Year Award to keep businesses under control: the winner of the 1989 Award was British Nuclear Fuels for its astonishing advertising claims that nuclear power was the most environment-friendly source of energy and the only possible answer to global warming!

Even with the best labelling scheme in the world, green consumerism is still consumerism. With the arrival of the new 'G' registration plates in August 1989, nearly 500 000 cars were sold in just that one month. The fact that most of them can run on unleaded petrol, and that a few of them will be fitted with catalytic converters, is obviously good news. But 500 000 cars, by any green stardards, are bad news for the environment.

There are now more 'green products' on sale than ever before, but they represent only a small step down the road to genuine sustainability.

Each of those cars will produce 3–5 tonnes of carbon dioxide every year, thus contributing to global warming. Each one will consume 1125–2250 litres of non-replaceable oil annually. And there's also the 1.2 tonnes of steel and aluminium needed to make the car; the 6.5 hectares per kilometre of paved-over farmland needed for it to run on; the chronic congestion it contributes to; the noise it makes; and the 40 000 people killed or injured by cars in the UK every year.

As we saw in Chapter 2, the 'green car' of the future will have to run on liquid hydrogen gas derived from solar energy, or on direct solar energy. Every single part of it will have to be completely recyclable; and motorists will probably have to drive no faster than 20 mph and pay a 'road-toll' if they want to travel in a built-up area.

Green consumerism is *not* a panacea for all our environmental problems. For one thing, it clearly discriminates against the less well-off. Many people today choose to buy organic produce, even if it costs them 50 per cent more. But most people simply can't make that choice, and depend on the Government setting, and enforcing, maximum residue levels for pesticides in all fresh foodstuffs. By the same token, many families may well be able to afford to insulate their houses, but many more depend on grants from their local authority, who in turn depend on support from central government.

At its best, green consumerism is a powerful lever for change, which is forcing some companies to adopt higher environmental standards and to produce more environmentally sound goods. The more people demand such goods, the greater will be the power of the lever. Companies which started off by turning the palest shade of green have been forced to go much further, as they begin to realise that 'going green' is not just a matter of image-building.

Five things are required if green consumerism is ever to become a truly effective catalyst for change:

1   A public which is well informed, vocal in its demands, consistently discriminating in its purchases, and willing to boycott companies which continue to endanger the environment.

2   Local authorities, schools, colleges, hospitals and other organisations which will do the same. In your own locality, you can write letters to key people in these institutions, asking what environmental standards they follow in their purchasing and operating policies. For instance:

Do they use recycled paper?

Do they use environment-friendly cleaning products?

Do they only buy timber that has been harvested in a truly sustainable manner, and avoid threatened tropical hardwoods?

Do they insist on lead-free petrol and catalytic converters for their car fleets?

Do they issue 'company bikes' (as Oxford City Council does), and encourage staff car-sharing schemes?

Do they avoid using disposable plastic and styrofoam mugs, plates, etc?

Do they minimise the use of pesticides on gardens and parks?

Do they recycle as much as possible of their own waste?

3   A government-backed 'eco-labelling' system, based on guidelines covering a product's whole lifespan, from manufacture to eventual disposal.

4   A law compelling companies to issue an annual environmental report, alongside their annual statement of accounts, backed by an established system of professional environmental auditing.

5   More rigorous local, national, EEC and international regulations, ensuring the highest standards of environmental conduct, and providing severe penalties for misconduct. Companies have been arguing for years that they need a 'level playing field', so that the same regulations apply in every

country. Without these laws, Company A, which pays to have its waste treated properly, will have higher costs than Company B, which simply dumps it into the sea.

Green consumerism should therefore be seen as an important step forward, but no more than that. It is a means to an end, not an end in itself. That 'end' is of course genuine sustainability. Much of the current froth about green consumerism may well serve to conceal critical home-truths about the sheer volume of current consumption patterns in the developed world. The goal of genuine sustainability is far harder to achieve than most companies realise. But some are at least coming to terms with a few of the implications of this colossal challenge.

THE GREENING OF INDUSTRY

66 *We believe very strongly that environmental policy – and by that I mean not just having one, but putting it into practice in all aspects of business – will be the single most important factor for a competitive company in the 1990s and beyond. In short, environmental ethics has to be the most important strategy a company can adopt for its long-term survival.*99

These words are taken from a speech made in 1989 by Robert Bringer, Vice-President for Environmental Engineering and Pollution Control at 3M. This huge manufacturing company, based in St Paul, Minnesota, is considered by its peers as *the* role model for good environmental practice, and it has certainly set the pace for the entire industry by its commitment in June 1989 to reduce emissions of all hazardous materials by 90 per cent before the year 2000:

66 *Existing programmes have already reduced our emissions to half of what they would otherwise be. A programme begun last year will reduce our emissions by another 70 per cent. Now we're making a commitment to a 90 per cent reduction for all emissions. Our ultimate goal is to come as close to zero emissions as we possibly can.*99

3M's track record is certainly impressive. Their managers realised way back in the sixties that their best response to an ever-increasing body of environmental legislation in the United States would be to reduce pollution *at source* rather than at the end of the production process. This led to the

141

development of their '3P policy' (Pollution Prevention Pays) in the mid-seventies. Pollution prevention at source depends on four complementary processes:

1 *Reformulating products* by changing the raw materials involved in the manufacture (e.g. eliminating the use of solvents or encouraging water-based products).

2 *Modifying the manufacturing process* to reduce harmful by-products and implement better control systems.

3 *Redesigning equipment* to perform under much more stringent operating conditions and to eliminate as much waste as possible.

4 *Designing for recycling* at the very start of the manufacturing process, including recovery of waste materials for re-use or sale.

The 3P programme has been very successful. Since 1975, it has reduced air pollutants by 120 000 tonnes, water pollutants by 15 000 tonnes, sludge and solid waste by 315 000 tonnes, and waste water by 6.75 billion litres every year. In addition, the company has saved more than $420 million by not having to buy pollution control equipment and facilities, by reducing consumption of materials and energy, and by retaining sales on reformulated products.

3M is of course big enough and prosperous enough to be able to afford high capital investment costs, knowing that it may take several years to see those costs paid back in full. Pay-back periods are often shorter than anticipated, but this sort of risk is very difficult for smaller companies to take on.

This may all sound pretty technical, but it's fascinating to see at first hand how this approach permeates the entire company. Admittedly, they do have a certain advantage in that 3M is primarily involved in developing *new* products (they have something like 60 000 products to their name), so staff at every level are already geared up to innovation and experimentation. But their commitment to pollution prevention is utterly genuine and *practical* – they were, for instance, the first major company to undertake to phase out almost all ozone-depleting CFCs by the end of 1990. What started out as a somewhat grudging compliance with increasingly stringent legislation (which, incidentally, they felt wasn't really necessary anyway!) has now become an object lesson in how to combine sound commercial practice with

**Pollution
Prevention
Pays**

Managing for a better environment

Another 'waste mountain' takes shape, an increasingly common sight as landfill sites become scarcer.

the pursuit of the highest environmental standards.

The interesting thing is the way they design for recycling at the earliest possible stage in the manufacturing process. Regrettably, this is still a very alien concept for many manufacturers who give little if any thought to what happens to their products at the end of their life. That, after all, is somebody else's problem. Indeed, built-in obsolescence, 'throwawayability' and over-packaging are essential components of an industrial strategy dependent on short life, low quality, high turnover and cosmetic appeal.

Friends of the Earth has been campaigning about recycling for so long that it's quite a relief to see our enthusiasm for it being diligently recycled by industry and government alike! But Britain's record on recycling is still appalling in comparison to other EEC countries, and insufficient attention is being paid to the *markets* for recycled products. For instance, it's all very well persuading everyone to recycle their newspapers, but it's even more important to ensure that the market for recycled products (especially the low-grade, off-white papers from recycled newspapers and magazines) is expanding. So serious did this problem become in the USA that in 1989 the federal government legislated to oblige every single federal agency to use recycled paper. That will eventually have a huge impact but, in the short term, the Americans are continuing to dump their subsidised recycled paper in Britain, which has devastated the British collection system.

143

What is lacking is any sense of strategic direction for industry as regards waste management, let alone any incentives or encouragement to pursue the *optimum* course. We need a quite explicit hierarchy of waste management, something along the following lines:

1 First, we should seek to eliminate waste *at source*, or at least reduce it to the minimum as in the example of 3M.

2 We should then design products for durability and ease of repair, so that shoes, for example, don't break or wear out after a few months, but last as long as they once used to do (even if they cost a bit more).

3 We should also be designing products for re-use. For instance, being able to re-use bottles, as with glass milk bottles, is much better than recycling them through a bottle bank scheme, although that in turn is much better than simply throwing them away.

4 If re-use is not possible, we should design for recycling, so that all soft drinks cans, for instance, whether aluminium or tin plate, would at least be *recyclable* – even if a few slipped through the retrieval system.

Recycling in the Nineties Charter for Action

PRODUCED BY FRIENDS OF THE EARTH

Recycling can play a vital role in environmental protection through the conservation of energy and finite resources as well as reducing the amount of waste we produce.

If recycling is to work, however, it is essential that parallel to the collection of recyclable waste, markets are developed for re-processed materials. Only by dis-playing a demand for goods made from recycled materials will we encourage the Government to take action on this issue, and persuade industry to invest in the technology required to recycle materials.

We believe that if action is taken in four main areas, real progress will start to be made. As individuals we must:

LOBBY OUR MPS
To demand that the Government legislates to ensure that local authorities and government departments, as part of their purchasing policy, positively discriminate in favour of recycled materials.

ENCOURAGE LOCAL COUNCILLORS
A To demand that all grades of recycled paper are used by all departments within the council.
B To demand the use of recycled plastics for municipal applications such as fence posts and road signs.

PETITION OUR PLACES OF WORK
To use recycled paper, particularly off white grades for photocopying, internal memos and unbleached recycled toilet tissues.

LOBBY OUR LOCAL SUPERMARKETS
A To use packaging made from recycled materials.
B To use packaging that has been designed so it is easy to reclaim.
C To stock recycled tissue and stationery.

5 Only then should we contemplate outright disposal, either in properly engineered landfill sites (with the potential for methane retrieval as an important energy source) or in state of the art incinerators (again, with the potential for electricity generation or heat production in combined heat and power schemes).

Recycling facilities at Hartley Wintney in Hampshire

As the costs of landfill and incineration rise (which they inevitably will, once the true cost of responsible waste disposal is fully internalised in the price paid per tonne), stages 1 to 4 will become far more attractive to industry. The new Environment Protection Act will go some way towards this, but it remains to be seen if it will entirely do away with the waste disposal cowboys who have so flagrantly disregarded their environmental responsibilities.

Waste disposal is just one of the environmental challenges that industry must come to terms with, and it would be foolish to expect this to happen without a great deal of external encouragement from at least three groups. Firstly, the government can speed the process of change by using its fiscal powers (as with the discount on unleaded petrol in Britain), enforcing existing regulations, and obliging industry to achieve higher environmental standards by imposing new pollution limits that can only be met through the introduction of new technology. Secondly, the Green Movement will continue to have an essential role as watchdog and whistle-blower on the real malefactors, while simultaneously encouraging those who are genuinely greening their companies. And lastly, individual shareholders and large investors, such as pension funds and unit trusts, can have an enormous influence through socially responsible investment.

Socially Responsible Investment (SRI), or Ethical Investment, as it is called in Britain, started life in the USA as a result of churches wanting to feel sure that their money was not being invested in companies dealing with alcohol or gambling. In the 1980s, a new generation, including some state pension funds, began to seek out investment portfolios in companies which had no involvement with South Africa, military production, nuclear power or tobacco products. A total of $600 billion is now being screened annually for socially responsible factors – about 10 per cent of the money passing through Wall Street. In Britain, there were 17 funds specialising in 'ethical investment' at the start of 1990, and interest is growing rapidly. With the right kind of advice, it is now possible to have a pension, house insurance, life assurance, a personal equity plan and an investment account all screened for socially responsible factors.

This is a crucially important development. The assumption that money is 'amoral' and will always seek the greatest rate of return, irrespective of other human values, is being overturned. The new socially responsible investment funds are enabling people to say 'I want greater control over how my savings are invested. I don't want my money to be invested in a way that will undermine the values I believe in.' Interestingly, in many instances these funds have been *outperforming* equivalent conventional funds.

More recently, people have also been demanding that their money be invested in companies which do not harm the environment. According to a 1989 poll in *Which?* magazine, 63 per cent of the people interviewed said that they were concerned about the ethical and environmental aspects of their investments. In the UK, the Merlin Ecology Fund has taken

the lead in this area. This unit trust fund was the first in Europe
to invest only in companies which are positively benefiting the
environment, rather than simply in those which are not
actually harming it. The fund has performed extremely well,
which comes as no surprise to its manager, Christopher Surtees:
'Companies which pay rigid attention to the environment,
will, by definition, have better management. If they are not
good enough to be aware of what is going down the drain,
they are not sound companies.'

Most importantly, their financial acumen is backed up by a
proper research unit, unlike a lot of ethical funds. All 32
companies in which they invest have been vetted against a
range of environmental criteria. None would claim to be
perfect, but the key test is proven commitment to improving
the environment and their own performance.

This is, inevitably, a somewhat subjective test. After all,
who is to judge what constitutes 'commitment', let alone
'improved performance'? Here again, the USA is well ahead
of the UK and other European countries. We spent a
fascinating morning in Boston with Gordon Davidson of the
Social Investment Forum, which has been at the forefront of
the drive for socially responsible investment in the United
States. Back in 1988, together with most of the leading
environmental organisations in the States, they set up the
Coalition for Environmentally Responsible Economies
(CERES) in order to tackle this issue of how best to assess
environmental performance. The initiative was already well
under way when the *Exxon Valdez* disaster in March 1989
provided the impetus they needed, and the Valdez Principles
were drawn up as a charter for US industry (page 148).

When the Principles were launched in September 1989, the
firms approached were in agreement with the first six
principles, but not with the last four, which are about
compliance. The intention is that the Principles should be used
as a screen for investment purposes. Each company that signs
up will be given a rating against the ten criteria and this
information will then be made available to potential investors
so they can make up their own minds about where they wish
to put their money. And CERES is not just talking about
small individual investors. The States of California and New
York (with $125 billion to invest) have both intimated that
they would only consider investing their pension funds in and

The Valdez Principles

PROTECTION OF THE BIOSPHERE

We will minimise and strive to eliminate the release of any pollutant that may cause environmental damage to the air, water, or earth or its inhabitants. We will safeguard habitats in rivers, lakes, wetlands, coastal zones and oceans and will minimise contributing to the greenhouse effect, depletion of the ozone layer, acid rain or smog.

SUSTAINABLE USE OF NATURAL RESOURCES

We will make sustainable use of renewable natural resources such as water, soils and forests. We will conserve non-renewable natural resources through efficient use and careful planning. We will protect wildlife habitat, open spaces and wilderness while preserving biodiversity.

REDUCTION AND DISPOSAL OF WASTE

We will minimise the creation of waste, especially hazardous waste, and wherever possible recycle materials. We will dispose of all wastes through safe and responsible methods.

WISE USE OF ENERGY

We will make every effort to use environmentally safe and sustainable energy sources to meet our needs. We will invest in improved energy efficiency and conservation in our operations. We will maximise the energy efficiency of products we produce or sell.

RISK REDUCTION

We will minimise the environmental, health and safety risks to our employees and the communities in which we operate by employing safe technologies and operating procedures and by being constantly prepared for emergencies.

MARKETING OF SAFE PRODUCTS AND SERVICES

We will sell products or services that minimise adverse environmental impacts and that are safe as consumers commonly use them. We will inform consumers of the environmental impacts of our products and services.

DAMAGE COMPENSATION

We will take responsibility for any harm we cause to the environment by making every effort to fully restore the environment and to compensate those persons who are adversely affected.

DISCLOSURE

We will disclose to our employees and to the public incidents relating to our operations that cause environmental harm or pose health or safety hazards. We will disclose potential environmental, health or safety hazards posed by our operations, and we will not take any action against employees who report any condition that creates a danger to the environment or poses health and safety hazards.

ENVIRONMENTAL DIRECTORS AND MANAGERS

At least one member of the Board of Directors will be a person qualified to represent environmental interest. We will commit management resources to implement these Principles, including the funding of an office of vice president for environmental affairs or equivalent executive position, reporting directly to the CEO, to monitor and report upon our implementation efforts.

ASSESSMENT AND ANNUAL AUDIT

We will conduct and make public an annual self-evaluation of our progress in implementing these Principles and in complying with all applicable laws and regulations throughout our worldwide operations. We will work toward the timely creation of independent environmental audit procedures which we will complete annually and make available to the public.

purchasing supplies from those companies who have signed. Shareholder action resolutions are also being raised across the States, asking if a particular company has signed, and if not, why not? In this way, the founders hope to bring considerable pressure to bear upon the corporate world. A similar charter is clearly needed in Europe.

One of the main problems for industry, as regards the Valdez Principles, is what to do about imports from countries which have lower environmental standards. Environmentalists are equally worried about multinational companies exporting their hazardous or heavily polluting production processes to Third World countries, or to the newly industrialised countries like Taiwan and South Korea, specifically to take advantage of lower environmental standards in those countries. In Taiwan, for instance, 30 years of undiluted industrial 'success' (with an average growth rate of 9 per cent per annum) has created desperate environmental problems, on a par with those in Eastern Europe: 90 000 factories, ten million cars and 20 million people are packed on to an island no bigger than the Netherlands; less than 1 per cent of human sewage receives any treatment whatsoever; air pollution in the capital, Taipei, is worse than in Los Angeles; landfill sites are largely unregulated; and water supplies seriously polluted.

They are only able to keep on churning out goods at a lower price than most of their competitors because they have written off their environment. The only viable mechanism for dealing with such an unfair trading advantage is some kind of 'green tariff' levied on imports from countries like Taiwan to restore the 'level playing field'. This would promote domestic environmental reforms *and* discourage multinationals from abusing the understandable desire of many Third World countries to encourage Western investment.

Such concerns are still a long way off. Though there are plentiful straws in the wind (epitomised by an incisive one liner from the *Economist* magazine in October 1989: 'Caring for the environment used to be a chore. It is now a marketing opportunity'), only a tiny percentage of British companies have even stepped on to the first rung of a very long green ladder.

The Chinese often say that the journey of a thousand miles starts with a single step, but as far as the greening of industry is concerned, consumer pressure, investor pressure,

OPPOSITE: The *Exxon Valdez* disaster: the clean-up goes on.

149

encouragement from local government, carefully controlled eco-labelling, national legislation, environmental taxation, and much no-holds-barred campaigning will all be needed before we can say that the journey has truly begun. And much of that pressure will need to be exerted at the *local* level.

BUILDING THE LOCAL ECONOMY

For many people, the most pressing problems are not the threat to the whales, or the difficulties of investing their savings in a way which will not destroy the Earth. In the UK, one person in eight depends on welfare as their only source of income. For them, unemployment, lack of money, poor housing and a run-down local environment are more immediate problems.

All around the world – whether in the grim housing schemes outside Glasgow, the shanty towns of Nairobi, the parched lands of Ethiopia, or the farms and factories of Poland or Mongolia – the dream of escaping from poverty and hardship is what keeps people going. So, as well as finding a way of living, working and trading which does not destroy the Earth's environment, we also need to find a way which does not produce grinding poverty and hunger alongside the wealth of the relatively few. That is intolerable, both to experience and to behold. As we'll see in Chapter 8, there's much that can be done at the international level, but our concern at this stage is primarily local.

One of the most inspiring examples of local economic regeneration is the Grameen Bank of Bangladesh. This is a financial institution dedicated to expanding credit opportunities among Bangladesh's rural poor. The Bank was set up in 1977 by Muhammad Yunus, and has since expanded to include over 140 000 borrowers, all of them people owning less than 0.2 hectares of land and 60 per cent of them women. Yunus describes the Grameen project as an attempt 'to reverse the age-old vicious circle of low income, low savings, low investment, low income'.

The key to breaking the cycle is the injection of credit, and the basic unit of the scheme is a group of five unrelated people, all of the same sex and from similar circumstances. They come together initially with a bank worker for training and to discuss ideas for generating income. They then pick which ideas, and which borrowers, hold the most promise. Initially, two of the five are given small loans (the average loan is $60, which may sound very little, but it is more or less half the average per capita income) with a short pay-back period. If payments are on schedule, the next two borrowers become eligible, and then the last borrower.

The loans finance a long list of small income-generating projects, including cows, small shops, sewing machines, weaving, food processing, and trading ventures of all kinds. Each group member thus has a very clear interest in the success of all the others – which not only adds peer pressure for prompt repayment, but also leads group members to keep a critical eye on the ideas and prospects of their colleagues. There is also a mandatory savings scheme, with each member contributing about one-third of a day's wage to the group savings each week. This money can be borrowed, interest-free, by group members for personal emergencies. Additionally, a 5 per cent 'tax' is taken out of each development loan, which then becomes the group's operating fund, and another small percentage is held for an insurance fund to cover emergency defaults.

Collections of groups in any one village gather at a 'centre' for weekly meetings. These centres scrutinise loan requests; and loan decisions, disbursements, and repayments all take place at these meetings, rather than in some distant bank.

The Grameen Bank has 328 branches and makes loans in 5600 villages. It has lent $54 million to 275 000 borrowers and continues to make small loans at the rate of some $2 million a month. Best of all, the repayment rate remains remarkably stable: more than 98 per cent.

The Grameen example shows what huge progress can be made when a different set of values is applied intelligently The key to success of this kind lies in *community organisation*. Instead of leaving economic initiatives up to individuals, a community must start to think collectively, and its members must find ways to help each other. If Third World lending had only been organised in the Grameen way (instead of lending money for the construction of nuclear power plants which never worked or the building of grand schemes which benefited only politicians and banks), we would now be living in a very different world.

In a wonderful reversal of the usual course of events, the Grameen experience has now been introduced into the United

Housing renovation schemes have been the key to the regeneration of the local economy in the South Shore area of Chicago. TOP: This is how much of it looked before . . . and (BOTTOM) this is how it looks now.

States. In the heart of rural Arkansas, a revolving loan fund (called the Good Faith Fund) has been set up to help small-scale businesspeople and farmers in a similar way to the Grameen system. Though many people were sceptical about this scheme working in the rather different culture of the United States, the same kind of peer group support techniques seem to be developing extremely well.

The scheme in Arkansas was actually set up by a bank in Chicago – the South Shore Bank. South Shore is a poor, and predominantly black, suburb of Chicago; in the early seventies it looked as it if was going into the final phase of a typical cycle of decline, with many abandoned apartments being used by drug dealers, or burnt out by arsonists.

At that point, a small group of 12 people bought out the South Shore Bank, which had long since ceased to serve the community in any meaningful sense. Right from the start, the Bank's new managers realised that the key to regeneration was community participation, and after an initial unsuccessful attempt to invest in small businesses in the area, they started to make loans to rehabilitate the decaying (but still soundly built and often very beautiful) buildings. By 1987, the Bank had given out 'development loans' for mortgages and rehabilitation work, totalling over $75 million, and had facilitated work on more than 200 buildings – nearly a quarter of all the apartment buildings in South Shore.

The next priority was job creation, and they duly set up The Neighborhood Initiative, which was affiliated to the Bank itself. This non-profit corporation has placed more than 2700 trainees in jobs, counselled more than 1000 entrepreneurs, and assisted roughly 70 new firms in starting up.

To achieve both these aims, the new management had to reverse a dramatic outflow of deposits from the Bank and confidence and credit from the community. It did this by making the Bank's services highly competitive, organising community meetings, extending credit, encouraging the participation of private mortgage insurers, inviting local residents on to its board, remodelling its facilities in the community, attracting public subsidies for development projects, retraining its staff, securing the services of a community-sensitive housing rehabilitation company, raising investment capital for community organisations, and generally heralding the revival of South Shore as a viable community.

American banks (which are able to do far more in this respect than their UK equivalents) are in a very good position to promote neighbourhood renewal. They can specifically set out to convert ordinary bank deposits into development credit, and by restoring local self-confidence, can release astonishing local energies that transform apathetic residents into fully engaged participants. I was deeply impressed with the commitment of the South Shore Bank staff, and the informal and supportive atmosphere within the bank itself. They modestly described all their achievements as nothing more than the regular business of 'a good old-fashioned bank', but it made me think about the extent to which most British high street banks have become alienated from their local communities.

With willingness to cooperate and to serve the local community, remarkable results can be achieved. In Modena, and elswhere in Northern Italy, local businesses have grouped together to form a Loan Guarantee Consortium, to underwrite loans from local banks, thus making it far easier to borrow, at lower rates of interest. Since it was founded in 1976, the consortium has underwritten £4.6 million in loans, and lost only 0.7 per cent.

Perhaps the best example of a fully cooperative economy is in Mondragon, in the Basque area of Northern Spain. In the early fifties, some local engineers bought out a manufacturing company that was about to close down, and turned it into a cooperative. Thirty years later, there are around 170 linked cooperatives in the area, run by 20 000 worker-owners, guided and sustained by their own bank, the Caja Laboral Popular. They run their own schools, training colleges, product development centres, and even their own social security fund.

Even during the difficult period from 1979 to 1983, when recession caused the market to fall by 10 per cent, they experienced zero business failures, and only 30 people were ever unemployed. The worker-owners decided to take a 10 per cent cut in wages, rather than sack 10 per cent of their own friends. Cooperative businesses which ran into difficulties were able to receive extensive help from the bank (which they also owned), and where necessary a business was closed down, with the workers moving to other cooperatives, or into training or education. New cooperatives are still being formed all the time, with continuing assistance from the bank.

In the UK, many people have been working hard since the seventies to pioneer new ways of regenerating local economies. In the process, they are massively improving the quality of life for local residents. Local enterprise agencies and cooperative development agencies have been successfully established to help local people start their own businesses. Many community marketing centres, credit unions, local innovation centres, youth enterprise centres and community development agencies have been set up.

In Scotland, over 100 'community businesses' have been started in low-income neighbourhoods with high unemployment. Local people own the voting shares, and set up and control these businesses, which are involved in everything from fisheries to building repairs, from community laundries to enterprise workshops. When the profits come in (which can take several years, if at all), they will then discuss how best they can be re-invested for the community's benefit. A sophisticated, coordinated back-up system provides training, support, advice and a range of grants and loans. Housewives are becoming company directors; local people are learning how to make business decisions and how, with a mixture of vision, determination, skill, finance, training and support, they can begin to revitalise their run-down economies.

The problem in the UK (and throughout Europe) is that there are not nearly enough of these community institutions or enlightened banks. For every neighbourhood which has a community economic development agency of some kind, there are 50 which have none, so the overall situation in poor and run-down areas is still generally negative and grim. The problem is not a lack of knowhow, or even of successful models to emulate – but a fundamental lack of commitment and financial resources from government and the banking sector.

NEW WAYS OF WORKING

It may well be possible, with some real commitment, to make the necessary adjustments to our lifestyles, and pass the necessary environmental legislation, to make our businesses and our lives environmentally sustainable. It may also be possible, if we can establish economic institutions which seek to develop the wealth and wellbeing of a local economy as a *whole*, to eliminate poverty, unemployment and most aspects of urban deprivation.

But what about the actual work that we do? Our nineteenth-century ancestors used to work an 80-hour, seven-day week in conditions that were dirty, noisy and dangerous. To that generation, the 40-hour week was a distinct dream. Today, most people work 40 hours or less a week. Many have no work at all, passing their days in poverty and personal difficulty. Of those who do have work, a large number feel that they are wasting their lives. Some are frenetically overstretched, commuting long distances to work in an office,

A red letter day for a West German green bank

FOR the 13,000 academics, professionals and even policemen who supported it, Monday was a red letter day. After almost four difficult years, West Germany's Oekobank (Ecobank), Europe's first ecologically-oriented bank, opened for business in the northern suburb of Frankfurt.

The idea of founding a bank 'with a more human face' to back environmental and women's causes is nothing new. The initiative dates back to the early 1980s, when Germany's Green movement was gaining momentum.

But collecting the DM 6m minimum capital required to set up a co-operative bank took time, as did finding the right people to run it. The first seven candidates put forward to the Federal Banking Supervisory Authority in Berlin were all turned down. Only last summer did the regulators finally give the nod to Mr Hans-Peter Schreiner and Mr Franz Laessig, both of whom won their banking spurs in the country's co-operative banking movement.

'Lending to companies making machines to help protect or clean up the environment is one of our main aims,' says Mr Schreiner. 'Biological' growers using ecologically-sound methods are also candidates.

But fighting sexism is also a priority. In its business Oekobank will be particularly sympathetic to women's projects and depositors will even be able to buy special savings bonds linked to them.

hardly seeing their children or friends. Many women rush out to work, and come in exhausted to grab an instant meal from the freezer to eat with the kids in front of the television. For all our labour-saving inventions, our working lives seem to be getting faster and distinctly crazier.

Martin Jacques, of *Marxism Today*, summed it up as follows:

> 66 *The truth is that on such issues we are locked into a deeply conservative culture which refuses to see things differently from the way it has always seen them. It assumes that paid work is still full-time and male, and that women do not work because their function is to do unpaid domestic work.*
>
> *The reality, of course, is different. Women comprise 40 per cent of the labour force, and one in four workers are part-time. The old model of work is dead, but it lives on in the national mind.*
>
> *Women have entered the labour force as dramatically in Britain as virtually anywhere else in Western Europe, and yet Britain has seen least movement in terms of childcare and weekly hours worked by men which, given the prevalence of overtime in manufacturing in this country, have in practice changed little over the past 20 years or so.* 99

A green way of working would look very different. The barrier which exists between formal paid jobs and unpaid formal work would be further eroded. Both men and women would share the housework and the childrearing more equally. Many would work close to home, in community and neighbourhood businesses, or in 'cottage electronic offices' from which they could be linked up to the entire world. Many would work from home, or work with others in specially converted houses or studios nearby. Working hours would be self-chosen, with people making individual contracts with their colleagues or employers concerning the hours, days and weeks they worked.

Commuting would cease, except for journeys to occasional meetings, and most long-distance communication would be via face-to-face telecommunications systems. There would be a strong emphasis on the local community, and some people might choose to devote some hours each week, paid or unpaid, to community service jobs, such as street-cleaning, childcare, or work in the recycling depot. If they wished, people might undertake voluntary community work in lieu of local taxes; such an arrangement already exists in Florida, known as 'service credits'. People might trade skills and produce with each other through community barter schemes, keeping track of their various credits and debits to the system as a whole through a central computer, as in the Local Employment and Trade System (LETSystem), 50 or 60 of which are running around the world. For some people, a typical working week might combine formal paid work for a local business, school or organisation, unpaid voluntary work for the community, household work and work paid through the LETSystem.

Too Utopian? Not necessarily. Such a way of life may not be such a distant dream, but in order to break down the strict nine-to-five, five-days-a-week routine of contemporary working life, let alone the environmental lunacy of long-distance commuting, we need to do some new political thinking. And at the moment British political parties seem to be totally lacking in imagination on this score.

In the USA, a range of different worksharing options are being encouraged through the work of a number of centres, such as San Francisco's New Ways to Work and Boston's Work Options Unlimited. Instead of automatically assuming that you have to work the hours you are told to work, people are encouraged to negotiate work patterns to suit them. Among the choices available are 'compressed' and 'modified workweeks' (four 10-hour days or three 12-hour days); 'V-time' (negotiated reductions in the working day, week or year); 'banked overtime' (allowing you to take longer holidays in lieu of overtime worked); jobsharing (where two people share one job); and flexitime (where you choose your own times to start and finish). In Winnipeg, Canada, teachers can choose a scheme called the 'deferred salary leave plan', which allows you to save up on a tax-free basis towards a year off, with your job being held for your return. By coordinating the number of teachers taking a year off at any one time, the Winnipeg school system is able to employ additional full-time staff on a permanent basis.

In Britain, only jobsharing is generally available as a choice, though it's estimated that no more than 10 000 people currently enjoy its benefits. The shortage of young people leaving school in the 1990s (the so-called 'baby bust') may yet persuade government and employers to contemplate a much wider range of worksharing options, to suit women with children who want to return to work, as well as the growing number

157

of men who want to work shorter hours in order to play a larger role in childcare. If such initiatives are to work, the government will need to establish the right to proper pension schemes and an end to discriminating pay practices for part-time workers, especially women. Community worksharing agencies could then play an important role in spreading the practice of worksharing among employers. And of course the development of worksharing would also play its part in reducing unemployment.

The second major development which could make a difference to the way we work is telecommuting – the practice of working from home, linked by telecommunications systems to your office or company. A number of Swedish villages have taken the idea one step further and established 'cottage electronic offices' or 'telecottages', fully equipped to enable local people to work from their village, in a work-oriented atmosphere, with support from other people. One of the current drawbacks is that telecommuters often feel isolated and cut off from the support, chatter and information flow at the office. A cottage office can provide all this, while enabling people to remain close to their homes and communities.

The first UK 'telecottage project' was launched in November 1989 when British Telecom and the Peak Park Trust set about the renovation of a group of derelict barns in Derbyshire, with funding coming from the Rural Development Commission and local councils.

A third change that is already in the air relates to the working atmosphere. With increasing pressure to reach ever higher targets, more and more people are beginning to wonder what it's all for. As we have seen, there is a direct link between the desperate, profit-obsessed nature of our economic culture and the destruction of our environment. The pressure and stress that people feel at work, or while commuting, is another direct result. There is not time to sit and reflect or appreciate the beautiful things of life. Our *doing* is destroying the Earth, while our souls are starving for a lack of *being*.

The 300 members of the Briarpatch Network, in San Francisco, who agree to help each other in their businesses, are clear that work is not just about money. Among the list of principles, which members must agree to, are the following:
● You have an insatiable curiosity about how the world works.

The Rural Revolution

WE may have to wait for history to tell us whether rural England is undergoing as profound a change as it did in the agrarian revolution of the 18th Century and the industrial revolution which followed that. But it may come as a surprise to many people that the 1980s can even be described in these terms.

The most obvious sign in the countryside itself of the new rural revolution is, without doubt, the spread of 'development' – a proliferation of new houses, housing estates, new roads and motorways, superstores and business parks which you will see, for example, on a drive northwards from London into East Anglia.

The 'revolution' this seems to portend has been brought about by many factors, though with two critical elements.

One is the astonishing growth of the new information technology which, with its computer, portable telephone and fax machine, has made it possible for many more people to live and work in the countryside.

The other is the decline of agriculture. No longer the mainstay of the rural economy, agriculture is releasing both land and people for new uses and employment.

The benefits of the revolution are considerable – as are the problems.

It is difficult to be sure precisely how many new jobs have been created countrywide, but the government-financed Rural Development Commission (RDC), whose function is to promote economic development in many of the more remote rural areas, is well placed to observe the trends.

In its 27 special rural development areas (RDAs), designated only in 1984 as areas of special need, it has charted population growth of up to 4 per cent in all but three and a dramatic drop in unemployment in virtually all.

There is a downside to these developments, as the RDC notes. Within the RDAs, services are subject to great pressure.

Village schools are still closing, and for the 15 per cent of rural families without use of a car, access to medical facilities, shopping and other services is difficult. Pockets of real poverty persist.

Above all, rurally concerned bodies such as the RDC draw attention to the inability of local people to afford to buy houses as prices rise with the competition from 'incomers.'

But important though it will be to make sure that the gap between rich and poorer rural areas is narrowed, the greatest challenge of the rural revolution is probably that posed by the extent and pace of development which, if it continues unabated and with as little control as in the recent past, threatens to overwhelm the countryside itself.

As the Town and Country Planning Association's journal put it recently: 'The challenge is to steer a course between the various visions of horror of the countryside as sterile food factory, noisy fun palace, concrete jungle, the preserve of the affluent or decaying museum piece, and find ways of widening the options for people to live and work in a healthy, sustainable and beautiful countryside.'

© THE FINANCIAL TIMES 8.12.1989

159

● You seek to do the work you love and to make a living at it.

● It is more important to you to provide the highest-quality product or service than to get rich.

● You prefer cooperation to isolation.

● You prefer honesty and openness to deceit and secretiveness.

● You believe in independence and responsibility.

● You believe in simple living and environmental preservation.

● Financial records are open to the community.

● You have been in business long enough to have a track record of your performance as a business.

The initiative as a whole took two to three years to develop, growing to around 300 members, and has remained stable since then. It has a business failure rate of less than 10 per cent in the first three years, which compares favourably with the national US average of 30 per cent failure in the first five years. Although the network's membership is generally small businesses of five employees or less, the largest business in the network employs 250 people.

In this chapter I have only been able to skim across the surface of a few of the economic issues we confront. The transformation of industry and a completely new approach to work are *essential* components of any serious strategy to achieve sustainability or a better quality of life. Sadly, they are also the areas about which the Green Movement feels least confident. The result is that most people simply do not realise that alternatives exist – and work.

Chapter 7

ONE
WORLD?

In May 1990, the BBC exposed the nation to a whole week of television programmes dealing with environment and development. They dubbed this green TV jamboree 'One World Week', which was probably somewhat irritating to all those church and development organisations who had been diligently staging their own unsung 'One World Weeks' year in year out. None the less, it made good viewing.

But what does the notion of 'one world' really mean? The Brundtland Report (published in 1987) drew an interesting distinction: 'the Earth is One, but the world is not', and went on to demonstrate this by depicting the massive disparities between First World and Third World countries. The BBC tried to reflect this distinction by dealing with environment and development issues from many different perspectives. A wide variety of programmes incorporated a green strand, including *Tomorrow's World, Blue Peter* and even *Wogan*. But only two stood out for me.

The first was Prince Charles's film on the environment which caused quite a stir, not least because it so courageously refused to pander to the 'quick-fix' managerialism that now dominates the environment debate. In this, Prince Charles seems to be well ahead of many mainstream environmentalists, and offers a challenge from which many still seek to avert their eyes. In his words:

> 66 *We have suddenly become aware of just what a devastating impact we have made on the world. In the last few decades, with our huge advances in technology, that impact has reached a point of crisis. . . .*
>
> *I have gradually come to believe that we cannot solve our environmental problems simply by coming up with yet more answers based on technology alone. Every so-called 'solution' seems to unleash a whole new generation of problems. What interests me is the debate going on beneath the actual issues. It's a debate about values; about what we mean by things like 'wealth', 'progress' and 'growth'. It has become apparent to me that we need to develop a new version of the Earth, and of the role that we humans have to play as stewards of the Earth.* 99

The other memorable and highly controversial programme was William Nicholson's 'March on Europe'. The storyline of this powerful drama was simple: instead of dying anonymously and unremarked in their famine-torn refugee camps in the Sahel, the poorest of the world's poor rose up and marched across the desert, intending to cross the Mediterranean and die in the sitting-rooms of Western Europe. With disconcerting candour, the film explored all sorts of racial prejudices, as in the following exchange between the two leading protagonists of the rich North and the poor South.

> 66 CLAIRE   Are you the one who speaks English?
>
> ISA EL-MAHDI   Yes madam.
>
> CLAIRE   I work with the European Community. I am the Commissioner for Development. I have come here to find out what we can do to help.
>
> ISA EL-MAHDI   You can do nothing. We are poor because God made us this way. Nothing can be done about it. You may go home.
>
> CLAIRE   I don't think we can blame it all on God.
>
> ISA EL-MAHDI   Then perhaps you think we choose to be poor of our own free will? We are lazy, and stupid, like all natives. You can do nothing.

The process of 'coco-colonisation'
(exporting some of our 'luxury goods'
to the Third World) creates wealth of
a kind, but brings no real benefits to
the poor and dispossessed.

ABOVE: One of the ultra-modern factories that make up the Mondragon Cooperative in the Basque country of Spain.

RIGHT: High-tech medicine at its best. The benefits of this electro-encephalograph are beyond dispute, but does it really represent the best use of limited resources?

x

ABOVE: A typical coffee plantation in Costa Rica, which has been particularly badly affected by the fall in coffee prices.

LEFT: Cattle ranching in Costa Rica, predominantly for the benefit of the hamburger-hungry Americans.

RIGHT: Chief Paulinho Paiakan of the Kaiapo people.

BELOW: To celebrate their twenty-fifth anniversary, the World Wide Fund for Nature organised an Interfaith Festival in Assisi, bringing together representatives of the world's major religions to discuss their role in protecting the Earth.

Churchyards can become lush and thriving nature reserves, home to an astonishing diversity of flora and fauna . . .

. . . alternatively, they can become sterile, chemical-drenched 'green deserts'.

RIGHT: The rainforests are the most prolific and genetically rich eco-system on Earth. More than 60 per cent of all species are to be found in the world's rainforests.

BELOW: A Swedish lake, incredibly beautiful to look at, but almost lifeless under the surface on account of acid rain.

ABOVE: Tree-planting in Kenya, organised by the Green Belt Movement.

RIGHT: Chandi Prasad Bhatt, one of the leaders of the Chipko Movement, addresses a meeting in Gahrwol. Their actions to defend the forests of Northern India have become an inspiration to environmentalists the world over.

The Earth from space.

CLAIRE   No, I don't think that either. Why don't you stop telling me what I think, and tell me what *you* think?

ISA EL-MAHDI   I think we are poor because you are rich.

CLAIRE   I'm sorry, but I don't agree. The situation isn't that simple. We spend a lot of money on aid to Africa, but most of it never reaches the people who need it. We're not the only problem.

ISA EL-MAHDI   They say that in Europe you have many cats.

CLAIRE   Cats?

ISA EL-MAHDI   Small animals that –

CLAIRE   I know what cats are.

ISA EL-MAHDI   They say that the cost of keeping a cat is more than $200 a year.

CLAIRE   I've no idea.

ISA EL-MAHDI   Let us come to Europe as your pets. We can drink milk. We can lie by the fire. We can lick your hand. We can purr. And we'd be much cheaper to feed.

CLAIRE   Mr El-mahdi – that may work on the Americans, and the British, and the Germans, but I'm *Irish*, and I say: phooey! My people have been colonised. Our land has failed us. We starved in our millions. So don't go pulling your guilt number on me. All right, so you've been exploited. I've got news for you. So has everyone else. It's a hard world.

ISA EL-MAHDI   The people here kill their own children, to save them a lifetime of pain. Some parts of the world are harder than others, madam.

CLAIRE   We've poured hundreds of millions of dollars into Africa. Where's it all gone? I'll tell you. Into presidential palaces, and tanks and fighter planes, and giant dams that don't work, and luxury goods for corrupt elites, and genocidal tribal wars. Isn't that right, Mr El-mahdi?

ISA EL-MAHDI   You will go home, and we will die. We live invisible lives. We die invisible deaths.

CLAIRE   What do you expect us to do about that? Watch you die?

ISA EL-MAHDI   If we must die, yes, I want you to watch us die.**99**

For some people, 'The March on Europe' gave powerful expression to the corrupting hypocrisy at the heart of most First World countries. We profess deep humanitarian concern about the people of the Third World; when confronted with shots of swollen bellies, stick-like limbs and fly-blown faces,

163

we may even, occasionally, make out a cheque or give a credit card donation by phone to prove how much we care. But on no account will we explicitly acknowledge that our own temples of affluence are partly built out of the bones of the Third World's poor and dispossessed.

Others reacted very differently, believing the film would reinforce fears of some swelling black/brown tide of humanity waiting to engulf the developed world. It was harshly criticised by some as exacerbating racial tension, and playing into the hands of the many racists who lurk so ominously within British society.

Either way, 'The March on Europe' exemplified the problems of moving from the warm and friendly abstraction of 'One World' to the reality of more equitable and sustainable development patterns. The many different meanings attached to the word 'development' only increase these difficulties.

LIMITING THE DAMAGE CAUSED BY DEVELOPMENT

Environmentalists have become increasingly concerned that much of today's development seems to be at the expense of the life-support systems on which the long-term wellbeing of Third World countries depends. Time after time, we've pointed out ways in which conventional development economics have actually *reduced* the capacity of poor people to improve their livelihoods and their chances of survival. The most important message of the Brundtland Report was that the number of dispossessed will continue to grow until such time as we radically reform our understanding of what development is all about.

A Bhopal here, a famine there, terrible flooding somewhere else: to us, these are the stuff of dramatic but short-lived images on the TV screen. But to millions of people such events are the stuff of their everyday lives. Despite all the evidence of very severe ecological breakdown in many parts of the world, the development lobby continues to follow the traditional path. Unfortunately this means that for every winner in the development process, there has to be a loser.

Because of their close proximity to many of the most serious environmental problems, the poor are often directly blamed for the destruction of their environments. Over-grazing, erosion, denuded forests, surface water pollution, mismanagement of natural resources – it is all laid at the feet of the poor. But this is a grotesque misrepresentation. As many have asked, why should farmers and settlers, who have harmoniously and successfully managed very difficult environments for hundreds of years, now so suddenly and wilfully choose to destroy them?

It is of course true that poor people today are having a greater impact on their forests and grazing lands than they did before. This is *partly* because their numbers have increased, but also because their forests have been cut down by logging companies or because their herds are now confined to far less and more marginal grazing land as a result of the 'development' of more fertile land elsewhere.

There are two main fly-wheels in this engine of destruction: one is externally driven through the unrelenting pressure of international debt. The other is internally powered by the corruption and incompetence of many governments in the South that have become impervious to the suffering of their own people. The poor, and the environment on which they depend, are remorselessly ground down by the interlocking teeth of these two fly-wheels.

The link between the state of the environment and economic pressures, such as debt or falling prices, can be easily illustrated. Imagine the situation of a peasant farmer whose crops fail. To tide him over, he borrows money from the village money-

The port of Lagos, Nigeria.

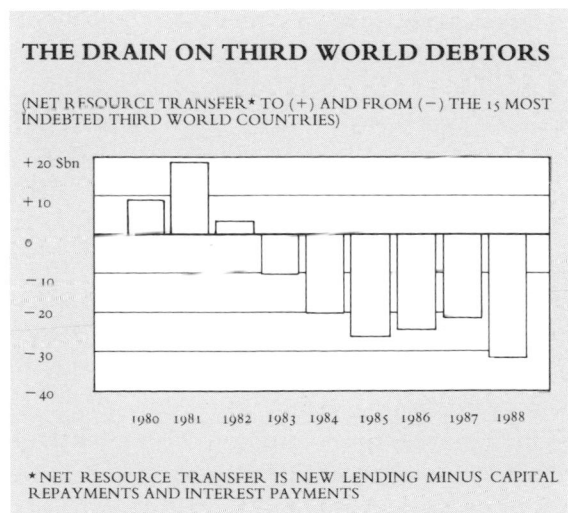

THE DRAIN ON THIRD WORLD DEBTORS

(NET RESOURCE TRANSFER★ TO (+) AND FROM (−) THE 15 MOST INDEBTED THIRD WORLD COUNTRIES)

+ 20 $bn
+ 10
0
− 10
− 20
− 30
− 40

1980 1981 1982 1983 1984 1985 1986 1987 1988

★NET RESOURCE TRANSFER IS NEW LENDING MINUS CAPITAL REPAYMENTS AND INTEREST PAYMENTS

Another plunge in price of cocoa

WE are eating more chocolate every year, but the price of cocoa plunges ever lower. On the London market yesterday, beans could be bought for May delivery at £613 a tonne, the lowest market price for more than 14 years and a new post-war low in real terms.

World consumption, about 2.2 million tonnes a year, keeps hitting new records; yet production is growing even faster. The result has been surpluses for the past six seasons.

Years of glut have helped chocolate makers keep their prices surprisingly stable worldwide, so boosting purchases. Oversupply of cocoa is therefore good news for big chocolate eaters such as the British, who on average get through about 2.5 kg of cocoa a year, second to the Swiss (4.3 kg).

However, the impact has been devastating for the economies of the big producers such as the heavily-indebted Ivory Coast and Ghana, which rely on bean exports as the main source of revenue.

© **ROBIN STAINER**
THE GUARDIAN 9.2.90

lender. The next year he has to devote more of his limited land to growing cash crops rather than food for his own family. He then sells the produce to the money-lender's cousin, at a pathetically low price, as the local market is flooded with similar crops from other equally desperate farmers. He just manages to pay off the interest, but still can't repay the loan. So the next year he cuts down the few remaining trees on his farm to sell as firewood, and tries to squeeze a bit more out of his tired soil – and so on and so on.

That, in a nutshell, is what today's world economic order comes down to for many Third World countries. Export earnings took a nosedive in the early eighties, and have never recovered. Debtor countries have therefore been obliged to convert more and more of their natural resources (forests, clean water, topsoil and pasture) into monetary resources. These natural resources are of course theoretically renewable, but only if managed properly and on a sustainable basis. And that is impossible if their monetary value is eroded year after year, further intensifying the pressure to try and get more out of already dangerously degraded natural systems. In its push for increased trade, the International Monetary Fund (IMF) has now imposed 'adjustment packages' on more than 40 countries, indiscriminately encouraging further investment in cash crops without any regard for future markets. The good old-fashioned laws of supply and demand then ensure that prices stay low.

The IMF measures the purchasing power of a basket of 30 primary commodities in terms of the manufactured goods they can buy. Starting from 100 in 1957, the trend has been gradually downward, and by 1985 the index plummeted to its lowest ever at 66. Many countries simply cannot diversify their way out of glutted markets as they have no capital to effect the necessary transformation – and there's no guarantee that new markets for different products won't be equally saturated by the time they've entered them.

Malaysia accounts for 60 per cent of the world's exports of tropical logs; most of the commercial forests in Sarawak and elsewhere will be completely logged out within a decade. But it is Japan that adds the value to, and gets the profit from, those Malaysian logs when it turns them into hi-fi cabinets for export to Europe. In the same way, it is the subsidised agriculture of Europe and the United States that keeps prices artificially low for Brazil's soybean exports. This in turn forces Brazil to grow more and more to keep revenues up in order to pay back $12–14 billion every year in interest on its huge loans.

On top of all that, many Third World countries become the victims rather than the beneficiaries of the massive borrowing that finances grandiose, ecologically destructive mega-projects. For instance, the cumulative impact of large dams financed by the World Bank and other multilateral lending agencies has been devastating. Millions of hectares of agricultural land and forest have been flooded (the infamous Tucurui Dam in Brazil, featured in the film *The Emerald Forest*, accounted for 216 000 hectares of rainforest). Longer-term costs include severe sedimentation, the salinisation of soils through poor irrigation projects, and greatly increased numbers of people suffering from malaria, schistosomiasis and other water-borne diseases. These costs, let alone the irreparable damage done to tribal people and peasant farmers, never appear in the cost-benefit appraisals of such projects. As a result of hydro-electric projects approved by the World Bank between 1979 and 1985, 450 000 people on four continents were involuntarily resettled.

But it's not all doom and gloom. Since 1985, the World Bank has been exposed to great pressure by environmental and development organisations in the United States and Europe. That pressure is now beginning to pay off. The number of environmentalists and ecologists employed by the Bank has risen sharply; more proposals are now turned down on the grounds of potential environmental damage; and they have begun to include some proper environmental criteria in their evaluations.

In truth, however, this is all largely defensive, designed to defuse criticism, particularly from the United States Senate and Congress. The concept of 'sustainability' means little to the Bank's decision-makers, and they find it almost impossible to use their vast resources genuinely to target the poor. For one thing, they are mandated to lend a certain amount of money every year, a sum that runs into many billions of dollars. They can only do this by investing in huge mega-projects rather than in the kind of grassroots, community-led and community-controlled projects without which *genuinely* sustainable development will continue to elude us.

167

At the moment, the only way the World Bank can claim a project has been 'successful' is by showing that it has achieved a certain rate of economic return. But their methodologies for assessing different rates of return remain incredibly primitive. They have also failed to promote the kind of research into different ways of assessing value detailed in this article about the Peruvian rainforest, taken from the 3.6.89 issue of the *Guardian*:

Scientists champion rainforests' harvest

DESTRUCTION of rain forests for cattle ranching or timber not only threatens the world's climate and environment but is also less profitable than reaping its harvests of rubber and fruit, a team of American scientists have calculated.

Researchers from the New York and Missouri botanical gardens and a forester at Yale University have calculated that a hectare (about $2\frac{1}{2}$ acres) of untouched Peruvian rain forest has a net economic value of $6,820 (£4,400) in its yield of fruit and rubber.

The same area farmed for cattle is worth $2,960 (£1,910) and was worth only slightly more as a managed timber plantation –

$3,184 (£2,055), according to a report in the magazine, Nature.

The scientists, led by Dr Charles Peters of the Institute of Economic Botany in New York, based their studies on an area near Iquitos in Peru, where people make a living by shifting cultivation, fishing and collecting fruits, latex and other forest products and selling them. The hectare they chose contained 275 species of tree and a total of 842 trees.

Of these, 72 species and 350 individual trees yielded edible fruits and rubber. Out of this hectare, local people collected roughly $700 (£452) worth of produce each year without harming the forest. The scientists did not count the value of the smaller medicinal plants that grew underneath the trees.

The same area contained 94 cubic metres of saleable timber. If all cleared at once it could fetch $1,000 (£645). But, the scientists argue, if the logging harmed only 18 of the hectare's fruit trees, the

damage would wipe out the logging gains.

The researchers based their calculations for cattle farming on Brazilian studies. They found that fully stocked pastures yielded $148 (£95) per year per hectare – before deducting weeding and fencing costs.

The research lends weight to ecologists' arguments that destruction of rain forests is not only a world environmental threat but a waste of economic potential. There have been studies of individual plant values – the rain forests are rich in unexploited pharmaceutical and food plants – but there have been few systematic value comparisons.

The researchers ask: 'Why has so little been done to promote the marketing, processing and development of these valuable resources?'

© **TIM RADFORD, THE GUARDIAN 3.6.89**

What is even harder for them to accept is that the ways in which their forests benefit the so-called 'poor' cannot easily be reduced to a dollar value at all. The World Bank has pumped vast amounts of money into what it calls 'social forestry', which tends to mean establishing plantations of exotic trees like eucalyptus, often in very unsuitable environments. These plantations are fast-growing and extremely useful for producing pulp and other products needed by industry. An economic return is derived, but rarely

in a manner that benefits the poor. Such plantations cannot provide the crops they get from native trees, the fruit or nuts or the fodder they need for their cattle or other animals, the timber they need for building materials or firewood. And how do you measure the more subtle benefits of forests in terms of ecological wellbeing, clean water and fresh air? Very simply, there is no way the World Bank can comprehend the notion of sustainable development in such a context.

These dilemmas are not by any means exclusive to the World Bank. The UK's bilateral aid programme (administered by the Overseas Development Administration) is not only woefully inadequate in financial terms, but places as much emphasis on benefiting UK industry (through arrangements 'tied' to the purchase of British products). Such aid can often compound rather than relieve the environmental problems from which these countries are suffering.

Admittedly, such aid is not forced upon them. Many Third World politicians are still keen to book their seats on the Western gravy train, and will fight tooth and nail to strengthen their over-developed élites and inappropriate infrastructures. But in doing this, they will receive every imaginable inducement from political and business interests in the West who stand to gain so much, in the short term, from the Third World following in our own polluted and suicidal footsteps.

Fortunately, it's not always down to governments. One of the most heartening aspects of the last decade has been the

The vast Carajas iron-ore project in Brazil, funded largely through the World Bank and the EEC.

169

£1 bn aid to India 'caused pollution'

BRITAIN'S £1 billion aid to India has caused dangerous pollution, the export of banned pesticides and civil unrest between local people and mine-owners, according to a detailed investigation published yesterday by the National Audit Office, Parliament's financial watchdog.

It exposes problems in four large projects into which Britain has poured more than £200 million but has been unable to control what happened.

The worst was the Amlohri open cast coal mine in Uttar Pradesh, the construction of which led to violence and criminal charges.

A visiting British High Commission team found serious environmental problems. These included 'considerable devastation of the landscape, spontaneous surface fires, the lack of a watering system for the mine', and severe pollution from dust and gas.

Another £73 million aid package to Hindustan Zinc to develop a zinc mine and smelter in Rajasthan also caused problems for 3,500 local villagers.

A £37 million aid programme to the Hindustan Fertilizer Corporation is also criticised. It aimed to help 200,000 farmers increase grain production.

The auditors said pollution was not considered and hazardous pesticides, banned in Britain because they were dangerous to people, were included in the initial aid package.

The report also criticises a £120 million aid programme to build a coal-fired power station in Rihand for being rushed through because the Department of Trade and Industry was anxious to get the work for British companies. The project attracted £285 million in British contracts.

© DAVID HENCKE, THE GUARDIAN
31.1.90

Grassroots growth – the only hope for Africa

SINCE most of Sub-Saharan Africa gained independence in the 1960s, the continent has received billions of dollars in foreign aid, more per head than any other region. Millions of pages of economic advice have been lavished on it, and it has been populated by armies of expatriate experts – there are 100,000 in Africa today, costing about $5 billion a year.

Yet for the past 20 years, Africa's crisis has steadily deepened. Most of its people are poorer and hungrier now than they were then. Food production has increased, but not as fast as a population doubling every two decades – a rate which puts tremendous pressures on soil and forests, schools, health services and job markets.

Critics on both right and left have concluded that aid has made things worse, deepening Africa's dependence, and financial misrule. Even those who agree that without further outside help, Africa faces what the World Bank calls 'a spiralling decline that can easily become politically explosive', ask what purpose can be served by pouring good money after bad.

A World Bank report published today breaks new ground for international organizations by addressing this question squarely. Ending the taboo on mentioning internal politics, which has made official debate on Africa so artificial, it identifies a 'crisis of governance' so great that 'ordinary people see government as the source of, not the solution to their problems'.

Authoritarian rule, it says, has allowed Africa's élites to 'serve their own interests without fear of being called to account'. Bureaucracies have been politicized and corrupted; judicial systems have been destroyed and debate has been stifled. Politicians have siphoned off fortunes into overseas accounts; foreign aid has 'expanded the opportunities for malfeasance'. Even more important than this waste of funds has been 'the profound demoralization of society at large'.

Africa's human potential, says the Bank, must be given absolute priority, through better education, health, infrastructures and communications, but also through better, more equitable government. African governments must learn to use their countries' 'best-trained minds, many of which are in exile or under-utilized', rather than relying on expatriates.

The Bank is advocating a high-risk strategy with this people-first approach. Much will depend on the depth of support it attracts among younger Africans and those politicians who acknowledge, like Nigeria's Olusegun Obasanjo, that Africa's post-independence rulers converted its revolution 'into one of fire and thunder against their own people'. To have posed the questions, however, does Africa signal service.

ROSEMARY RIGHTER, © THE TIMES
22.11.89

extraordinary upsurge of grassroots organisations and groups throughout the Third World. Many of these groups have been set up and organised by women, despite the vast burden of work they shoulder in so many Third World countries. It is these groups who are planting the seeds of hope for the future. Their focus is local and cooperative, regenerating wealth from the bottom up, nurturing the natural systems on which their livelihoods depend. And they are increasingly suspicious of the huge development schemes that so often exacerbate rather than relieve their poverty.

There are many organisations or development schemes that now provide beacons of hope for those who might have been persuaded that there was no hope left for the world's poor. In an overview of this kind it's impossible to go into detail, but organisations like the International Institute for Environment and Development, Panos, Oxfam, War on Want and the Catholic Fund for Overseas Development have all produced stirring books portraying one inspiring case study after another. Collectively, they give the lie to the weary fatalism and patronising attitudes with which so many government officials and 'aid experts' set about 'the business of helping the Third World'.

Though these case studies certainly justify aid programmes of the right kind, no one would claim that they constitute a sufficient response to the overwhelming poverty of many Third World countries. The talk today is therefore of a 'new bargain' between North and South, to be shaped as much by ecological as by economic considerations.

It has gradually begun to dawn on world leaders in the North that the future wellbeing of humankind depends as much on the Third World as it does on anything that we in the North can achieve. This may sound obvious, but prior to the publication of the Brandt Report in 1980, the Third World was, in practice, held to be largely irrelevant to the great struggles being fought out between the superpowers or between the West and the burgeoning economic power of the Far East and the Pacific Basin. Willy Brandt in his Commission argued that the self-interests of the North could best be served by promoting massive development in the South, and the Brundtland Report in 1987 went one step further by asserting the need for this development to be achieved sustainably.

171

GRASSROOTS ORGANIZATIONS IN SELECTED DEVELOPING COUNTRIES, LATE EIGHTIES	
Country	Description
INDIA	Strong Gandhian self-help tradition promotes social welfare, appropriate technology, and tree planting; local groups number in at least the tens of thousands; independent development organizations estimated at 12,000.
INDONESIA	600 independent development groups work in environmental protection alone.
BANGLADESH	1,200 independent development Organizations formed since 1971, particularly active with large landless population.
PHILIPPINES	3,000–5,000 Christian Base Communities form focal points for local action.
SRI LANKA	Rapidly growing Sarvodaya Shramadana village awakening movement includes over 8,000 villages, one third of total in country; 3 million people involved in range of efforts, particularly work parties, education, preventive health care, and cooperative crafts projects.
KENYA	16,232 women's groups with 637,000 members registered in 1984, quadruple the 1980 number; 1988 estimates range up to 25,000; many start as savings clubs.
ZIMBABWE	Informal small-farmer groups throughout country have estimated membership of 276,500 families (2.3 million people); active women's community gardens multiplying.
BURKINA FASO	Naam grassroots peasant movement has 2,500 groups participating in dry-season self-help; similar movements forming in Senegal, Mauritania, Mali, Niger, and Togo.
BRAZIL	Enormous growth in community action since democratization in early eighties: 100,000 Christian Base Communities with 3 million members; 1,300 neighborhood associations in São Paulo; landless peasant groups proliferating; 1,041 independent development organizations.
MEXICO	Massive urban grassroots movement active in squatter settlements of major cities; at least 250 independent development organizations.
PERU	Vital women's self-help movement in Lima's impoverished shantytowns with 1,500 community kitchens; 300 independent development organizations.
SOURCE: WORLDWATCH INSTITUTE, BASED ON VARIOUS SOURCES.	

But only in the last few years have our politicians begun to acknowledge that reversing ozone depletion depends as much on countries like India and China as it does on us phasing out ozone-depleting chemicals; that saving the world's rainforests depends on rainforest countries realising that it is in their interests to protect rather than burn the forests; that efforts to reduce the release of carbon dioxide and other greenhouse gases will ultimately depend on how far the Third World decides to play its part.

Northern politicians do not like it, but the South has suddenly acquired massive new bargaining powers. Their line (and it is one with which I greatly sympathise) goes something like this:

> 66 *You in the North got rich by doing what we now aspire to do: using your land, raw materials and energy sources to fuel a process of economic growth and industrial expansion. In the process, you have caused untold ecological damage in your own countries and in ours. You now expect us to hold back from a pattern of development that has served you so well because you fear that in the process we will exacerbate the pollution you have already caused and accelerate the process of ecological collapse you first set in train. And you apparently expect us to do this out of the goodness of our hearts when millions of our people are dying of malnutrition or preventable diseases, or living in grinding poverty. Well, you can get stuffed – unless you are prepared to pay up. After all, don't you all subscribe to the idea of the 'polluter pays principle'? If so, put your money where your mouths are, and give us the means to provide for our people sustainably and without doing further damage to the global environment.* 99

And in truth, even if you are not moved by the appalling disparities in wealth between North and South, there is really no alternative to paying up. Only the South can deliver what we now want: reductions in ozone-depleting chemicals in as short a period of time as possible; intact rainforests; a ceiling on the use of fossil fuels; patterns of development that are genuinely sustainable. The original, somewhat sentimental interpretation of 'One World' takes on a much more realistic meaning once we realise that we really are all in it together. It would therefore be very foolish if OECD countries became so obsessed with the idea of new aid packages to Eastern Europe that the substantial support still required in the Third World was further delayed.

173

REDEFINING NATIONAL SOVEREIGNTY

To achieve any new bargain with the South requires not only the perception of self-interest (which is gradually dawning in even the most unenlightened political circles), but the appropriate means to put such a bargain in place. New agencies, protocols, conventions and treaties have all been called for, to remedy the inadequacy of our existing international institutions and agreements.

Much has been made of the Montreal Protocol, negotiated in 1987 and reviewed in June 1990, which limits the production and consumption of ozone-depleting chemicals. It was indeed a milestone in international affairs (inadequate though environmentalists now consider its phase-out timetables to be), and has done much to restore the credibility of the United Nations Environment Programme (UNEP), under whose aegis it was negotiated. But UNEP has always been ludicrously under-resourced – the British contribution to UNEP in 1990 amounts to about 0.0001 per cent of our projected budget surplus for the year!

Essentially a scientific and advisory body, UNEP has no real power. In comparison, for instance, with the EEC, with its supra-national powers for obliging autonomous nation-states to incorporate internationally agreed standards and agreements into their own national legislatures, UNEP is nowhere. From that perspective, those who hope that UNEP in its current shape will be able to play a more dynamic and interventionist role in shaping international solutions to today's problems are, I think, misguided.

That is certainly the perception of most Third World countries, who remain extremely sceptical about both the effectiveness and the fairness of the Montreal Protocol. At least 95 per cent of the damage done to the ozone layer to date is from the release of CFCs in the West. They rightly point out that the developing world contributes no more than 16 per cent of total CFC usage today. Not a single Western leader has made any specific commitment or pledge to abide by clauses which are already contained within the Montreal Protocol concerning the transfer of technology and financial assistance to developing countries to enable them to introduce the more expensive alternatives which we are advocating.

In the same mean spirit, many OECD countries, particularly

the UK and the United States, are fighting shy of the idea of a 'special global fund' to ease the impact of global warming on Third World countries. The debate about how best to restrict emissions of greenhouse gases will start in earnest in 1991, once the Inter-Governmental Panel on Climate Change has made its official report at the end of 1990. All sorts of ideas are being considered, but they are all going to entail some kind of preferential arrangements for the Third World.

It's probably unfair to be too critical, since as yet the Green Movement may not have come to terms with these developments any more than the mainstream of politics and society. The Green Party, for instance, argues that Britain should immediately withdraw from the EEC, because of the EEC's inherently unecological nature. But at the same time, it is important to assess the role that EEC directives have played in shaping and strengthening UK environment policy over the last ten years. Without these directives, Britain would be in a far worse state than it is now. Even though the Green Party is actually more 'internationalist' than any of its rivals, apart from the Liberal Democrats, it has ended up looking very parochial.

The reason for this sort of confusion is that the Green Movement has not been able to articulate an alternative vision of international affairs, in which 'giving up' certain areas of autonomy and national sovereignty to supranational bodies (such as the EEC, a strengthened UNEP, or even a new United Nations Environment Council working in parallel with the existing Security Council) is balanced by 'passing down' economic and political power to regions, districts and parishes.

At the moment, we are getting the worst of both worlds. Not only are most politicians still superficially obsessed with outmoded notions of national sovereignty, but they also seem utterly unconcerned by the creeping 'homogenisation' of culture being perpetrated in the guise of 'economic progress'. This international economic steam roller flattens the regional variations and cultural diversity which are as essential to the wellbeing of our extended human family as they are to the stability of all ecosystems. Our national identity is being stolen from us by stealth, even as our politicians dig in against any erosion of our so-called national sovereignty.

Personally, I believe that a sense of national identity is just as important as a sense of belonging to one human family or indeed to one immediate and intimate community. Looking at events in Eastern Europe and the USSR, it seems that countries need to feel secure in their own nationhood before they feel able or inclined to give up any part of their sovereignty in the interests of a greater whole. Western European countries are only now stumbling towards that kind of internationalism after 40 years of stable nationhood.

A green approach to these matters involves accepting our international obligations (and adapting our laws and institutions accordingly), while simultaneously defending our regional and cultural diversity. There is no contradiction between accepting minimum standards for water purity throughout Europe, and simultaneously refusing to have our beer served in litres rather than pint pots. Likewise, one does not have to bicycle on the right-hand side of the road to help reduce global warming!

Whatever our attitude might be to national sovereignty, there's a vast amount that we can still do in terms of promoting and assisting the right kind of development in Third World countries. Through the transfer of new and environment-friendly technologies, which are currently being developed for our own use, we can enable the Third World to generate higher levels of sustainable, self-reliant prosperity, thus leapfrogging decades of earth-bashing 'progress' of the old kind. The 1922 United Nations Conference on Environment and Development, when North and South come together to agree such a programme, will be a crucial turning-point.

ECOLOGICAL SECURITY

The only pot of money that is sufficiently large and potentially available for reallocation to cover the costs of any 'new bargain' between North and South or East and West is that currently set aside for military spending. With the Cold War definitively over, and disarmament talks proceeding more optimistically than ever before, even quite cautious commentators have begun to talk of 'the peace dividend', and the liberating of financial and human resources hitherto tied up in military budgets.

Even without such propitious omens, we are desperately in need of a new definition of security. It long ago ceased to make any sense to interpret security exclusively in terms of size of arms budget or number of tanks or nuclear weapons. Security has to be defined in civil, economic and ecological terms, as well as military. There's little point investing billions in further arms spending, if, for lack of those very resources, one's economy is fundamentally weakened or one's life-support systems are heading for environmental bankruptcy.

And yet that's exactly what's been happening, both in the North and South. Between 1960 and 1988, global military expenditure more than doubled (in real terms), going from $400 billion to $980 billion. Yet few countries would claim to feel twice as secure, for the simple reason that military security is all but unattainable: an increase in the military capability of one country inevitably decreases its neighbours' sense of security; they in turn feel obliged to increase their military commitments, and so on. Resources are drained out of the economy, needs go unmet, ecosystems go unprotected, and security is threatened far more powerfully by civil unrest or ecological collapse than by any armed aggressor.

In a most helpful discussion paper on ecological security, Professor Norman Myers has begun to put some flesh on the bones of this relatively unfamiliar concept:

> 66 *If a nation's environmental foundations are depleted, its economy will steadily decline, its social fabric deteriorate, and its political structure become destabilised. The outcome is all too likely to be conflict, whether conflict in the form of discord and insurrection within the nation, or tension and hostilities with other nations. We can surely expect that this new scope for conflict will expand as increasing numbers of people seek to sustain themselves from declining resource stocks.* 99

There are all too many examples of potential conflicts over natural resources (Britain once went to war with Iceland over the humble cod). Norman Myers lays particular emphasis on shared water resources and river systems, highlighting the potential for conflict over access to the Nile, Jordan, Tigris, Euphrates, Ganges and many other major rivers.

Of the world's 214 most important rivers, 155 are shared by two countries, and 59 by more than two. These rivers support 40 per cent of the world's population.

Gorbachev call for UN 'Green Cross' unit

A TOTAL 'once and for all' nuclear test ban is essential for preserving the environment as well as for military security, President Gorbachev said yesterday.

'We say again the Soviet Union is ready anytime to end tests if the United States and others agree,' he said.

In his first major speech devoted to the environment, Mr Gorbachev proposed an 'international Green Cross' under the United Nations to help countries which were in ecological distress.

He was elaborating on an Austrian proposal, which he approved, for a UN force of 'green berets' to intervene in ecological disasters.

Calling for the 'ecologisation of politics' Mr Gorbachev proposed that the UN's conference on the environment and development in Brazil in 1992 should be held at 'the highest level'.

The conference should elaborate an 'international code of ecological ethics binding on all states, laying down criteria for a civilised attitude to nature.'

© WALTER SCHWARZ, THE GUARDIAN 20.1.90

INTERNATIONAL RIVERS IN DISPUTE		
RIVERS	COUNTRIES INVOLVED IN DISPUTE	SUBJECT OF DISPUTE
NILE	EGYPT, ETHIOPIA, SUDAN	Siltation, flooding, water flow/diversion
EUPHRATES, TIGRIS	IRAQ, SYRIA, TURKEY	Reduced water flow, salinization, (constraints on irrigation & hydropower)
JORDAN, YARMUK, LITANI, WEST BANK	ISRAEL, JORDAN, SYRIA, LEBANON	Water flow/diversion
INDUS, SUTLEJ	INDIA, PAKISTAN	Irrigation
BRAHMAPUTRA, GANGES	BANGLADESH, INDIA	Siltation, flooding, water flow
SALWEEN/NU JIANG	BURMA, CHINA	Siltation, flooding
MEKONG	KAMPUCHEA, LAOS, THAILAND, VIETNAM	Water flow, flooding
PARANA	ARGENTINA, BRAZIL	Dam, land inundation
LAUCA	BOLIVIA, CHILE	Dam, salinization
RIO GRANDE, COLORADO	MEXICO, UNITED STATES	Salinization, water flow, agrochemical pollution

Iraq warns Turks on Euphrates dam

Iraq yesterday warned Turkey that the commissioning of a hydroelectric dam across the Euphrates river seriously threatened their relations and followed up the warning by dispatching a high-level delegation to Ankara.

On Saturday President Ozal pushed a button to cut the flow of the Euphrates and fill the new Ataturk Dam, said to be the ninth largest in the world, outside Bozova, 340 miles south-east of Ankara. The 1,750-mile Euphrates flows through Turkey, Syria and Iraq to the Gulf.

But Syria and Iraq rely heavily on the Euphrates for hydroelectric power and irrigation, and the Iraqi Baath Party daily *al-Thawra* said yesterday that diverting its waters could cause a long-term agricultural disaster. In a front-page leading article, it said relations could suffer if Turkey does not relent.

The drastic reduction in the Euphrates' flow would affect 3.2 million acres of prime farmland in the river basin and force Iraq to shut four power plants in the western region which produce about 40 per cent of the country's electricity, the paper said.

Syria, in severe economic trouble and almost totally dependent on the river for irrigation and hydroelectricity, has not officially reacted to Saturday's commissioning, but has condemned the plan in the past.

© THE TIMES 15.1.90

Some of the trade-offs that emerge from Professor Myers' paper are fairly startling:

• An action plan for tropical forests would cost $1.3 billion a year over the course of five years. This annual sum is the equivalent of less than half a day of military expenditure worldwide.

• One of the greatest environmental hazards in the Third World is the lack of clean water for household use, contributing to 80 per cent of disease. This could have been countered by the UN Water and Sanitation Decade which was denied all but a small fraction of the $30 billion needed every year during the 1980s. This is the equivalent of ten days of military spending.

• To supply contraceptive materials to all women who already have family-planning motivation, and thus to reduce the ultimate global population by some two billion people, would cost an additional $2 billion per year on top of the $1 billion spent today. This is the equivalent of 16 hours of military spending.

• The military build-up in both Pakistan and India has been so extensive that by 1985 the two countries were spending almost $10 billion on military activities each year. Two per cent of these outlays would have been enough to establish tree plantations in 96 000 square kilometres of Pakistan and 300 000 square kilometres of India.

• A single Trident submarine costs around $1.4 billion. This is the equivalent of a global five-year child-immunisation programme to prevent one million deaths a year. Reducing infant mortality would help to foster family-planning motivation among multitudes of Third World parents.

Investing in ecological rehabilitation and sustainable development programmes is far more likely to bring lasting security than further investment in weapons. In view of the dramatic changes in Eastern Europe and the USSR's evident desire to reduce military spending in order to redirect resources into economic regeneration and meeting consumer demand, the opportunity now exists for the United States and Western Europe to reduce their own arms budgets massively.

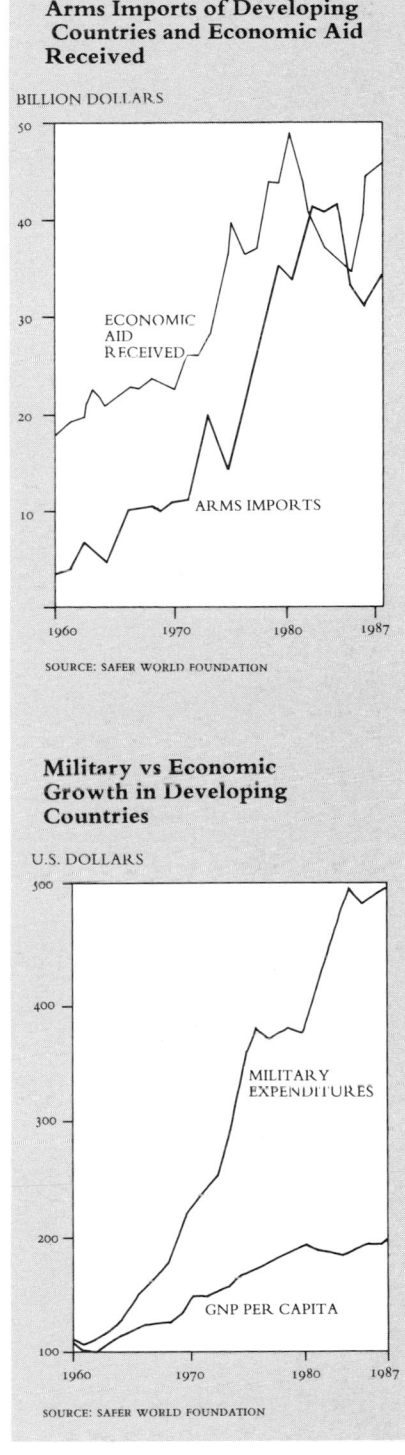

Arms Imports of Developing Countries and Economic Aid Received

BILLION DOLLARS

ECONOMIC AID RECEIVED

ARMS IMPORTS

1960   1970   1980   1987

SOURCE: SAFER WORLD FOUNDATION

Military vs Economic Growth in Developing Countries

U.S. DOLLARS

MILITARY EXPENDITURES

GNP PER CAPITA

1960   1970   1980   1987

SOURCE: SAFER WORLD FOUNDATION

These changes were prefigured in an extraordinary but little-reported speech to the UN General Assembly, by Mr Shevardnadze, the Soviet Foreign Minister in September 1988:

> 66 *For the first time today we have clearly realised that, in the absence of any global control, man's so-called peaceful constructive activity is turning into global aggression against the very foundations of life on Earth. Faced with the threat of environmental catastrophe, the dividing lines of the bi-polar ideological world are beginning to recede. The biosphere recognises no divisions into blocs, alliances or systems. All share the same climatic system and no one is in a position to build his own isolated and independent line of defence against any ecological crisis. Man-made or second nature has turned out to be dangerously deficient. In a situation like this it is suicidal to try to rein in progressive natural developments, to wear down the enemy through economic pressures. Much more sensible, as we are proposing to the United States and other countries, would be to abolish planned or on-going military programmes and to channel the funds thus released towards instituting a new international regime of ecological security.* 99

In its pamphlet, 'Security After the Cold War', the organisation Safer World has mapped out an incremental disarmament strategy that should satisfy all but the most die-hard of Cold War warriors. This is based on the twin pillars of 'non-offensive defence' (ensuring that the *defensive* capability of one's non-nuclear forces is superior to the *offensive* capability of any potential adversary, so that both parties have the capacity to repulse an attack, but not to mount one) and 'minimum deterrence' (in which the superpowers' nuclear weapons are reduced to the minimum level necessary to deter the first use of nuclear weapons by the other side, and undertakings of no-first-use are given on both sides as part of a transitional process to eliminate *all* nuclear weapons).

Current talks on both conventional and nuclear disarmament confirm the viability of such an approach. Robert McNamara, former US Defense Secretary, sees it like this:

> 66 *I believe that within six to eight years the United States could cut its defense budget in half in relation to GNP, from 6 per cent to 3 per cent. That would free up, in 1989 dollars, $150 billion per year. If I were Defense Secretary today I would be considering how that could be done six to eight years from now, without endangering security in the West.* 99

One only wishes that the UK had something positive to offer in this exciting context other than an entrenched commitment to maintain current levels of arms spending, and an almost nostalgic attachment to the iron-clad idiocies of the Cold War.

One final threat to global security needs to be addressed with the utmost urgency: the sheer increase in human numbers.

POPULATION PRESSURES

Just to remind ourselves of the likely increase in human numbers: 5.3 billion in 1990; 6 billion by 2000; and 8.5 billion by 2025. (This is an increase of 3.2 billion over 35 years, 3 billion of them in developing countries.) Beyond that point, there are varying estimates, before world population 'stabilises' at around 11 or 12 billion towards the end of the next century.

Even if the planet's life-support systems turn out to be more resilient than anticipated; even if new technologies enable us to get more out of less with minimum pollution; even if those technologies are geared to meeting human needs rather than generating additional profit, so that wealth is distributed far more equitably; and even if world leaders suddenly find the political will to make all these things stick, those standard population projections spell untold misery for millions of people and the steady elimination of ecological diversity across the entire planet. I find it inconceivable that so many development experts do not seem to realise that all their work could simply be swept away by the rising tide of humanity.

In most African countries, for instance, and even in parts of Latin America, per capita food consumption is falling and living conditions are deteriorating. As Lester Brown puts it in the 1989 *State of the World Report*:

> 66 *Given the trends in per capita food production and income, many countries may have delayed too long in implementing effective family-planning policy. They may now face a choice: adopt a one-child family goal or accept a decline in living standards. It is hard to imagine anything more difficult for a society than striving for acceptance of a one-child family goal, except suffering the consequences of failing to do so.*
>
> *Countries that have made the shift to small families typically have four things in common: an active notional population education programme, widely available family-planning services, incentives for small families (and in some cases, disincentives for large ones), and widespread improvements in economic and social conditions.* 99

Education is the most critical element in any family planning programme.

181

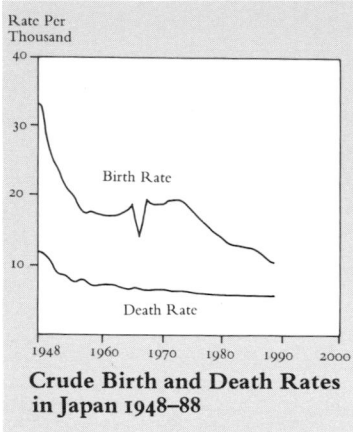

Rate Per Thousand

Crude Birth and Death Rates in Japan 1948–88

Between 1970 and 1976, China's population growth rate dropped from 2.6 to 1.3 per cent, but population pressures in China are still critical.

As examples of what can be done, he details the experiences of China (between 1970 and 1976, China's population growth rate dropped from 2.6 per cent to 1.3 per cent) and Japan, which cut its population growth rate from 2.2 per cent to 1 per cent between 1944 and 1956 in the fastest ever recorded decline in fertility.

If we were able to replicate these success stories (and those of South Korea, Taiwan, Singapore, Java, Sri Lanka, Zimbabwe, Cuba, Tunisia or Thailand) with some rapidity and political determination, the world's population could stablise at around eight billion. If things start to get worse in certain countries (such as the Philippines), we could well end up with more than 12 billion. That differential of four billion gives a fair indication of what can be achieved if we genuinely get on top of the population problem before it gets on top of us.

The World Fertility Survey has demonstrated that about one-third of the 140 million women who become pregnant every year in the Third World do not want to have another baby. And, contrary to what one might think, many countries simply can't get adequate funding from the developed world for their *existing* family-planning programmes. That's the real tragedy.

But the example of Japan referred to above is equally important, for it is clearly incumbent upon us to reduce our own numbers, given the relative impact each one of us in the developed world makes on the Earth's resources in comparison to people in the Third World. In 1989, the Green Party was rubbished in the press for daring to devote a major part of its annual conference to discussing population. How long will it be before their basic common sense on this matter is echoed by other politicians, just as it has been on so many other issues?

COSTA RICA

Making the television programme on the international dimension of the Green Movement presented us with a particular problem. It would have been impossible to give any kind of overview in a 25-minute programme, and to hunt out cases of 'best practice' from one continent to the next would merely have produced a frustratingly incoherent picture. So we decided to home in on just one country, and settled on Costa Rica, knowing that this tiny Central

American republic, squeezed in somewhat unnervingly between Nicaragua at one end and Panama at the other, probably has more going for it than any other developing country. By assessing the extent to which the Costa Ricans are successfully moving towards sustainable development, one can begin to appreciate the huge problems that less favoured nations are likely to encounter during the nineties.

The first thing to say about Costa Rica is that it is a very small country (just 51 000 square kilometres, about the same as Denmark) with a population of 2.8 million. It was discovered by Christopher Columbus in 1502, and earned its name (the 'rich coast') from rumours of vast gold reserves – which never materialised. But it is an astonishingly fertile country, and the Costa Ricans rightly take pride in the fact that a combination of sun, rain and good topsoil means they can grow almost anything.

What they grow most of now is cows, for export to the hamburger-hungry citizens of the United States. In 1950, cattle ranches covered just one-eighth of the country; now it's up to a third. Beef production quadrupled during that time, but per capita consumption in Costa Rica itself fell by more than 40 per cent during the same period. (The average American cat eats more beef a year than the average Costa Rican citizen!)

As so often in Central America, the forests paid the price for this agricultural expansion; it is now predicted that by 1995 Costa Rica will have forests on no more than 10 per cent of its total land mass – and much of that will be within the National Parks. All its commercial forests will be exhausted by that time, and Costa Ricans will almost certainly be importing timber products from their Central American neighbours, although it's possible that careful forest management and extensive reafforestation schemes may have been introduced just in time to avoid this.

Costa Rica has earned a justifiable reputation for its National Parks. The 13 parks and 15 nature reserves comprise about 8 per cent of its territory; as a developing country with good environmental intentions but no spare cash, it has no hesitation in seeking financial assistance from foreign governments. The Netherlands has given $30 million and Sweden $25 million towards the National Parks Scheme, and at least 30 per cent of the running costs come from the United States, a substantial

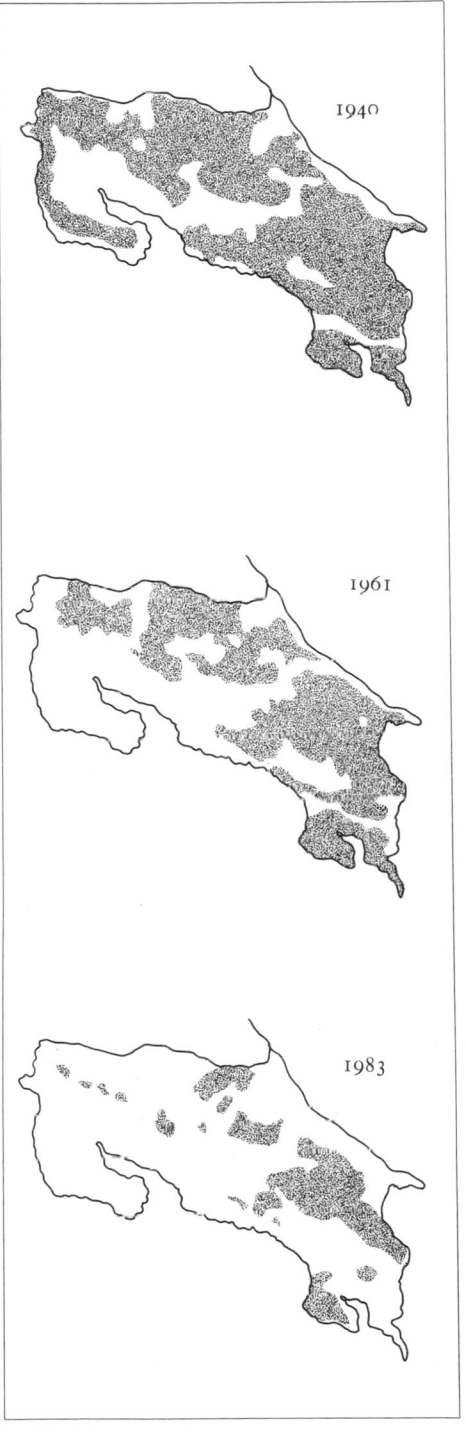

1940

1961

1983

Deforestation in Costa Rica.

part of it via a highly imaginative Debt Swap for Nature Programme. This is all in stark contrast to other Central and South American countries, such as Brazil, who often react negatively to any initiative from the developed world to help protect their forests.

One highly beneficial consequence of the National Parks Scheme has been the dramatic increase in 'eco-tourists', visitors coming to Costa Rica specifically to enjoy the wildlife and beautiful scenery. This has helped to create many new jobs in the parks and hotels, thus boosting the country's foreign reserves. Fortunately, the expansion of the new facilities is being handled with considerable sensitivity in order to avoid the problems of intensive tourism in countries like Kenya.

I can certainly vouch for Costa Rica being a wonderful country to visit as an ecologically minded tourist, though there are obviously tensions inherent in the very notion of 'eco-tourism'. Thousands of tourists jetting in from all over the world is not exactly a cost-free process from an ecological standpoint! However, it's clearly preferable that the cash they bring with them should help to protect the environment rather than systematically destroy it, as has happened in so many Mediterranean countries and in many parts of the Far East.

The business of bringing in foreign exchange is a constant struggle for countries like Costa Rica. It's a big importer of oil (costing around $80 million per annum) and other industrial goods, and has found that more and more has to be exported every year in order to pay for the same level of imports. Costa

Eco-tourists hunting down the big game in Kenya's Masai Mara National Park. Congestion is becoming quite a problem!

Rica exports coffee, bananas, sugar and tropical fruits like pineapple, melons, mangos and paw-paws.

Land distribution is biased towards cattle ranching and cash crops for export. Just 2000 ranchers control *half* the agricultural land in use, and the best of the rest is given over to large plantations. Production of staple foods such as rice, corn, beans and sorghum has not been keeping pace with population growth, and the bill for food imports has been steadily rising. This situation is fairly standard throughout Central America.

The answers to such problems are likely to emerge from Costa Rica itself, which is home to two fascinating initiatives aimed at establishing more sustainable patterns of agricultural production. The first of these is ANAI, a non-governmental organisation operating in one of the poorer regions of Costa Rica, and working very closely with local farmers to encourage agricultural diversification, conservation and sustainable management techniques. With a budget of around $500 000, they run a wide variety of projects over a 3000-square-kilometre area, including community tree nurseries, agro-forestry, the introduction of little-known tropical fruits, and, most recently, organic fruit-growing for export.

The use of agro-chemicals is increasing rapidly in Costa Rica, all of them imported by multinational companies like ICI. Growing crops on a large scale in a hot and humid climate is difficult, due to the great speed at which weeds, pests and other insects can multiply. Traditional methods of minimising this are intercropping (raising low-growing plants which shade the soil and thus deter weed growth) and planting mixtures of crops to prevent any one kind of pest from having a field day. Once the monocultural plantations take over, those natural defences can no longer be counted on. A 'need' is created for vast amounts of costly and often dangerous pesticides.

ANAI believes that this is a dangerous path for Costa Rican farmers, encouraging dependency and agricultural techniques that simply don't translate from temperate to tropical climates. With organic mangos selling at $5 each in Miami supermarkets, they may well be right – yet here again, concern about the sustainability of such trade inevitably recurs.

The other place we visited in Costa Rica was the Tropical Agriculture Research and Education Centre (or CATIE, as it is known in Spanish). CATIE is a non-profit-making

Heavily subsidised sugar beet production in East Anglia and throughout the EEC has severely damaged sugar exports from countries like Costa Rica.

185

association which promotes research, training and technical cooperation in agriculture and forestry. Its brief is simple: to find ways of increasing agricultural yields without damaging natural resources or life-support systems. While we were there, we visited a dairy project, to increase yields by selective breeding; an extensive project in Integrated Pest Management, partly funded by the UK's Overseas Development Administration; and a fascinating agro-forestry scheme to introduce 'woody perennials' such as Erythrina, which is a nitrogen-fixing tree and thus helps to build up the fertility of the soil.

But perhaps the most important aspect of CATIE is the fact that it is co-funded by seven countries: Costa Rica, Panama, Nicaragua, Honduras, Guatemala, El Salvador and the Dominican Republic. It is perhaps the most effective example of international cooperation in a region that is notoriously difficult to bring together. There is indeed a regional trading bloc in the area (the Central American Common Market), but it accounts for only a small proportion of the imports and exports into the region. In 1987, for instance, 48 per cent of Costa Rica's exports went to the US, 25 per cent to the EEC, and just 14 per cent to Central America; 43 per cent of its imports came from the US, 13 per cent from the EEC and 24 per cent from Central America. The notion of regional self-reliance, as outlined in Chapter 5, has a long way to go.

Much of the pressure to increase both Costa Rica's traditional and non-traditional exports arises from its huge burden of debt. Until recently, its debts stood at $4.6 billion. With a population of just 2.8 million, that made it one of the most heavily indebted nations in the world. In 1988, the cost of servicing that debt amounted to well over 30 per cent of the total value of Costa Rica's exports.

However, some relief would now seem to be on the way; together with Mexico, Costa Rica is to be the first beneficiary of the so-called Brady Plan. With the help of the World Bank and the IMF, about $1.6 billion of its debt will be 'bought back' (at its discounted value on the secondary market) or swapped for an equivalent stake in Costa Rica's industry. This is the first time that the World Bank has put money directly into helping to pay off old debts, rather than rescheduling those debts or even providing new money. The Brady Plan offers a small ray of hope, but Costa Rica is an exception.

Despite not paying much of its interest over the last few years, the banks consider Costa Rica one of the 'good boys'. A lot more help is still needed for countries that don't fit into that category.

Costa Rica is also fortunate in that it does not suffer from the problem of 'flight capital' – large amounts of money loaned by the West being creamed off by corrupt officials and politicians and deposited in personal bank accounts abroad. Repatriating flight capital remains a major stumbling block in the debt forgiveness schemes proposed for other countries.

The most important effect of the Brady Plan for Costa Rica will be to reduce the annual cost of servicing the debt, thus ensuring that a higher proportion of GNP can be directed into sustainable development and maintaining already impressive standards of health care and education. Between 1960 and 1980, life-expectancy in Costa Rica increased from 60 to 74, infant mortality fell from 76 deaths per thousand to 15 in the same period, and per capita income doubled. Costa Rica was one of the first countries in the world to adopt free primary, secondary and university education *for all*. As a result, illiteracy almost disappeared, and its highly educated workforce has been able to move into manufacturing and industrial markets such as electronics, jet engine servicing and plastics.

This provides a good example of what I referred to earlier as 'civil and economic security'. In Costa Rica's case, it is all the more significant that the army was abolished way back in 1949 after a short but extremely unpleasant civil war. While many of its neighbours in Central America have poured billions of dollars into expanding arms budgets, Costa Rica has been able to invest in education, health care and social security.

And this process has in turn been facilitated by the fact that Costa Rica is the oldest and one of the most stable democracies in Latin America. Voting first took place in 1866, but regular elections actually date from 1889. Men and women over 20 have the right to vote to determine the members of the 57-strong legislative assembly for a four-year term. The president is also elected for a four-year term of office, after which he is obliged to stand down and is not eligible for re-election. The two major parties do not have strikingly different policies, and the Costa Rican electorate quite happily changed over from one to the other in the February 1990 elections.

187

Costa Rica is justifiably proud of its long-lived and stable economy. It has brought immense social and economic benefits to the people of Costa Rica.

The one fly in this social ointment is a population growth rate of 2.8 per cent, which means that the current population of 2.8 million will double in 25 years. That is already causing considerable pressure within the capital, San José, and other towns, to which displaced farmers have been steadily gravitating over the last 20 years. Although it sounds bad, Costa Rica has already done an immense amount to reduce its population growth rate from a high point of 5.6 per cent, with an extremely effective family-planning programme. But it is of course a Catholic country, and there are cultural and social limits to what can be achieved.

All in all, Costa Rica's is an impressive story, though even the most sympathetic analysis of the extent to which its economy is 'sustainable' would produce a very mixed verdict. There is an obvious clash between sustainability and the interdependence that characterises its economic relationships with the developed world. In terms of the continuing burden of debt, the promotion of chemical intensive cash cropping, the inequitable distribution of land among cattle ranchers and plantation owners, low commodity prices, restrictive tariffs, other forms of protectionism in the United States and the EEC, and the difficulty it has had in building up regional markets, Costa Rica tends to lose out one way or another.

If this is the case with Costa Rica, it is a much greater problem with many other less-favoured developing countries. In the end, the pursuit of sustainability and the achievement of conventionally measured success in our current world economic order are *mutually exclusive*. Asking Third World countries to do both at the same time is like asking a farmer to protect wildlife on the farm while simultaneously increasing yields, or asking a travelling salesman to get from A to B more quickly while simultaneously cutting back on petrol consumption. The confusion is ours, but the consequences of it are felt most painfully by the Third World.

It must by now be clear, when dealing either with broad generalities or specific case studies, that there are no environmental problems *per se*, but rather massive political and economic problems that have extremely serious environmental repercussions. By the same token, there are no environmental solutions *per se*, but only political and economic solutions. It is to the murky world of politics that we must now turn.

Chapter 8

BODY POLITIC, IMMORTAL SOUL

THE NEED FOR CHANGE

I would like to think, by this stage of the book, that I had succeeded in establishing three basic principles:

1 That radical and lasting change is absolutely *necessary* and that if we don't make such changes over the next decade, we're in for a pretty grim time in the next century.

2 That such change is technically and economically *feasible*, and that most of the necessary measures are already being implemented somewhere in the world, albeit in a desperately inadequate and uncoordinated way.

3 That such change is socially *desirable*, in that it will allow us to achieve a better quality of life, to spread the benefits of our wealth more fairly, and to live in the knowledge that we are not destroying the prospects of future generations.

If change is necessary, feasible and desirable, what's the problem? Short-sighted politicians? Wicked multinational companies? Ivory-tower economists? Over-cautious scientists?

Or we ourselves? The answer is all of us, as we painfully and grudgingly come to terms with the fact that this wonderful industrial civilisation of ours has been built on shifting, increasingly polluted sands. And the process of change, even in building up that basic awareness, is agonisingly slow.

Over the last few years, however, things seem to have speeded up at long last. Back in the late sixties and early seventies, the debate was all about the limits to growth, with the emphasis on the physical constraints to our ability to exploit the Earth's raw materials and natural wealth. These outer limits remain crucially important, but it's encouraging to see a new emphasis on the inner limits which now confront us at every turn.

In *The Inner Limits of Mankind*, Irvin Laslow has written powerfully of what he calls 'the obsolescence of modernism', and the inability of much of what poses as intellectual thought today to provide any kind of solution to the human dilemma. In his words: 'it is not the finitude of the planet, but the bounds of human will and understanding that now obstruct our evolution to a better future'.

THE AGE OF REASON

Achieving a better future seems to me to be wholly dependent on properly interpreting the past. Political principles and ideologies do not emerge from an intellectual vacuum; they are shaped, consciously and unconsciously, by the prevailing philosophical beliefs and values of the age. Exponents of capitalism and communism, for instance, justifiably refer back to Adam Smith and Karl Marx as their most formative influences, but neither of these two were just sitting at their desk, when suddenly, one bright and sunny day, 'Eureka, Capitalism! Communism!' They are, of course, important historical figures, but it's *their* sense of history that really matters.

The question we need to ask is a simple one: at what point in the human adventure did we become wedded to the value system (and its attendant notion of progress) which still dominates our lives today? To me, there's a clear divide: the years between 1600 and 1700, when Francis Bacon, René Descartes and Isaac Newton were laying down the law (and a new law it was too) about the relationships between God, human beings and the Earth. Sean McDonagh explains the contribution of Francis Bacon:

> 66 *Bacon brushed aside much of the metaphysical speculation which had preoccupied Western thought for almost 2000 years. Knowledge was not about insight and understanding, but rather about power. Power should be used to transform the Earth's capital resources. The Earth was no longer endowed with mystery. It was not something to evoke awe in the enquirer, or something to be communed with in love. Rather, its secrets were to be stormed, to be prised open with increasing violence, no matter what the cost to animal or plant worlds or to a large section of the human community.* 99

In a similar vein, René Descartes talked about 'making ourselves the lords and possessors of Nature'. He believed that the laws of Nature could best be revealed by utterly objective, quantifiable measurement, and that a mathematical method should be developed to reduce the whole of life to a systematic process of quantification. Thus was born the all-powerful idea that life can be interpreted as a machine, governed by universal mechanical laws, an idea developed in some detail by Sir Isaac Newton, the 'father of modern science'. God might very well have made the machine, but we human beings were the mechanics, and all the little cogs and wheels were there for us to play with for our own benefit.

All these men, each in his own way, were still deeply religious, and fell back on the biblical injunction to exercise 'dominion over the Earth' as the rationale for their ideas. But they set in train the great Age of Reason, which gradually undermined religion as comprehensively as it did Nature. From that point on, in a series of leaps and bounds, a world view developed which rested on four crucial notions:

TOP: Francis Bacon

BOTTOM: René Descartes

1 That the workings of the planet and of life itself could only be understood as a strictly mechanical process.

2 That it was the task of scientists and philosophers to reduce those workings to the smallest possible measurable units, and that the progress of the human species depended on their success in this venture.

3 By virtue of our ability to perform these intellectual feats, Man should be seen as something quite separate from the rest of life on Earth, and what's more, the Bible said so.

4 That all living creatures and all living matter existed solely to serve Man's purposes and it was up to us to 'tame' them as best we could in order to maximise the benefits of this unlimited source of wealth.

It was against that philosophical backdrop that Adam Smith and, later, Karl Marx delivered up their great economic theories, which have in turn shaped the two dominant ideologies of the modern age, capitalism and communism. These are the left and the right legs of the staggeringly powerful colossus that now crushes life on Earth at every step. The ecological horrors outlined in Chapter 1, which we've seen so much of on our TV screens over the last few years, flow as inexorably from that prevailing world view as night follows day.

THE POISONED CHALICE

I'm sure they and their successors never wanted it to be like that. Indeed, I'm sure they were motivated purely by a desire to benefit humankind – and that world view has certainly brought enormous benefits in its wake, enriching many millions of people. I do not therefore believe that politicians today are wicked people, intent on maintaining power and privilege for their own, for as long as possible, even if it ends up costing us the whole Earth. The more one studies their reactions to a collapsing world, and shares their confusion and consternation, the more they are revealed as the victims of a 300-year-old mindset that has got them so firmly by the intellectual short-and-curlies that they don't know which way to turn.

Nor do I believe that our spiritual leaders have deliberately and systematically misinterpreted their own scriptural texts in order to make life easier for themselves. Rather, they've been metaphorically mugged by a vision of progress which seemed to allow for an honourable compromise between their obligations to God and their equally pressing obligations to their fellow human beings. There has, since then, been no turning back, even as they have found themselves failing in their duty to both.

But while awareness may gradually be dawning for some, defiance and the wilful disregard of reality (now that we really *do* know what's happening to the planet and its atmosphere) remain the last resort of many others. The history of humankind has been characterised by sustained bouts of what the Greeks called *hubris* (overweening pride and arrogance). And, sadly, there are, as yet, few signs of people relinquishing their faith in our thrusting, technologically driven concept of progress.

In that respect, our understanding of evolution is still unapologetically human-centred, as is our vision of the future. The most that the Green Movement has been able to achieve (by way of what Fritz Schumacher called 'metaphysical reconstruction') is to displace the macho terminology of 'conquering', 'governing' and 'taming' the Earth with a more opportunistic array of green jargon: 'managing our natural wealth', 'sustainable growth' or 'stewardship' of Planet Earth. The focus is still human-centred, but at least our exploitation of the Earth can now be presented as much more environment-friendly.

The scope for such 'green packaging' is nowhere more evident than in the burgeoning field of genetic engineering. No self-respecting gene splicer would dream of presenting a proposal that didn't somehow, miraculously, benefit the environment. They all play down the significance of their work, implying that it's little more than an extension of selective breeding. Yet there are clear limits to selective breeding, limits set by Nature itself. Genetic engineering takes us way beyond those limits, reducing all living creatures to a few lines of genetic code. The most effective campaigner against genetic engineering in the United States, Jeremy Rifkin, puts it like this: 'our children will view all of nature as a computable domain. They will redefine living things as temporary programs that can be edited, revised, and re-programmed'.

From such a perspective, genetic enginering is the epitome of humankind's defiant reflex, the collective endeavour to keep ourselves alive by gradually extending our control over every facet of life on Earth. The promise of a genetically engineered cornucopia is but the latest of technical fixes, tantalisingly waved in front of us, guaranteed to dispel gathering apprehension that our very understanding of progress may be fatally flawed.

We are all, in varying degrees, trapped by images of our own power and superiority, by a centuries-old failure to

193

balance our rights and entitlements as the dominant species on Earth with the all-important obligation to protect and value the rest of life on Earth *for its own sake*, and not just for its usefulness to us.

For many people, all this moral philosophy may put a rather different slant on the notion of green politics. But environmental issues like acid rain or global warming are just symptoms of a much deeper malaise. That's why the Greens quite rightly go on and on about the need to deal with causes, not symptoms. And that's why the answer to acid rain, for instance, has to involve a lot more than sticking a bit of fancy, state-of-the-art technology on our power-station chimneys. The answer has to be both political and philosophical, and the vague outline of this is just becoming discernible.

But before we get into all this too deeply, let's start by looking at the foundations of this bold new human venture: the organisations that make up today's Green Movement.

THE GREEN MOVEMENT IN THE UK

Over the last few years, there have been scores of articles and half a dozen definitive studies of the Green Movement, all of which have found it immensely difficult to cope with its astonishing breadth and diversity. Literally thousands of organisations are involved, both nationally and locally, some so well known that they have become household names, others so obscure that their existence is known only to their own members.

And there's still considerable confusion between the *conservation movement* (which, technically, describes only those organisations involved in nature conservation itself, such as the Royal Society for Nature Conservation and the British Trust for Conservation Volunteers), the *environment movement* (still widely used to describe *all* activities concerned with the environment, not just nature conservation), and the *Green Movement* (which embraces the totality of groups and organisations dealing with anything that's even vaguely green, not just the environment).

Though still predominantly middle-class, well-educated and relatively affluent, there are clear signs that the Green Movement is gradually broadening its case, becoming an increasingly representative cross-section of society. It is also expanding rapidly, both in terms of membership and income, as the table below reveals. This was produced by Michael McCarthy, Environment Correspondent of *The Times*, in June 1989, and gives a very fair indication of the prospects of the Green Movement over the next few years. Paid-up membership of the major environmental organisations rose from around 1.8 million in 1980 to nearly 4 million in June 1989, and is likely to be nearer 6 million by 1992.

These figures need to be taken with a substantial pinch of salt: for instance, 1.6 million of that 1989 total were accounted for by members of the National Trust, the majority of whom are almost certainly in it for the fantastic service it offers through its historic houses rather than for its performance as

GROWTH OF CONSERVATION ORGANIZATIONS

SURVEY OF BRITISH ENVIRONMENTAL AND CONSERVATION BODIES AT WORLD ENVIRONMENT DAY (JUNE 5, 1989)

† Estimate ★ 1987	Membership				Income (£ million)			
Organization + standard membership (£)	1980	Now	Est 1992	% Incr	1980	Now	Est 1992	% Incr
1. The National Trust (£16)	949,000	1,660,000	2 million	21	22.80	*87	100.00+	—
2. The National Trust for Scotland (£15)	105,000	179,000	250,000	39	5.60	7.90	7.60+	—
3. World Wide Fund for Nature (£20)	70,000	170,000	500,000	128	2.00	13.0	35.00	169
(with supporters):		(1,045,000)	(3 million)	200				
4. Royal Society for the Protection of Birds (£12) (incl Young Ornithologists Club)	421,000	556,000	940,000	69	2.46	15.40	22.00+	42
5. The Civic Trust (£ various) (Civic Amenities groups)	n/a	400,000	450,000	12½	n/a	1.30	1.75	34
6. Greenpeace (£12)	15,000	252,000	+500,000	100	0.10	6.00	12.00?	100
7. Royal Society for Nature Conservation (£9–12) (County trusts and urban wildlife groups)	138,000	215,000	300,000	39	2.50	9.00	12.00	33
8. Friends of the Earth (£12)	†10,00	98,000	300,000	200	0.20	6.00	20.00	230
9. Ramblers' Association (£9.75)	36,000	71,000	85,000	16	0.15	1.10	1.50	36
10. Woodland Trust (£8)	5,000	62,000	100,000	61	0.20	3.00	6.00	100
11. British Trust for Conservation Volunteers (£10)	15,000	51,000	75,000	47	0.40	8.70	12.00	37
12. Council for the Protection of Rural England (£8)	27,000	39,000	60,000	53	0.10	0.60	0.60+	—
13. Wildfowl Trust (£12)	19,000	31,000	45,000	45	0.60	2.80	3.00+	7
14. Green Party (£15)	4,500	11,000	35,000	227	0.03	0.18	0.25	28
15. ARK (£10)	—	6,000	250,000	4,000	—	†1.25	3.00+	140
TOTAL:	1,805,000+	3,801,000	5.8 million	52	38.04	163.25	236.7+	—
(with WWF supporters) (less Nat Trust Income):	—	(4,846,000)	8.8 million	—	(15.24)	(78,25)	(136.7+)	79

an environmental pressure group – though this role is not to be discounted. And the 1 million 'supporters' of the World Wide Fund for Nature (to be distinguished from their fully subscribing members) are probably more interested in good bargains from their glossy trading catalogue than they are in saving the world's wetlands from further damage. There are also huge overlaps in terms of the same person being a member of more than one organisation. Some Greens seem to collect organisations like yuppies collect credit cards, with each one adding an extra layer of security in a troubled world.

Lastly, some of the estimates for 1992 are distinctly ambitious. Internal ructions inside Ark (the newest of the groups founded in 1989, and one which still can't decide between selling washing powder or becoming a fully fledged pressure group) make it extremely unlikely that they will hit 250 000 supporters by 1992. Indeed, in the first half of 1990, many of the other organisations (including Friends of the Earth) were surprised to see how directly their financial fortunes were tied to the state of the economy; as interest and mortgage rates stayed high, financial forecasts were gradually revised downwards.

For all that, the figures add up to a picture of one of the most influential social and political movements in the UK today, especially as they do not include any of the smaller groups, nor the strictly local groups (whose members often have no time for what they see as unwieldy national organisations), let alone the non-environmental organisations that would still loosely describe themselves as part of the Green Movement. To put it in context, it's worth remembering that the combined membership of the British trades unions is around 8 million, and still falling, with a total income of around £40 million.

The extent to which the Green Movement can genuinely wield lasting political influence remains a moot point. At the very least there will be 6 million people at the next election who are sufficiently clued up and interested in the environment to demand as much from their candidates on that score as on the economy or defence or any other issue. Many marginal constituencies are going to be highly vulnerable to swings among these 'green voters' (though this is by no means the same thing as saying that they will all be voting for the Green Party), especially when controversial issues are involved like the Channel Tunnel, new development proposals, nuclear facilities and so on.

It's worth adding that the Green Movement in the UK is not unique in this pattern of expansion. Most Western European countries have experienced similar (though less dramatic) growth throughout the eighties, and even the Southern European countries, such as Spain and Greece, are beginning to witness a real surge in environmental awareness and commitment.

THE GREENING OF EASTERN EUROPE

Not surprisingly, the most fascinating developments have been taking place in Eastern Europe. In one country after another, environmental protest has emerged as a crucial factor in the democratisation process.

• In the Baltic republics (Latvia, Estonia, and Lithuania), massive resentment at the terrible damage done to human health and the environment by heavy industry and chemical plants, deliberately located in these countries by the USSR in the fifties and sixties, has fuelled the call for independence. They quite rightly feel that they have had to suffer all the costs of the USSR's industrialisation, but have received few of its benefits.

• In the USSR itself, the policies of perestroika and glasnost have ensured the emergence of a genuinely independent environment movement. There are now around 40 people from environmental groups serving as Deputies in the Supreme Soviet. Access to long-suppressed information about environmental problems has made a huge difference, and the Chernobyl disaster served as a catalyst for millions of people who until then had simply not been aware of the importance of the environment. After all, they had been brought up on the idea that environmental pollution was just another symptom of the 'inherent contradictions of capitalism'.

• In East Germany, before the Wall came down, environmental groups provided a focus for dissent and were often imprisoned by the hard-line government. Many of these environmental groups are now at the forefront of building a new Germany.

Green image for Bosnia's discredited Reds

TAKING a leaf out of Mrs Thatcher's book, the Bosnian Communists have gone green.

For the first time in 43 years of Communist rule in Yugoslavia, a party branch in one of the country's six republics, Bosnia and Herzegovina, hired a marketing agency last week to promote its three-yearly Congress in Sarajevo, hoping to stem the resignations of thousands of disillusioned members each week.

The design team from the agency – itself a rarity in Socialist Yugoslavia – came up with a new green theme which downgraded the party's emblem, a giant red star, to an exclamation mark alongside a green question mark.

Other innovations were 20-second advertising spots on radio and television, paid for by the party, and a free information pack in a recyclable green paper carrier bag instead of the usual expensive yellow wallet.

'The green theme symbolises the growing concerns with the environment here in Bosnia,' said Mr Nenad Fischer, one of the Congress organisers.

© THE DAILY TELEGRAPH 15.12.89

● In Romania, Bulgaria and Czechoslovakia, equally hard-line regimes ensured that environmental protest was harshly suppressed, despite mounting evidence of desperate environmental damage. As yet, environmental groups in these countries are very thin on the ground, though the main Bulgarian group, Eco-Glasnost, seems to sum up in its name all the hopes and ambitions of Eastern Europe.

● In Hungary, by contrast, lobbying by environmental groups was instrumental in changing legislation way back in the seventies. But the real breakthrough came in the late eighties, when the campaign against the series of dams on the Danube was finally successful. The Blues (as the Greens in Hungary are known!) are a diffuse but vital part of the emerging political scene.

● In Poland, Solidarity and the Polish Ecological Club kept the torch burning for environmental issues during the dark days of the mid-eighties, and there is now an almost uncontrolled flowering of grassroots groups, which are gradually coming to terms with the devastating legacy of 40 years of communist corruption and incompetence.

An article by Michael Redclift in *The Ecologist* magazine explained the significance of these events:

> 66 *The emergence of Green Movements in Eastern Europe has significance for a number of reasons: these movements expose problems in orthodox Marxist analysis; they remind us that ecological politics cannot simply be understood in terms of Western capitalism; and they serve to illuminate the way in which the ecological crisis is bound up with questions of human rights, freedom of information and participatory democracy.* 99

THE POLITICAL RESPONSE

It's quite clear that environmentalism has moved decisively out of the wings and on to the centre of the political stage over the last few years. Whether or not it will stay there would seem to depend on how rapidly and effectively today's rather motley Movement develops a style and practice consistent with its new-found status. That may not be easy.

In Britain, for instance, most people have a very nebulous understanding of environmentalism. The environment is 'somewhere out there', constantly under assault, increasingly degraded and polluted, squabbled over by politicians and eloquently popularised by David Attenborough or David Bellamy. Environmentalism is seen as an imprecise amalgam of protest, lifestyle advocacy and a somewhat apologetic, anti-industrialist vision.

Quite rightly, people do not see environmentalism as a wholly new political loaf, but rather as a new and important way of leavening existing loaves, which have recently fallen so very flat. In its most basic form, it is a vote-grabber for opportunistic politicians who, if nothing else, know how to read an opinion poll. At its best, it can permeate both the policies and the values of mainstream political parties in a way that is beginning to surprise even the media's most cynical commentators.

The fact that much of this recent surge of interest in the UK has been *partly* the result of Mrs Thatcher's tumultuous arrival on the green scene remains deeply offensive to many Greens. Yet her speeches in 1988 and 1989 achieved what she herself must have failed to anticipate: they gave credibility and stature to many organisations that had previously been considered dangerously radical, dismissed indeed as part of 'the enemy within'. For Mrs Thatcher to declare (in her 1988 Party Conference speech) that 'we Conservatives are not merely friends of the earth – we are its guardians and trustees for generations to come', not only astonished many members of her own party, but made Friends of the Earth appear reassuringly (perhaps disturbingly?) respectable.

But voicing these sentiments also achieved what she *did* anticipate: consternation among the opposition parties, who suddenly saw Mrs Thatcher wipe the floor with their hitherto strangulated utterances on the environment. Having dismissed years of environmentalist lobbying by Friends of the Earth, Greenpeace and a host of other organisations as 'special pleading', they had only themselves to blame when they found this item on the agenda (like so many others) dominated by the Prime Minister's rhetoric.

The big question now is whether the rhetoric will be converted into genuine policy reform. The Environment Protection Act was a reasonable start, and the development of a system of Integrated Pollution Control is a genuine and important innovation. But the success of this new legislation depends entirely on providing proper funding for Her Majesty's Inspectorate of Pollution, and the Government's record to date on funding its environmental agencies has been appalling. Moreover, there's an important distinction between things that look good on the statute book, and what is then actually implemented. The Conservative Party's main prior claim to environmental credibility is the 1974 Control of Pollution Act, but some of the most important elements of this have still not been implemented!

The Labour Party is unlikely to let Mrs Thatcher off the green hook. It has now built up an impressive new team under Bryan Gould, and the environment sections of the Labour Party Policy Review provided a comprehensive and reasonably far-reaching statement of its intentions. Indeed, compared with its policy statements on the environment as recently as the 1984 general election, one might be talking about two quite different political parties.

Unfortunately, however, no real effort has been made to integrate environmental concerns with economic policies in the policy review, and many in the Labour Party are still genuinely fearful of going too far down the green road. They are anxious to keep 'the environment' neatly compartmentalised to ensure that there is no erosion of its conventionally expansionist industrial and economic policies. Back in 1989, Michael Meacher gave an interesting indication of the continuing ambivalence of the Labour Party on green issues:

> 66 *we must set a low priority on larger environmental issues which, however forcibly pressed by their advocates, do not impact on people's daily lives in the same way. After ten years of Thatcher, we should be more concerned with taking the grey out of people's lives than putting the green in.*99

It would be unwise to dismiss such unreconstructed nonsense as a foible peculiar to Mr Meacher; the landscape of socialism is still well populated with dinosaurs of all shapes and sizes, and many Labour spokespersons still sound rather embarrassed when talking about the environment, as if it constituted some fundamental betrayal of the working class.

The Democrats, by contrast, seem to be united in their determination to turn a darker shade of green. This makes a lot of sense, given that it has proved totally impossible to build

Who are the new ecology voters?

THE rise of the Green vote over the last year has been dramatic, writes David Lipsey. In December 1988, ICM – The Sunday Correspondent's pollsters – first detected a measurable 'Green' vote, then amounting to only one per cent of the electorate. From there it rose to a peak of eight per cent in June – the month the Greens stunned the political establishment by polling 15 per cent of the votes in the European elections.

Today, it stands at five per cent – but students of public opinion do not believe the Green voter is about to disappear. 'One thing certain about the Green vote is that it will never go down to its pre-1989 level,' says Professor Roger Jowell, of Social and Community Planning Research.

The rise in Green voting follows an even more striking rise in the proportion of voters rating the environment among the most important issues facing the country. Last December, the polling firm Mori found only five per cent of voters rated green issues among the top two facing Britain. By August this had risen to 30 per cent, second only to the National Health Service.

ICM analysis shows that
- Green voters tend to be younger, with 43 per cent under 34, compared with 34 per cent of voters generally. And although 20 per cent of voters are 65 or over, only eight per cent of Greens are.
- The Greens do better among the top (AE) social classes, with 27 per cent of Green voters in this group, compared with 17 per cent of the electorate generally.
- The Greens tend to be southerners: 57 per cent of Green supporters live in the South, compared with 40 per cent of the electorate.
- Contrary to myth – which has it that woman are more environmentally concerned – the Greens draw their support almost equally from men and women.

© THE SUNDAY CORRESPONDENT 17.9.89

an authentic political alternative in the UK by merely attempting to split the difference between Right and Left, and that they are unlikely to make any kind of breakthrough without proportional representation. It's clear that the Democrats can only establish themselves by developing a quite distinct political vision, and, now that the far Left has been eclipsed by events, the only visions on offer are those of the Green Movement.

Paddy Ashdown was one of the first to acknowledge this, as the Centre crumbled around the Alliance after their disastrous 1987 general election campaign. Like many Liberals, he must then have been thinking rather wistfully of the late seventies when the Liberal Party flirted quite enthusiastically with the notion of going green just before throwing in its misbegotten lot with the Social Democrats. Green politics

201

The UK Green Party celebrates after its 15 per cent breakthrough in the 1989 European Election.

reinforces and reinvigorates that old Liberal core. Alliance apparatchiks may not like it, but Paddy Ashdown is surely right in seeking to rescue his colleagues from middle-of-the-roadism by emphasising a long-term green vision at the expense of short-term grey expediency.

So, as they all go greener, is there still a role for the Green Party? That question was emphatically answered by the 1989 European election results when the Green Party won 2.3 million votes, 15 per cent of votes cast. This was the best election result for any Green Party anywhere in the world.

Considering some of the curmudgeonly comments in the press since then, it's worth stating that the whole Green Movement owes that doughty band of Green Euro-candidates and workers an enormous debt of gratitude. It may well be that many of the 2.3 million thought they were voting for Friends of the Earth or Greenpeace; it may well be that they didn't know what all the policies of the Green Party were, due to the pre-June shut-out by the media; and it may well be that the Green Party vote will now stick at the 4 to 6 per cent mark. For all that, the Green Party's result will probably do as much to advance the cause of the environment as anything the 4 million members of the various environmental organisations will be able to do over the next few years. The reason for that is simple: now that real votes are involved, it's got the politicians really thinking.

All this has provided new lobbying opportunities for the environmental organisations which they have not been slow to exploit. But if the Green Movement is now able (for the first time, it has to be said) to turn the electoral success of the Green Party to its own ends, the Green Party is in an even more advantageous position to turn today's unprecedented environmental awareness to *its* own ends. Very few people turn dark green without having been light green along the way. The Green Party now has the credibility and the media platform (if it knows how to use it) to explain precisely why old-fashioned environmentalism, let alone newfangled 'green consumerism', simply aren't up to the job of rescuing humankind from its terminal folly.

The Euro-election result has also ensured that the Green Party can dare to be green and nothing but green. It doesn't have to be red-green or orange-green, or even blue-green – just green. I've always thought that the Green Party was badly served by those who put their own brand of Socialism or Liberalism up front. Many may indeed draw on those political traditions in different ways, and some may even have the courage to acknowledge their occasional indebtedness to the Tory tradition. But, in the long run, no one is going to be very impressed if the Green Party is seen as the stalking horse for some other faltering ideology. If it genuinely aspires to be of some service to *all* people in the UK, let alone in the rest of the world, then there must be no compromise in its renunciation of what the Left, Right and Centre still stand for.

THE EUROPEAN GREENS

Each and every one of the Green Parties in Europe has a slightly different view on this issue, and when they all get together for their regular meetings, as the European Greens, there is no less political controversy than one would expect at gatherings of the Left and the Right. There may even be rather more, because all Green Parties, whatever their level of electoral success, are still very young, and most are having to 'learn on the job' at a time of tempestuous change throughout Europe. Several political commentators have claimed that electoral success has come too early and too easily to some of the Green Parties. But, however painful the birth pangs may have been, these parties have already had a very considerable impact on the political scene. There are now Green MPs in 11 European countries and 24 Green MEPs in the European Parliament, where their influence is gradually increasing.

The British press is notoriously bad about covering other Green Parties; indeed, they've only just got round to covering the Green Party in the UK! Not surprisingly, they continue to home in on Die Grünen in West Germany, the largest and best-known Green Party in Europe, though they are by no means the most representative. They weren't the first Green Party, nor indeed the first to get an MP elected (the Swiss Greens claimed that honour back in October 1979), but they were the first to cross the visibility threshold with a combination of radical policies and highly imaginative electoral tactics. Their breakthrough came in the 1983 federal elections, when their 5.6 per cent vote earned them 27 seats in the Bundestag. This was indeed one of the most catalytic

Radical saplings present a political challenge

NO green party in Europe has yet matched the 15 per cent vote chalked up by the British Greens in the Euro-election. But almost everywhere they are on the march; in most European countries there are now Green Members of Parliament, seven out of the 12 EC states elected Green MPs in June, and their success in forcing a green agenda on more established political parties has been remarkable.

Within the past year, there has been a surge forward, first signalled last September when the Swedish Greens stormed into Parliament for the first time. The Greens won 20 seats, with 5.5 per cent of the vote, and also won representation on more than 90 per cent of Sweden's 284 local authorities, holding the balance of power on 40.

Three months earlier, the Greens had mounted a more disciplined challenge in the elections to the European Parliament, and they were rewarded with sharply increased support. France, Germany and Italy each elected seven or eight Green MEPs, and with further successes in Belgium, Holland, Spain and Portugal, the Greens became the fifth largest group in the Parliament, with 30 members.

© **DICK LEONARD, THE SUNDAY CORRESPONDENT 14.2.90**

events in the development of green politics, and one which put the whole international movement on the map for the very first time. In 1987, they raised their vote to 8.3 per cent, increasing their seats to 42.

The importance of the different electoral systems in Europe immediately becomes apparent. In those countries with proportional representation, the Greens have a real chance of breaking through. In those without (such as the UK and France), there is almost no chance at all. The French example is a particularly telling one. In the European elections of 1989 (for which a proportional representation system operated), les Verts did extremely well, and ended up with nine MEPS; in the 1988 elections for the National Assembly (a winner-takes-all system, over two rounds of voting) they did extremely badly, and won not a single seat.

The growth of new Green Parties is not confined to Western Europe. There is an excellent Green Party in Tasmania (which now holds the balance of power in the State Parliament), great activity elsewhere in Australia, in the United States and Canada, and even a couple of nascent Green Parties in Poland and Hungary. For those who are interested in the worldwide picture, by far the best (and in fact the only) reference work is *Green Parties* by Sara Parkin.

THE GREENS IN SWEDEN

Each country has a different story to tell. For the television series, we decided to concentrate on the Swedish Green Party, or Miljopartiet. In many ways, Miljopartiet is a very typical Green Party. It wasn't actually founded until 1981 (ten years after the UK Green Party, which was the first out of the starting gate) but, as in Germany, this was preceded by a prolonged period of debate about energy policy, and nuclear power in particular. The controversy came to a head in 1980, when the Swedes organised a referendum on the future of their ten nuclear reactors. The result was very inconclusive: 18.9 per cent voted to continue with the nuclear power programmes; 39.1 per cent to dismantle it over a 30-year period; and 39.7 per cent to dismantle it over a ten-year period.

Oddly enough, this was interpreted by many environmentalists as a real setback, and the dominant role of the Social Democrats (by far the largest party in Sweden) in supporting nuclear power persuaded many that the time had come for a proper green alternative. Inspired by an erstwhile Liberal Party MP called Per Gahrton, Miljopartiet was set up in September 1981.

At first the going was very hard despite the fact that in Sweden the threshold for getting MPs elected is just 4 per cent of the vote. In the 1982 general election, they won just 1.7 per cent of the vote, but at least succeeded in establishing themselves on many municipal councils. Things weren't much better three years on, in 1985, when they got pretty well the same miniscule vote. Though by then they were hoping to emulate the growing success of the German Greens, they were ruthlessly squeezed by the major parties. Again, however, they increased their vote at the local level, ending up with more than 250 seats on various municipal councils, and holding the balance of power in Göteborg and Uppsala.

This increased credibility at the local level greatly strengthened Miljopartiet's national profile, as did the subsequent ruling by the Swedish broadcasting authority that it had been unfair not to give Miljopartiet a separate listing in the opinion polls in the run-up to and during the election. This may seem a trivial matter but, as the UK Greens have also discovered, you simply have to appear in the polls on a regular basis if you are to be taken seriously.

In September 1988, they at last met with success, becoming the first new party to enter the Swedish Parliament since 1918! A vote of 5.6 per cent gave them 20 MPs, despite increasingly ferocious attacks and 'dirty tricks' from the other parties, particularly the Social Democrats, who were playing the time-honoured game of pretending to be as green as the Greens. Given the rather poor record of the Social Democrats on basic environmental issues, Swedish voters were not taken in. (Will they be, I wonder, in the UK?) Miljopartiet also did extremely well in the local elections, and now hold the balance of power on 40 of Sweden's 284 local councils.

The Swedish Greens are essentially anti-establishment and non-authoritarian, and it hasn't proved particularly easy to accommodate 20 MPs in their midst. There's already been some criticism from the grassroots that they've become too middle of the road. But the most important decision they took (after a furious pre-election controversy) was not to support any of the major parties in Parliament on a permanent basis:

205

Environmental concerns run high in the Netherlands, not least because of the threat of increased sea levels (through global warming) overwhelming their current sea defences.

they decide on each individual issue which way their vote will go. More than 18 months on, they are providing powerful opposition to the ruling Social Democrats, who in turn continue to play all sorts of games with green issues, not least on the future of nuclear power.

This tactic of 'stealing the clothes' of the Green Parties is pretty well standard throughout Europe. It usually induces a state of apoplectic rage among fully paid-up members of these Parties, but it's interesting to reflect that the green influence to date, at least at the national level, has largely been achieved by scaring other political parties into the very business of stealing their clothes! Indeed, it's possible to imagine a point at which so many clothes have not only been stolen, but actually worn, that the justification for the existence of a separate Green Party disappears. Paradoxically, that has to be our hope, for we serve little purpose working out our days as faithful servants of a permanently beleaguered minority.

THE DUTCH ENVIRONMENT PLAN

Perhaps something of the kind is already going on in the Netherlands. Dutch politics is *very* complicated, so one hesitates to make any definitive judgements, but it is surely significant that in the country which has the lowest electoral threshold required to win a seat (less than 1 per cent!), the Dutch Green Party has failed to make any impact whatsoever at national level.

Yet the Dutch can rightly lay claim to having one of the most effective Environment Movements anywhere in Europe, and the same could be said of their Peace Movement *and* their Development Movement. They have a long history of environmental concern, and many of the 15 political parties (at the last count!) have consistently emphasised environmental policies in their manifestos. At different times, for different elections, some of these parties (including the Radicals, the Pacifist Socialists and the Communists) have cobbled together an ad-hoc 'green alliance' in order to advance their own political fortunes.

But throughout 1989, environmental attention in the Netherlands was focused neither on these pseudo-Greens, nor on the genuine (but still very weedy) Greens, but on the Government itself. At the start of the year, the Centre Right coalition (made up of the Christian Democrats and the Liberals, with Mr Ruud Lubbers as Prime Minister) came up with a major new initiative: the National Environment Policy Plan. This represents by far the most comprehensive policy statement from any Western European government, and contains all sorts of radical ideas about a carbon tax, massive investment in public transport, increased expenditure on pollution control, and the removal of tax breaks from company cars in order to cut the number of cars on the roads.

It was this last item that precipitated a crisis for the Liberals, for they hadn't been properly consulted about it as coalition partners, and suddenly saw a lot of their most secure voters disappearing in a cloud of exhaust fumes. In May the Government fell, and an election took place in September, dubbed by some 'the Environment Election', as the National Environment Policy Plan featured so prominently in it. Lubbers and the Christian Democrats retained their share of the vote, but the Liberals were punished by an increasingly green electorate and lost a lot of ground. After eight weeks of tough negotiations, a new coalition was put together, made up of the Christian Democrats and the Labour Party (these things are possible in a civilised country with a sensible electoral system!). The Labour Party has promised to support the Environment Plan and pledged to spend even more on it than the Christian Democrats themselves intended to do. Since then, it would seem that the wily Mr Lubbers has already began to water down some of the proposals in the Plan, and the Dutch Environment Movement is girding its loins for another bout of sustained pressure. But for all that, there would seem to be quite a lesson here, and I for one can't wait for the day to dawn when a government in the UK can be brought down over an environmental issue!

Enthusiastic tree-planters in Tower Hamlets!

THE LOCAL SCENE

I am very conscious that, for many Greens, this emphasis on national politics is wholly misplaced. There's just as much going at the local level, where much more direct pressure can be brought to bear on local councillors. In the UK, councils as different as Sutton, Tower Hamlets, Sheffield, Kirklees, Leicester and Oxford have been quietly working away at improving their environment policies, with growing support from bodies like the Association of Metropolitan Authorities and the Association of District Councils. Sutton and Oxford deserve special mention. Despite frustrating limitations on the remit of their activities and very damaging expenditure controls imposed by central government, they have succeeded in integrating environmental initiatives across the confusing mosaic of different departments and committees which make up local authorities. Such models are important for others to follow, and in 1989 Friends of the Earth launched its Environmental Charter for Local Government specifically to encourage best practice at every level of local government.

The Charter sets out how local authorities can integrate environmental concerns into their policies and services. In adopting the Charter, councils give an undertaking to review all their policies and to develop new ones that meet standards set by Friends of the Earth in energy, recycling, pollution, transport, planning, health and environmental protection. At the time of writing, four local authorities – Milton Keynes, Lincoln, Southend and Ipswich – have committed themselves to the terms of the Charter. This is an encouraging sign that local government is rising to the environmental challenge.

But beyond that, many have lost faith in the whole political process, be it local or national. They simply prefer to get on with living their lives in as environment-friendly a fashion as possible. A commitment to putting green theories into practice is, as we've seen, essential in today's Green Movement, and there are millions of people in the UK now engaged, in varying degrees, in doing just that – whatever the politicians choose to get up to.

This aspect of the Green Movement is even more pronounced in the United States, where the concept of voluntary simplicity ('living more simply that others may simply live') is well established. Running parallel to the great explosion of materialism in the twentieth century, there has been a much more subdued tradition of pursuing the simple life: more self-reliant, less consumer-oriented and less wasteful.

By the same token, the American Green Movement has always laid much greater stress on the spiritual aspects of achieving a sustainable and equitable society, drawing heavily on the inspirational writings and lives of people like Thomas Jefferson, Henry Thoreau, Ralph Waldo Emerson, John Muir, Lewis Mumford and a host of less well-known characters.

EXPLORING THE SPIRITUAL

I've been accused by some in the Green Movement of 'always going on about the spiritual bit', as if this were some terrible crime! It's true that I am firmly of the opinion that a Green Movement without a spiritual dimension isn't ever going to move anywhere, and if anything, I feel guilty about not 'going on about it' more often. Indeed, so conscious am I at public meetings of the secular sensibilities of some in the Green Movement, that I usually relegate the spiritual bit to the end, as a rather apologetic, ethereal postscript.

Half the trouble is that people mean so many different things by the word 'spiritual'. For some, it is a strictly religious concept, implying adherence to one of the world's major faiths; for others, it's a semi-religious notion, a vague belief in something mystical or divine, but free of the dogma and fusty tedium of the established churches. For some, it's a full-blown love affair with nature, worshipping trees and rivers and even the hills themselves as manifestations of the divine; for others, it's a sense of reverence and awe at the astonishing beauty and diversity of the living world, an uplifting, inspirational communing with God and nature. For some, it's a state of transcendental meditation, a complete withdrawal from the material world in pursuit of righteousness, right livelihood or wholeness; for others, it's access to moments of unanticipated tranquillity, the finding of a still centre in the hurly-burly of modern life. Spirituality, in short, means as much or as little as we want it to.

But the problem with almost all Western notions of spirituality is their very separatedness and special nature. Spirituality is differentiated in principle and practice from all the other complex relationships that make up the rest of our lives. It often requires a different venue, a change of clothes, a suitably respectful demeanour, a special mindset, a hushed voice and so on. And when people actually do slip effortlessly from secular mode to the spiritual, those they're with seem to get embarrassed or even irritated.

I was powerfully reminded of this in November 1989 when Paulinho Paiakan, a Chief of the Kaiapo people in the Amazon, visited the UK to protest at the proposed construction of a series of new dams on the Xingu river, a tributary of the Amazon, which were to be partially funded by UK banks. He addressed the Friends of the Earth Annual Conference with these words:

> 66 *I'm here to fight for the forests where my people have always lived. We live now as we lived yesterday, using only what we need and what we make with our hands.*
>
> *Today, everybody wants to make money out of the Amazon, and we are scared: scared by the burning that is taking place, by the destruction, by the pollution. These are our enemies, the enemies of the forest and of the Indians. I speak as a person who has lived all his life in the forest. Without the forest, we have no life. Without the forest, we won't be able to breathe, our hearts will stop and we will die.*
>
> *The exchange with the white man has put us in terrible danger. We are losing our land, our culture, and many of the medicinal plants we used before we had any contact with the white man.*
>
> *We know now that the Brazilian government plans to build several new dams on the Xingu river with funding from the World Bank. Many banks in Britain and Europe are collaborating in this act of destruction. Why should countries that are living well and enjoying a good life want to destroy the lives of other people in other countries? Why do these banks wish to exterminate us – the Indians, the forest, the flowers and the rivers? We question such values. We are not against Brazil getting loans, but the loans must not destroy people or forests.*
>
> *If the Brazilian government gives permission to destroy the forest, we will fight against them. As warriors we're used to fighting. And in fighting to save the forest, we're fighting to save everybody.*
>
> *For saying these things, and for seeking your help, I am being prosecuted as a 'foreigner' in my own country. This prosecution turns the world on its head, for is it not the white man who should be prosecuted for destroying the forest, rather than the Indian seeking to protect it?*
>
> *We have decided we are not going to leave our land. We are going to stay there. And if it comes to it, we shall die there. We are simply trying to save the knowledge that the forests are alive, and to give it back to you, who have lost the way.* 99

That kind of statement could be replicated a hundred times by other indigenous people the world over. Not once is the word 'spirituality' actually mentioned, and yet the whole speech breathes the spirit of the forest, and is more powerfully and inspiringly spiritual than any Sunday sermon.

It is not my intention to romanticise tribal people. It's just as important to think in the same way about our own countryside and our own urban environment. But most of us have simply lost the knowledge of how to commune with God in nature; indeed we've almost lost the capacity to see nature as it really is.

> 66 *The tree which moves some to tears of joy is in the eyes of others only a green thing which stands in the way. Some see nature as all ridicule or deformity. Some scarce see Nature at all. But in the eyes of the man of imagination, Nature is imagination itself.* 99
>
> (William Blake)

> 66 *One of the first conditions of happiness is that the link between Man and Nature shall not be broken.* 99
>
> (Leo Tolstoy)

A GREEN CHURCH?

This kind of approach is offensive to some Christians, who are increasingly apprehensive of what they see as the 'paganism' of the Green Movement. And these fears indicate the extent to which Christianity long ago parted company with an interest in the living Earth, and in the process marginalised those who believed that God's Earth should be joyfully celebrated as the miracle of creation that it is. Even William Temple, one of the greatest Anglican archbishops, got short shrift when he wrote in the following terms:

> 66 *The treatment of the Earth by man the exploiter is not only imprudent, it is sacrilegious. We are not likely to correct our hideous mistakes in this realm unless we recover the mystical sense of our oneness with nature. Many people think this is fantastic. I think it is fundamental to our sanity.* 99

How ironic that the world's religions (whom one might think would be the first in the lists against the forces of

Mammon) should, until recently, have proved to be an even more impermeable membrane than the obsolete political ideologies with which we are still encumbered. In some respects, I still feel as I did back in 1984 when I wrote:

> 66 *I can't help but be astonished at the sheer lack of urgency among church leaders today. Ours is a world crying out for leadership, for some kind of spiritual guidance. And yet, as the winds of change whistle up their richly caparisoned copes, where on Earth are they? Can't they see the green shoots creeping up between the flagstones of their deserted cloisters?* 99

However, in 1989, things began to change here too, and it would seem that there is at last a genuine green stirring within the established religions. Before the end of the year, both the Archbishop of Canterbury, Robert Runcie, and His Holiness the Pope had delivered major statements on the state of God's temporal kingdom:

WE know that humans are acting imprudently, polluting and squandering the riches of the earth at a pace which far exceeds the rate of natural renewal. We are impoverishing our habitat. We have begun to realize, fearfully, that if we go on this way, we are capable of making of this earth a place dark and cold and uninhabitable. The initially endangered species has become the endangering species. Whether our attention is focused on the seals, the tropical rainforest or the ozone layer, the cause of the crisis is the same – men and women have demanded more than the planet can give. Prudence, and concern for our own future demand that we exercise our dominion over nature with less extravagance and self-indulgence.

But there are motives other than prudence for doing so – motives which since they are formed at deeper levels of the human spirit are likely to be more dynamic, more effective and compelling than prudence.

It is, I believe, at these deeper levels that some people risk themselves in trying to save the whale or the white rhino or any other endangered species from extinction. It is at this deeper level that some people accept for themselves considerable restraints of diet or lifestyle for the sake of sparing pain or stress to non-human creatures. The common motive of these endeavours is the conviction that nature does not exist simply and solely for the benefit of humankind: that nature is much more than the necessary infrastructure for our human survival and prosperity, that it has an intrinsic value by no means reducible to its benefit to human beings.

This conviction – I have heard it described as 'this new sensitivity' – is becoming increasingly widespread and articulate. Because it finds its source at such deep levels of the human spirit, it must, I think, be called a *religious* conviction. But it is not a conviction unique to any one religion in par-

ticular, and it is shared by some who would profess no religion at all.

The Bible teaches us that this is no cheap universe, no throwaway world in which everything except humankind is readily expendable. The world cannot be cheap: for it is the very creation of him whom Christ disclosed, whose very nature and name is love, and nothing made or done in love is made without cost or done without purpose. To Christians the intrinsic value of the world of nature lies in the cost of its creation, in the fragment of the love of God which is expended in and for every fragment of its being. The care and restraint and thoughtfulness with which we exercise our stewardship of nature is nothing less than an expression of our duty and obedience to Him who is the loving creator both of nature and of ourselves.

THE ARCHBISHOP OF CANTERBURY 17.9.89

Together we can save the world

BY HIS HOLINESS
POPE JOHN PAUL II

WE are all aware that peace in the world is threatened by the arms race, by conflict and by inequalities between people and between nations.

But it is threatened too by the lack of respect for nature, the disordered abuse of her resources and the progressive deterioration of the quality of life. This generates a sense of insecurity, which in its turn encourages egoism.

In the face of widespread environmental damage, humanity is beginning to realise that we cannot continue to use the riches of the earth as we have used them in the past.

Responsible politicians are worried. A variety of scientists from many disciplines are examining the causes. An ecological conscience is being formed.

If man is not at peace with God, the earth itself is not at peace. For this reason the world is in mourning – and those who inhabit it languish, along with the animals of the earth and the birds of the sky. Even the fish in the sea will die.

Our anxious question is what remedy can we find to restore the damage that has been done? Some elements of the present ecology crisis are at heart moral problems. First among these is the indiscriminate progress in science and technology.

Many recent discoveries have brought benefits to humanity. But the application of some of them in industry and agriculture has, in the long term, produced negative effects.

In some cases the damage is by now irreversible. In many others there is still time to stop. It is therefore necessary that the entire human community – individuals, states and international organisations – seriously assumes its own responsibilities.

But the most profound moral question behind the environmental crisis concerns the lack of respect for life. Our delicate ecological equilibrium is being disturbed by the uncontrolled destruction of whole species of animals and vegetation and by a careless use of resources.

All these things are done in the cause of progress. But they do not give advantages to humanity.

The earth is an inheritance whose fruits must benefit all. It is unjust that a few privileged people continue to accumulate superfluous wealth, depleting the resources available, when multitudes of people live in conditions of misery, barely above the minimum level of survival.

The ecology crisis is proof of the urgent moral need for a new solidarity, especially between developing nations and highly-developed industrialised countries.

Today the ecological problem has assumed such dimensions that it demands a universal response.

To end this message I wish to say directly to my brothers and sisters of the Catholic church that they must remember their important obligation to take care of all that has been created.

THE EVENING STANDARD 27.12.89

Moreover, there's an immense amount of good work now being done by thousands of individual Christians and countless church communities. The inspirational writing of Matthew Fox and Sean McDonagh (whose book, *To Care For The Earth*, was one of the great discoveries of the eighties for me); the pioneering and courageous work of ICOREC, the International Consultancy on Religion, Education and Culture (yet another initiative to benefit from the often unsung enlightenment of the World Wide Fund for Nature); the gradual transformation of the Industrial and Agricultural Chaplaincies; a score of bishops going greener by the day, and at last beginning to make the links with the liberation theology practised by so many of their counterparts in the Third World: these are surely more than a few chance straws blowing in the wind?

If it is the destiny of this generation to become the stewards of God's Earth (and it had better be, for we are the last generation likely to be given such a choice), then Christianity is going to have to be comprehensively reinterpreted, and its long-suppressed sacramental vision sung out anew. We do not need to invent any new religion – but Christianity assuredly needs to rediscover much of its own very old and resolutely earthbound wisdom.

For many spiritually minded people, whatever the churches do remains wholly irrelevant. For them, the general appeal of what has become known as 'deep ecology' is far more attractive.

The single most important aspect of deep ecology is its challenge to the human-centred perspective with which most of us still view the world, obliging us to recognise the intrinsic value of all life on Earth, regardless of its usefulness to our own species. It seems reasonably clear that our sense of separation from Nature is culturally determined, leaving us with a distressingly warped and diminished sense of what it is to be a human being.

Personally, though I find this very stimulating, I also find it hard to go all the way down the road with the deep ecologists. I have no difficulty whatsoever in accepting and indeed celebrating our oneness with the rest of life on Earth, but I cannot ascribe the same value to other creatures as I do to human beings. I suppose this goes back to the somewhat unorthodox Christianity which provides my own spiritual

214

The term 'deep ecology' was coined in 1973 by Arne Naess, a Norwegian philosopher. The principles of deep ecology have been summarised as follows:

1   The well-being and flourishing of non-human life on Earth have value in themselves, independent of the usefulness of the non-human world for human purposes.

2   Richness and diversity of life-forms contribute to the realisation of these values and are also values in themselves.

3   Humans have no right to reduce this richness and diversity except to satisfy *vital* needs.

4   The flourishing of human life and culture is compatible with a substantial decrease of the human population. The flourishing of non-human life requires such a decrease.

5   Present human interference with the non-human world is excessive, and the situation is rapidly worsening.

6   Policies must therefore be changed. These policies affect basic economic, technological and ideological structures. The resulting state of affairs would be deeply different from the present.

7   The ideological change is mainly that of appreciating *life quality* rather than adhering to an increasingly higher standard of living.

8   Those who subscribe to the foregoing points have an obligation either directly or indirectly to try to implement the necessary changes.

bedrock, in as much as I do not believe that evolution is a purely random process, but rather the purposeful unfolding of a purposeful creation. 'The Earth is the Lord's, and the fullness thereof'; for me that simply means that the spirit of God is at work in every cell of every living creature on Earth, *including* the human species. Sean McDonagh sums it up rather more poetically: 'In a human being, endowed as we are with self-awareness, the whole universe reflects upon itself and celebrates its own wonderful journey.'

Even now, the cynics among you must be thinking: 'what possible connection can there be between all this spirituality stuff and the hard-edged radical message of the Green Movement?' The answer is simple. If we are indeed just one strand in the web of life, then we are obviously unable to protect our species without simultaneously protecting the entire web. Furthermore, a crudely utilitarian ethic ('protect it only if it benefits us') will ensure that we go on losing as many battles as we win. For who is to define 'usefulness'? Only if we ascribe intrinsic (though not necessarily equal) value to all life forms are we likely to find both the means and the collective will to protect the living Earth on any kind of sustainable basis. One cannot sustain that which one does not value in its own right. And from a Christian perspective, one cannot sustain that which one does not revere.

The Green Movement without a spiritual dimension is like a plant which is kept indoors and not given enough sunshine or water. It doesn't have to be a Christian dimension; it can just as easily be Hindu, Sikh, Muslim, Jewish, Buddhist or Baha'i, and the inter-faith ceremonies organised by the World Wide Fund for Nature and ICOREC at Assisi, Winchester and Canterbury have laid great stress on the need for *all* faiths and religions to carry out their own process of rediscovery and renewal. As I've said, the spiritual dimension doesn't even have to be religious, just so long as it allows us not only to hear again the Song of the Earth, but to learn to sing it anew.

Chapter 9

DEFENDING
THE
FUTURE

OF ALL THE many questions I get asked at public meetings, none recurs more regularly than the one about 'whether or not there's still time' – time to achieve all the changes that we now know to be necessary. It's no easier to answer that question today, in the midst of an unprecedented surge of interest in all things green, than it was ten years ago when few people seemed to care very much one way or the other.

Environmentalists tend to tread much more cautiously these days than they once did. Gone are the cut and dried certainties of the Club of Rome's *Limits to Growth* (published in 1972), which confidently predicted exactly when key minerals and raw materials would run out. Gone are the blistering diatribes of the so-called 'New Jeremiahs' of the 1960s, the likes of Paul Ehrlich, Barry Commoner and Garrett Hardin. Only Teddy Goldsmith, founder and editor of the evergreen *Ecologist* magazine, keeps telling it as it *really* is, fulminating prophetically from on high against the economic and philosophical errors of our ways. His gloom is depressing, but his honesty and clarity of thought utterly compelling.

The rest of the Green Movement seems to have lapsed into an uneasy acceptance that the planet is apparently far more resilient to the assault of humankind than was once thought, and that there are too many variables and unknown feedback mechanisms for us to be able to predict the point at which some ecological apocalypse might begin. A progressive decline in life chances for millions in the South, together with a decline in the quality of life and genuine material hardships in the North, is considered a far more likely outcome *if* we continue with the same old policies.

All we can really say is not whether there's enough time, but whether we're on the right or wrong path when it comes to achieving genuinely sustainable development. And here the answer is clear: however much it may look as if politicians and institutions like the World Bank are going green, let there be no doubt that we are still very much on the *wrong path*, which will lead at some point in the future to a pretty grim outcome.

So much for the bad news. The good news is that more and more people know we're on the wrong path, and more and more people are beginning to discern both the existence and the direction of an alternative path. In addition, increasing numbers of people are actively engaged in shaping that path and persuading others to join them on it.

What it really comes down to is a race with ourselves. Our future as a species, and indeed of life on Earth, depends on four major factors:

1   Critical thresholds of the Earth's life-support systems
2   Changes in technology
3   Political will
4   The evolution of the human spirit

CRITICAL THRESHOLDS

Since the United Nations Conference on the Environment in Stockholm in 1972, we've accumulated a vast amount of knowledge about the Earth and its life-maintaining systems. But the more we know, the more we discover how little we know. For instance, the vast computers now engaged in modelling the greenhouse effect will always be working on inadequate information simply because we will never fully understand all the different feedback mechanisms and interactions that take place in the natural world. This obviously makes for a great deal of uncertainty. It means that we cannot rely on science to predict accurately at what point we are approaching or even crossing certain critical ecological thresholds. Indeed, we may have already crossed them without knowing they were there.

This is particularly true of the greenhouse effect, partly because of the number of different gases involved in accelerating global warming, and partly because of the way they interact. We all know about carbon dioxide but we hear relatively little of the other greenhouse gases: chlorofluorocarbons (CFCs), methane, nitrous oxide and ozone. It may very well be that the severity of the impact of global warming is dependent on one or all of these, rather than on carbon dioxide itself. For instance, one thing on which the climatologists all agree is that any temperature change will be greater at the poles than at the equator. John Gribbin and Mick Kelly explain why:

> 66 *There is no mystery about this. In regions where the surface of the Earth, the land or the sea, is covered by snow or ice, it is reflective, and a lot of the heat coming in from the sun is bounced back into space without warming the surface at all. But the bright snow or ice cover is lost as temperatures rise, and the dark surface of the land or sea is exposed, absorbing more energy and amplifying the initial warming.*
>
> *That's not all. The polar oceans contain heat trapped in the form of warm water beneath the ice, and this will be released into the atmosphere once the ice cover disappears, again boosting the original rise in temperature. As a result of these feedback processes, the greenhouse effect will be felt most strongly during the long polar winter. A global rise in temperature, of say, 3 degrees centigrade could be accompanied by warming of over 10 degrees centigrade in the Arctic winter.* 99

Furthermore, methane (which is 30 times more effective as a greenhouse gas than carbon dioxide, and increasing in the atmosphere at a rate of 1 per cent each year) is now trapped in vast quantities beneath the frozen wastes of the Arctic, locked in by the permafrost which usually remains frozen solid even during the brief Arctic summer. As the permafrost begins to melt, that methane will gradually be released – but no one knows at what point, how fast or with what kind of impact.

In such circumstances, we have to act as if the worst might happen, adopting what the House of Lords Select Committee

Report on Global Warming referred to as the 'no regrets approach'. When suitable preventive measures *can* be introduced without any serious social or economic penalties, then caution and common sense tell us that they *should* be introduced as soon as is reasonably possible. Such preventive, 'no regrets' action is likely to become necessary in more and more areas as the steady accumulation of pollutants or the sheer weight of human numbers bring critical thresholds nearer for different eco-systems. In the face of continuing ignorance and scientific uncertainty, it would be inexcusably complacent to congratulate ourselves on the fact that the Earth has turned out to be 'a great deal more resilient' than some feared it might be. Such resilience has given us a breathing space to get things right; it has not given us a licence to continue as if nothing had gone wrong.

CHANGES IN TECHNOLOGY

New technologies may also give us some breathing space. The changing climate (both meteorological and political) is giving unprecedented impetus to new, environment-friendly technological developments. Some of these will be 'defensive', limiting the damage which would once have been condoned but is now considered unacceptable.

As we saw in Chapters 2 and 6 in particular, other technologies will open up all sorts of opportunities to reduce pollution, increase energy efficiency, minimise waste and cut back on the volume of raw materials required. An information-intensive economy is clearly going to impact less damagingly on the Earth than a resource- and energy-intensive economy.

But there's one huge stumbling block in all this: whether or not they're environment-friendly, new technologies emerge only when new profit centres are identified or when national governments are intent upon establishing a lead in some high-profile area such as space exploration, next-generation computers or fusion energy. Profit-led market forces ensure that rich nations are able to get richer by virtue of their consumers' infinitely greater purchasing power, while the poor, with insignificant purchasing power in the market place, remain unable to attract the necessary investment to meet even their basic needs. More often than not, market forces promote the wrong kind of development in Third

World countries (for example, soft drink bottling plants, international airports, cigarettes, Western medicines and armaments) because that's where the profit lies, while neglecting the real needs of poor people.

POLITICAL WILL

A lot depends on politicians changing their ways. The relative speed with which green issues have burst on to the political scene does not necessarily make it any easier for mainstream politicians. Having spent all their working lives encouraging people to concentrate on getting richer by producing and consuming more, it's a little tricky to have to tell them, almost overnight, that it's all been a terrible mistake and that our future wellbeing depends on achieving higher quality, not greater quantity. Suddenly the politicians find themselves trying to get people to accept the humdrum realism of 'enough', rather than the subversive escapism of 'more and more'.

Each of the mainstream parties in the United Kingdom faces its own particular ideological dilemma in coming to terms with an ecological analysis. For the Tories, excessive dependence on market forces is unlikely to achieve a healthy and properly protected environment. Those who derive the benefits of production often fail to pay the true costs. Individual motorists may benefit from car ownership, for example, but many non-motorists pay the costs in terms of congestion, noise, pollution, accidents and the government's continuing reluctance to invest in a properly integrated public transport system.

There is also a deep antipathy within the Tory Party to intervening in the market by means of proper regulation. In her famous Bruges speech in 1988, Mrs Thatcher said: 'Our aim should not be more and more detailed regulation – it should be to de-regulate and remove the constraints on trade.' This is often coupled with a deep resentment of international agreements and regulations being 'foisted on the British people' by foreigners in Brussels or in the United Nations. One way or another, the greening of the Tories will be a peculiarly complex affair!

It is, of course, infinitely easier to be green in opposition, and some of the deeper-seated ideological conflicts between

The dumping of sewage sludge in the North Sea will now be phased out in 1998 after intense pressure from Greenpeace and North Sea countries.

green politics and socialism, Social Democracy and Liberalism can be easily papered over by well-drafted, all-things-to-all-people manifestos. But the Labour Party has yet to confront the ecological problems associated with its uncompromising commitment to economic growth and further industrial expansion. When set against the original Socialist principle of production for *use* (to meet human needs), the Labour Party's adherence to production for *exchange* (i.e. increased wealth and full employment through increased trade) is not necessarily any better than the Tories' attachment to production for *profit*: from an ecological point of view, the same productive – and often destructive – processes are set in train. There comes a point where the history and basic ideologies of all the mainstream parties come into conflict with the dark green approach to politics and economics.

When Mrs Thatcher declared on 5 June 1989, in a fascinating interview with Michael Buerk on the *Nature Programme*, that all the UK's environmental problems 'would be solved within the next five years or so', one could only be amazed at such

The price of affluence is effluents

THE tyrants of Central Europe have been toppled but a worry remains: it could be a long time before the goods start to arrive in the shops. If the political gains are to be firmly rooted, the revolution must be swiftly followed by economic transformation.

I have another worry. What if economic transformation succeeds? What if free enterprise, with help from the World Bank, the IMF and the EC, triumphantly supplants Communist central planning? What if Europe, from the Urals to the Atlantic and from Lapland to Crete, becomes an affluent consumer society?

Your local supermarket in Kolno, Eastern Poland, now offers as many brands of shampoo as my local one in Colchester. (At my last count: 34.) The goods that stack the trolleys for 100 million new consumers, with their wrappings and their waste products, are shunted back and forth from Cardiff to Cracow and from Bucharest to Birmingham. Forty-ton diesel lorries pound the six-lane Lisbon–Leningrad motorway, competing with extra traffic generated by the Single European Market. For every 100 new lorries there are 10,000 new private cars. The motorway is jammed most of the way, on most days of the year 2010.

All right, it will not happen quite like that, not east of East Germany anyway. The Balkans will be back in business, impeding modernity with muddled politics, and the old bureaucrats will get in the way of business.

Even if there is progress to a free market, the recent greening of politicians, from Mr Gorbachev to Mrs Thatcher, should save Europe from the worst excesses. They will sign agreements and harness technology to make the new industrial revolution more wholesome than the old.

At the very least we can expect enlightened governments to ensure that every new car is lead-free, reducing its potential pollution by 25 per cent. And so, mercifully, a thousand-fold increase in cars might multiply poisonous fumes only 750 times. With luck, all the new power stations will have filters that will reduce their sulphur emissions by 30 per cent. So, mercifully, nine times as many power stations might generate only six times as much acid rain.

The special horrors of Marxist-Leninist pollution in the Soviet Union, Poland, East Germany and Czechoslovakia will no doubt be excised. But if the automatic pilot is set on endless growth, the filth will surely creep back over the years.

Much of the 1989 revolution began as green protest in citizens' movements. In Armenia this was nationalism in revolt against murderous pollution imposed from outside for the benefit of strangers. The green strand is still prominent in the opposition in East Germany, Hungary, Bulgaria and Czechoslovakia. One hopes it will not be lost from view in the coming power struggles, and that it will help shape some of the strategic choices ahead.

© WALTER SCHWARZ, THE GUARDIAN 3.1.90

political bravado! However, Mrs Thatcher's assertion is justified to some extent, in that most of the UK's *pollution* problems can indeed be solved. As we've already seen, one gets a very different impression when considering the problems faced by Eastern European countries. A massive programme of aid and technology transfer, along the lines of the Marshall Plan after the Second World War, is clearly needed to help clean up the terrible damage already done and to bring further damage to a halt as soon as possible.

Meanwhile, we have to realise that all this damage has been done *despite* the chronic failure of those countries to raise living standards and meet consumer demands. With Western companies and governments positively licking their lips in anticipation of increased business and expanding markets, it

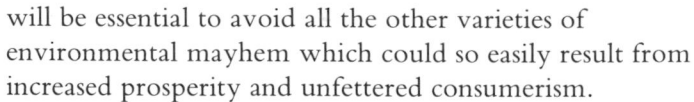

will be essential to avoid all the other varieties of environmental mayhem which could so easily result from increased prosperity and unfettered consumerism.

In an issue of the *Guardian*, in one of the very few articles to question the understandable euphoria at the process of democratisation in Eastern Europe (quoted on page 223), Walter Schwarz rightly raises the spectre of those long-oppressed countries replicating the environmental and social errors of our own Western economies.

THE EVOLUTION OF THE HUMAN SPIRIT

The human spirit is not some fixed, static entity. It is constantly changing, constantly evolving to reflect our changing cultural and political circumstances. It's not hard to see how different we are from our original forebears, but it's much harder to keep track of the speed with which we are now obliged to adapt if we wish to survive.

I like to think of the history of humankind in terms of the changing horizons of ordinary men and women. What is the point beyond which the imagination cannot reach? Around 100 000 years ago, an intensely hostile and dangerous environment must have meant that individual safety and survival were the foremost concerns of our Neanderthal ancestors. Gradually, our survival chances were enhanced by learning to work with others, by hunting together, sharing new experiences, bringing up our offspring in small family groups, and so on. As language evolved, those groups became larger and more sophisticated, with extended families providing for the first time a sense of community and tribal loyalty.

Of course, this is all just speculation – I'm always somewhat surprised at the confidence with which anthropologists and archaeologists trace the inner workings of the human mind right back to the origins of our species! But from the time when hunter-gatherer tribes gradually gave way to settled agricultural communities, it's possible to trace how our horizons as a species gradually widened. As the size and resources of our communities increased, and our ability to explore steadily extended, so the borders of the unknown and the wild were inexorably pushed back.

The development of permanent armies, and the capacity to

feed and organise very large numbers of people in expanding city states, widened our horizons yet further. Empires came and went, forcing people into unfamiliar and shifting alliances. But throughout most of this time their immediate loyalty was still to family, village, county or region, and only under duress to their king or emperor.

It took centuries for the concept of the nation state, as we more or less know it today, to take hold of that infinitely complex web of local and regional loyalties. Only slowly did it become more natural to think of oneself as 'English' or 'Scottish', and many of today's nation states (including Germany and Italy) were not brought together until the nineteenth century.

The next step, and the most recent in historical terms, was the aggregation of different nation states into huge political and military alliances such as NATO, the Warsaw Pact or the European Community. Though the British are notoriously insular, most Britons now see themselves as part of Europe, even though our very understanding of Europe is rapidly changing. In 1989, the East/West divide began to dissolve before our very eyes, allowing us to contemplate the notion of friendly co-existence with those who a few years before were castigated as 'the enemy'.

Beyond that, spurred on by our development of weapons so lethal that they cannot be used without the users destroying themselves, and by our growing awareness that the workings of planet Earth recognise no boundaries between different countries, we can begin to talk realistically of one world, a world in which the vastly extended human family can start to cooperate and work together.

Every stage in this process, from primitive individuals pitting themselves against the world, to global interdependence in the next century, has come upon us with gathering speed. And the human spirit has had less and less time to adapt to each progressive widening of our mental horizons. Through education, travel and mass communications, we have advanced in proverbial leaps and bounds.

But there's one more leap to go. It will be by far the hardest, and we shall have even less time to achieve it than with all the others which have gone before. I say it is the hardest because it entails widening our horizons *beyond our own species*:

to stop seeing ourselves as somehow disconnected from the rest of life on Earth, but rather, embedded within that life process and still so dependent on it that our very survival now rests on being able to cross this conceptual divide. In the words of Albert Schweitzer: 'Until he extends the circle of his compassion to all living things, man will not himself find peace.'

Albert Einstein expressed the same thought:

> 66 *The human being is part of the whole, called by us 'The Universe', a part limited in time and space. He experiences himself, his thoughts and feelings, as something separate from the rest – a kind of optical delusion of his consciousness. This delusion is a kind of prison for us, restricting us to our personal desires and to affection for a few persons nearest to us. Our task must be to free ourselves from this prison by widening our circle of compassion to embrace all living creatures and the whole of nature in its beauty. Nobody's able to achieve this completely, but the striving for such achievement is in itself a part of a liberation and a foundation for inner security.* 99

We can only widen 'our circle of compassion' by retracing our evolution as a species back to the formation of the very first living organism on Earth; and then, as John Seed does in this wonderful meditation, by reinterpreting that evolutionary process from a perspective freed of our narrow, man-centred, life-denying values:

> 66 *Within the Milky Way, our sun was born about five billion years ago, near the edge of this galaxy, while the cosmic dust and gas spinning around it crystallised into planets. The third planet from the sun, our own Earth, came into being about four and a half billion years ago.*
>
> *The ground then was rock and crystal beneath which burned tremendous fire. Heavier metals like iron sank to the centre; the lighter elements floated to the surface, forming a granite crust. Continuous volcanic activity brought up a rich supply of minerals, and lifted up chains of mountains.*
>
> *Then, about four billion years ago, when the temperature fell below the boiling point of water, it began to rain. Hot rain slowly dissolved the rocks upon which it fell and the seas became a thin salty soup containing the basic ingredients necessary for life.*
>
> *Finally, a bolt of lightning fertilised this molecular soup, and an*

adventure into biology began. The first cell was born. You were there. I was there. For every cell in our bodies is descended in an unbroken chain from that event.

Through this cell, our common ancestor, we are related to every plant and animal on the Earth.

First we were algae, the original green plants, then the first simple animal. The algae started to produce oxygen as a by-product of photosynthesis, and this over a billion years or so created a membrane of ozone, filtering out some of the fiercest solar rays.

Now I am a creature in the water. For two and a half billion years, simple forms of life washed back and forth in the ocean currents. This was followed by the evolution of fish and other animals with backbones. How does it feel to have a flexible backbone?

Finally about 450 million years ago, the first plants emerged from the water and began to turn the rock into soil, preparing the ground for animals to follow. The first animals to emerge from the seas were the amphibians. It wasn't until the evolution of the reptilian amniotic egg that we were liberated from our dependence on water, unable to move completely onto dry land. And by 200 million years ago, we had successfully moved onto the land.

As mammals, we became warm-blooded. Living in holes, alert, sense of smell, sampling molecules from the air. To breathe before being consumed. All of us are descended from this pedigree for four billion years. At every step, billions fell by the wayside, but each of us was there. In this game to throw tails once is to fall by the wayside, extinct, a ghost. **99**

And from there, of course, our particular species evolved through the monkeys, and then the great apes, and then the early hominids, and then Neanderthal man, to where we are today, unwisely thinking of ourselves as Homo sapiens.

SHADES OF GREEN

It is around ideas like these that the most important green debate for the nineties is now gathering pace. On the one hand, there is the conventional, utilitarian, man-centred approach to managing the environment more efficiently. On the other hand, a more radical, holistic ethic, which recognises the rights of all living creatures, has begun to gain ground. In short, we are dealing with conventional environmentalism versus 'deep ecology'.

For example, the argument for protecting the rainforests by attributing a measurable (and, ultimately, monetary) value to wild species is crystal clear. It makes it much easier for the governments of hard-pressed Third World countries to opt for conservation rather than ecologically damaging development, if they can show at least some financial return.

But evaluating wildlife in this way is a double-edged sword, for if a plant or animal is not considered to have some utilitarian function or economic value, then might one not be tempted to treat them as both useless and valueless? As Charles Secrett wrote in his book *Rainforest*:

> 66 *Paying one's own way must not become the sole yardstick for species preservation. The structures of ecosystems are too complicated and interwoven to treat conservation like the annual stocktaking exercise of a department store, where old lines are discarded and new ones approved strictly according to the dictates of the market place. In the words of Paul Ehrlich, an American environmentalist, every extinction is like popping a rivet from an aircraft: at some point a critical threshold is crossed and the wings fall off. One absolute value is the survival of life on Earth. If we rationalise a single extinction, where is the line then drawn? How soon before we allow central planetary life-support systems to begin irreversibly breaking down?* 99

This is the nub of the challenge posed by deep ecology: because of the interdependence of all living things, the natural world has certain rights, including the right to existence, which are quite independent of its utilitarian value to humankind. Such an ethic transcends conventional scientific approaches, in that conventional science invariably depends on 'man' and 'nature' being regarded as two separate entities.

Grafted on to this new ethic, one increasingly finds people subscribing to the notion that the Earth is a living, self-regulating organism, the constituent parts of which operate in such a way as to ensure the maintenance of life on Earth. This theory was first proposed by James Lovelock, a British scientist, in his *Gaia: A New Look at Life on Earth*.

Understandably, this debate has begun to create friction in the Green Movement. The deep ecologists argue (with a great deal of conviction and all the weight of industrial history behind them), that by giving in to the dominant values of our industrial culture, conventional environmentalists have been

The Penan people in Sarawak, Malaysia, have fought courageously to keep the logging companies out of their land. Many have been prosecuted and imprisoned.

bought off with the occasional marginal improvement while the overall position continues to deteriorate. Meanwhile, the conventional environmentalists argue that the deep ecologists are just a bunch of unworldly dreamers whose political naïvety will accelerate the rate of destruction rather than slow it down!

Polarities are rarely as polar as they appear, and there may be a middle road to be carved out. For some time, for instance, Henryk Skolimowski has been trying to explain what would happen if we listened more carefully to 'an ecological-evolutionary imperative'. This would involve behaving in such a way as to:

● Enhance life, which is a necessary condition for carrying on evolution

● Preserve and enhance the ecosystem, which is a necessary condition for further enhancement of life and consciousness

● Preserve and enhance the capacities which are the highest-developed form of the evolved universe: consciousness, creativity and compassion

● Preserve and enhance human life, which is the vessel in which these most precious achievements of evolution are contained.

A GREEN VISION

This all sounds very grand, but so what? It's still hard for people (including any of those on the front line!) actually to envisage what life would be like if all the different 'greenprints' put forward in this book were to be adopted. We have no role models, at a national level, with which to substantiate such extensive speculation, and it's very hard to predict how the small, mostly local examples of best practice that we've looked at would actually work out nationally or internationally. Understandably, many people choose to remain faithful to 'the devil they know', even though they feel increasingly apprehensive at the direction in which this particular devil seems to be taking them.

In January 1990, I had to do an interview for Jonathan Dimbleby's programme, *On the Record*. To make a change from the swathe of reviews of the eighties, it was a somewhat premature review of the nineties, based on 'best bets' as to what was likely to happen over the next decade. The green component of this 'glimpse of the future' was pretty gloomy: in England, Epping Forest had been destroyed through uncontrollable contamination of surrounding groundwater after a major leak from a toxic waste dump; worldwide, skin cancer was increasingly dramatically, owing to ozone depletion; worst of all, two successive years of severe drought in the United States in the mid-nineties had eliminated world food stocks, caused the price of food to soar, and left millions on the brink of death throughout the Third World. Following violent food riots in a dozen UK cities, the first Green MP was elected in a by-election in Finchley in 1998!

Such gloomy projections are not uncommon. Progressive ecological decline, punctuated by the occasional out and out disaster, is how a lot of people see the future. In this scenario, if we're lucky, we gradually get greener not because we've enthusiastically opted for a different way of life and different ways of creating wealth, but almost by default – grudgingly, unwillingly – because there's nowhere else to turn. If we're not so lucky, we go green because we're told to, and the disturbing spectre of eco-fascism becomes a terrible reality.

I might add that this has nothing to do with the approach of the millennium. The fact that the year 2000 happens to be around the corner is utterly immaterial, but it is true that *some* of the language, imagery, and philosophy of the Green Movement seems to place it in the millennarian tradition. According to historians, 'the-end-is-nigh' predictions were rife around the turn of the last millennium. Many a monastery was given over to full-time preparation for the onset of Armageddon! Linda Bilmes and Mark Byford did an excellent piece on this in the *Financial Times* in December 1989:

> 66 *The green agenda harkens back to such a theme. The very events which were supposed to presage Armageddon are the ones we now call 'green'. Ozone depletion and the greenhouse effect will melt the ice caps (floods), shift agriculture patterns (famines), and increase skin cancer, cataracts, and weaken the immune system (plagues).*
>
> *Global warming is a new topic supported by old fears. In the same way that AIDS evokes fear of a plague, and nuclear weapons conjure up Armageddon, the prospect of drastic climatic change makes us recall biblical prophecies such as Noah's Ark.*
>
> *The philosophy of the Green Movement is deeply religious; consumption is sinful, simplicity virtuous. Like the Garden of Eden, the Earth is said to be ruined by human folly. The green message appeals to our deep-rooted fear of retribution; environmental blight is a punishment for excessive consumerism, lack of spirituality and wastefulness. We should repent, and mend our ways.*
>
> *The message that over-indulgence has led us into environmental hell is easy to digest and propound. At the same time, the Green Movement has failed to win universal support, partly because it accuses ordinary people of being materialistic in a somewhat holier-than-thou way.* 99

Perhaps this is fair comment. There is indeed a holier-than-thou, hairshirt tendency among some Greens which is not particularly attractive. I am also very aware that the Green Movement's collective reluctance to map out a full-blown vision of the future has left it very exposed. We hear a lot about 'progressive decline' or 'apocalyptic collapse', but very little of lives saved, habitats restored, livelihoods secured, wealth sustainably created and resources properly managed.

Maybe we've all become just a little too pragmatic, too rational, too wrapped up in coping with 'the real world' through the exercise of *realpolitik*. 'Where there is no vision, the people perish' – that Old Testament warning applies as much to the Greens as to mainstream political and spiritual leaders. Ultimately, the green alternative will only come about because people *feel* that it's right, even without the final stamp

231

of approval from the scientists or the media pundits.

If nothing else, I hope this book will have struck a chord with those who are sympathetic to the green alternative but have until now doubted its viability, its coherence or its vision. I've deliberately avoided concentrating too much on the visionary; instead, I've tried to ask the practical questions. What's actually happening? Who's out there doing it? What does that mean for the rest of us? What are the chances of making such changes?

My conclusion is a simple one; I believe we *do* have a real choice, and that the Green Movement's analysis of the factors involved in that choice is sound and increasingly significant in conventional political circles. I hope I've also demonstrated that the direction in which the Green Movement is now pointing is one which offers genuine, realistic hope for a better future.

Sitting here at my desk, looking at a photo of Eleanor, our one-year-old daughter, that matters even more to me now than it did when I set out on this road nearly 20 years ago. When it comes to defending her interests, and those of all future generations, there simply has to be a better way.

INDEX

USEFUL ORGANISATIONS

GENERAL

FRIENDS OF THE EARTH
26–28 Underwood Street
London N1 7JQ
Tel: 071 490 1555

Currently running campaigns on energy, global warming, tropical rainforests, countryside and agriculture, air pollution (including ozone depletion), water pollution, toxics, urban and transport issues and recycling.

FRIENDS OF THE EARTH INTERNATIONAL (SECRETARIAT)
26–28 Underwood Street
London N1 7JQ
Tel: 071 253 0201

Co-ordinates activities and campaigns between the 35 FoE groups worldwide. The groups are autonomous and deal with issues specific to their country, but work on international campaigns on air pollution, tropical rainforests and marine pollution.

FRIENDS OF THE EARTH, SCOTLAND
15 Windsor Street
Edinburgh EH7 5LA
Tel: 031 557 3432

An independent group under the FoE International umbrella, the only environmental group with a wholly Scottish membership. Current campaigns include forestry, fish-farming and lead in drinking water.

THE GREEN PARTY
10 Station Parade
Balham High Road
London SW12 9AZ
Tel: 081 673 0045

GREENPEACE
30–31 Islington Green
London N1 8XE
Tel: 071 354 5100

Involved in non-violent direct action and hard-hitting campaigns on a variety of issues including

nuclear disarmament and nuclear power, toxic wastes, marine mammals and the Antarctic.

POPULATION CONCERN
231 Tottenham Court Road
London W1P 9AE
Tel: 071 637 9582

Raises funds for population and development programmes around the world, and concerned to raise consciousness about the nature, size and complexity of world population.

WORLD WIDE FUND FOR NATURE (WWF)
Panda House
Weyside Park
Godalming
Surrey GU7 1XR
Tel: 0483 426444

An international organisation concerned with a wide range of issues ranging from the protection of endangered species to acid rain and tropical rainforests.

CHAPTER TWO:
ENERGY WITHOUT END

ASSOCIATION FOR THE CONSERVATION OF ENERGY
9 Sherlock Mews
London W1M 3RH
Tel: 071 935 1495

BRITISH WIND ENERGY ASSOCIATION
4 Hamilton Place
London W1V 0BQ
Tel: 0753 882447

CENTRE FOR ALTERNATIVE TECHNOLOGY
Llwyngwern Quarry
Machynlleth
Powys, Wales SY20 9AZ
Tel: 0654 2400

ENERGY EFFICIENCY OFFICE
Eland House
Stag Place
London SW1E 5DH
Tel: 071 273 0680

CHAPTER THREE:
THE FRUITS OF THE EARTH

COUNCIL FOR THE PROTECTION OF RURAL ENGLAND
Warwick House
25 Buckingham Palace Road
London SW1W 0PP
Tel: 071 976 6433

ELM FARM RESEARCH CENTRE
Hamstead Marshall
Nr. Newbury
Berks, RG15 0HR
Tel: 0488 58298

PARENTS FOR SAFE FOOD
Britannia House
1–11 Glenthorne Road
Hammersmith
London W6 0LF
Tel: 081 748 9898

SOIL ASSOCIATION
86 Colston Street
Bristol BS1 5BB
Tel: 0272 290 661

CHAPTER FOUR:
BUILDING A NEW SOCIETY

BRITISH HOLISTIC MEDICAL ASSOCIATION
179 Gloucester Place
London NW1 6PX
Tel: 071 262 5299

CENTRE FOR GLOBAL EDUCATION (YORK)
University of York
Heslington
York YO1 5DD
Tel: 0904 433444

CENTRE FOR THE STUDY OF COMPLEMENTARY MEDICINE
51 Bedford Place
Southampton
Hampshire SO1 2DG
Tel: 0703 334752

HEARTBEAT WALES
Brunel House
Fitzalan Road
Cardiff CF2 1EB
Tel: 0222 472472

NATIONAL FEDERATION OF CITY FARMS
The Old Vicarage
66 Fraser Street
Bedminster
Bristol BS3 4LY
Tel: 0272 660663

WWF (EDUCATION)
Panda House
Weyside Park
Godalming
Surrey GU7 1XR
Tel: 0483 426409

CHAPTER FIVE:
A WORD ON ECONOMICS

NEW ECONOMICS FOUNDATION
Universal House
2nd Floor
88–94 Wentworth Street
London E1 7SA
Tel: 071 377 5696

CHAPTER SIX:
INDUSTRIAL FUTURES

E.I.R.I.S
401 Bondway Business Centre
71 Bondway
London SW8 1SQ
Tel: 071 735 1351

MERLIN ECOLOGY FUND
Knightsbridge House
197 Knightsbridge
London SW7 1RB
Tel: 071 581 3020

NEW ECONOMICS FOUNDATION
Universal House
2nd Floor
88–94 Wentworth Street
London E1 7SA
Tel: 071 377 5696

NEW CONSUMER
52 Elswick Road
Newcastle upon Tyne NE4 6JH
Tel: 091 272 1148

CHAPTER SEVEN:
ONE WORLD?

INTERNATIONAL INSTITUTE FOR ENVIRONMENT AND DEVELOPMENT
3 Endsleigh Street
London WC1H 0DD
Tel: 071 388 2117

INTERNATIONAL PLANNED PARENTHOOD FEDERATION
Regents College
Regents Park
London NW1 4NS
Tel: 071 486 0741

OXFAM
274 Banbury Road
Oxford OX2 7DZ
Tel: 0865 56777

PANOS
9 White Lion Street
London N1 9PD
Tel: 071 278 1111

POPULATION CONCERN
231 Tottenham Court Road
London W1P 9AE
Tel: 071 631 1546

CHAPTER EIGHT:
BODY POLITIC, IMMORTAL SOUL

CHRISTIAN ECOLOGY GROUP
58 Quest Hills Road
Malvern
Hereford & Worcestershire
WR14 1RW
Tel: 06845 2630

FRIENDS OF THE EARTH
26–28 Underwood Street
London N1 7JQ
Tel: 071 490 1555

GREEN DEMOCRATS
73 Barnsdale Road
Orpington
Kent BA5
Tel: 0689 28999

THE GREEN PARTY
10 Station Parade
Balham High Road
London SW12 9AZ
Tel: 081 673 0045

ICOREC
Manchester Polytechnic
Didsbury Site
Wilmslow Road
Manchester M20 8RR
Tel. 061 434 8374

SERA
(Socialist Environment and
Resources Association)
11 Goodwin Street
London N4 3HQ
Tel: 071 263 7424

TORY GREEN INITIATIVE
19/21 Great Portland Street
London W1N 5DB
Tel: 071 637 2281

BIBLIOGRAPHY

DIRECTORIES AND REFERENCE WORKS

John Button *New Green Pages* (Optima, 1990). A directory of natural products, services, resources and ideas.

Environmental Information Bureau *The Green Index* (Cassells, 1990). Environmental organisations in Britain and Ireland.

ed. Monica Frisch *Directory for the Environment* (Greenprint, 1990). Organisations in Britain and Ireland.

CHAPTER ONE: WHERE ON EARTH ARE WE GOING?

John Button *How to be Green* (Century Hutchinson, 1989)

FoE *Friends of the Earth Handbook* (Optima, 1990)

Worldwatch Institute, Ed. Lester Brown *State of the World Reports* (Norton; produced annually)

CHAPTER TWO: ENERGY WITHOUT END

Christopher Flavin and Alan B. Dunning *Worldwatch Paper 82* 'Building on Success: the age of energy efficiency' (Worldwatch Institute)

Mick Hamer *Wheels within Wheels: a study of the road lobby* (Routledge & Kegan Paul, 1987)

Cynthia Pollock Shea *Worldwatch Paper 81* 'Renewable Energy: today's contribution, tomorrow's promise' (Worldwatch Institute)

CHAPTER THREE: THE FRUITS OF THE EARTH

Mike Birkin *C For Chemicals* (Greenprint, 1989)

Richard Body *Agriculture: The Triumph and the Shame* (Gower, 1982)

Geoffrey Cannon *The Good Fight* (Ebury Press, 1989)

Friends of the Earth *Off the Treadmill* (FoE, 1990)

Tim Lang and Tony Webb *Food Irradiation* (Thorsons, 1990)

Mark Gold *Living without Cruelty* (Greenprint, 1989)

CHAPTER FOUR: BUILDING A NEW SOCIETY

Joe Collier *The Health Conspiracy* (Century, 1989)

Patrick Pietroni *The Greening of Medicine* (Victor Gollancz, 1990)

Damian Randle *Teaching Green* (Greenprint, 1989)

Jeremy Seabrook *The Race for Riches* (Greenprint, 1988)

WWF *Earthrights* (Kogan Page, 1987)

CHAPTER FIVE: A WORD ON ECONOMICS

Guy Dauncey *After the Crash* (Re-issued by Greenprint, 1989)

ed. Paul Ekins *The Living Economy* (Routledge & Kegan Paul, 1986)

ed. D. Pearce *Blueprint for a Green Economy* (Earthscan, 1989)

Ted Trainer *Developed to Death* (Greenprint, 1989)

World Commission on Environment and Development *Our Common Future* (Oxford University Press, 1987)

CHAPTER SIX:
INDUSTRIAL FUTURES

Guy Dauncey *After the Crash* (Re-issued by Greenprint, 1989)

John Elkington and Julia Hailes *Green Consumer Guide* (Victor Gollancz, 1988)

John Elkington and Tom Burke *The Green Capitalists* (Victor Gollancz, 1989)

James Robertson *Future Wealth* (Cassell, 1989)

CHAPTER SEVEN:
ONE WORLD?

Czech Conroy *The Greening of Aid* (Earthscan, 1988)

Susan George *A Fate Worse Than Debt* (Penguin, 1988)

Paul Harrison *The Greening of Africa* (Paladin, 1987)

Teresa Hayter *Exploited Earth: Britain's Aid and the Environment* (Earthscan/FoE, 1989)

Ronald Higgins *Plotting Peace* (Brasseys, 1990)

Bertrand Schneider *The Barefoot Revolution* (Intermediate Technology, 1988)

Lloyd Timberlake *Only One Earth* (BBC Books/Earthscan, 1987)

14 case studies by African and Asian journalists *Towards Sustainable Development* (Panos, 1987)

CHAPTER EIGHT:
BODY POLITIC,
IMMORTAL SOUL

Ian Bradley *God is Green* (Darton Longman & Todd, 1990)

Erich Fromm *To Have or to Be* (Abacus, 1979)

John McCormick *The Global Environment* (Bellhaven Press, 1989)

Sean McDonagh *To Care for the Earth* (Geoffrey Chapman, 1986)

Martin Palmer *Genesis or Nemesis* (Dryad, 1988)

Sara Parkin *Green Parties* (Heretic Books, 1988)

Alec Ponton and Sandy Irvine *A Green Manifesto* (McDonalds, Optima 1989)

Jonathon Porritt *Seeing Green* (Blackwells, 1984)

CHAPTER NINE:
DEFENDING THE FUTURE

Fritjof Capra *The Turning Point* (Wildwood House, 1982)

James Lovelock *Gaia: A New Look at Life on Earth* (Oxford University Press, 1979)

Jonathon Porritt *The Coming of the Greens* (Fontana, 1988)

Walter and Dorothy Schwarz *Breaking Through* (Green Books, 1987)

John Seed *Thinking like a Mountain* (Heretic Books, 1988)